Oh! The Coal Branch

a chronicle of the Alberta Coal Branch

By Toni Ross

Standard book number 0-919212-51-4
Published in 1974
by Mrs. Toni Ross
2nd Printing, 1975
Third Printing, 1984
by Shannon Ross and Rebecca Leonty
Box 3006, Hinton, Alberta T0E 1C0
© June 28, 1974, 252345 Register 78
Printed by D. W. Friesen and Sons Ltd.
5720 Macleod Trail South, Calgary, Alberta T2H 0J6
Head Office: Altona, Manitoba R0G 0B0

Dedication

This book is dedicated to the pioneers — their bravery (particularly those who could not even understand the language) in coming to unknown land is almost beyond comprehension. I wonder how many of us would be equal to such a challenge.

— Toni Ross

Oh! The Coal Branch

Acknowledgements

Someone should write a book on the Alberta Coal Branch. This sentence has been repeated over and over again. Before many years have passed I believe this will be only one of a dozen books published about the various camps on the Branch and when these books have been published, they still will not have told all the story.

Where to start with acknowledgements — First the PEP Program of the Department of Culture, Youth and Recreation, under Hon. Horst A. Schmid. Without this Government of Alberta grant of six months. I could not have compiled this chronicle.

One must earn a living and not spend hours delighting in browsing through newspaper files in the Provincial Legislative Library, while patient employees haul dusty files out of basement storage, and then zerox countless requested copies.

Then the equally congenial employees of the Provincial Archives who for weeks on end set up audio and microfilm equipment so that I could listen and read, and read and read . . . who hauled out Alberta Provincial Police files to browse through. Much of these I used, much of it passed over. There were a fair number of suicides, mostly bachelors or men separated from families in Europe. No purpose would be served by recording these.

I am grateful to David W. Lake, who from the United Republic of Cameroon gave permission to use any or all of his thesis on The Historical Geography of the Coal Branch; to Andy A. den Otter who wrote "The Social Life of a Mining Community; the Coal Branch," and to both of these men who turned their taped interviews over to the Archives; to the Historian, RCMP, Ottawa, who dug up the earliest recorded case of the area; to the CNR Public Relations — Edmonton who also went through their files and contributed much.

Most of all I am thankful to have talked to many former residents of the Alberta Coal Branch, and shall be eternally sorry I did not start sooner, as the pioneers die, one by one.

I am grateful to the editors, reporters and correspondents of the early Edson papers, the *Edmonton Daily Bulletin,* which became the *Edmonton Bulletin* and the *Edmonton Journal.* Their records were invaluable. I appreciate very much the help given by the publisher and staff of the *Edson Leader,* and my neighbor Bobby Hooper, a steno who thought she was to spend the winter months knitting away, and instead found herself at a typewriter retyping marked, coffee-stained pages of this chronicle.

I am grateful too, to the encouragement of other neighbors and friends, and to my children, who for months have tried to eat at the kitchen table which has been continuously strewn with files, notes, photographs and general upheaval.

I shouldn't like to forget the Librarian at Edson or the office staff of the Town of Edson, who cleared desk space so I could scribble away. The list is endless, and of this I am much aware. To those not mentioned, thank-you.

This is a chronicle, a recording of events. Research could have gone on for years, and still not covered everything. Research probably will go on for years. Once I faced the fact that I couldn't hope to cover it all, I began to put it on paper. My children state that sometimes it is discordant. This I know, but little events were part of the life there as they are everywhere, and deserve mention.

Is it accurate in detail?

It is as accurate as the recorded written word, or man's memory can be ... no man is infallible.

Toni Ross.

Early Grand Trunk Pacific Map.

Provincial Archives of Alberta

Table of Contents

1912 GTP Pack Train at Edson   Provincial Museum & Archives

The original construction of the Big Eddy Bridge took place in 1909 and 1910 at a total cost of approximately $99,000. The bridge was 2,343 feet in length and 81 feet high. Timber used in the original structure was poor bridge material, possibly hewed on the site, and in the span of 10 to 12 years, the complete structure had to be rebuilt. The rebuilding cost, in 1922, spiralled to $103,500.

CNR Public Relations — Edmonton

Prologue

The country west of Edmonton was raw and beautiful. As survey teams penetrated further and further west, a little log cabin sprang up here, now there. Defineable trails began to appear as one pack-horse after another plodded along, picking the easiest path for the heavily-laden loads they bore. The pack-horse was purveyor of goods, transportation, and its strength a portal to things a man feels he must do.

Men came west on pack-trains or smaller groups. A trading post sprang up here and there where travellers stopped, receiving hospitable welcome and learned of the trail ahead.

Local legend has it that one such traveller, name of Hornbeck, pushed west in the late summer of 1906. Accompanied by only one fellowman, the two prodded a large number of horses owned by Hornbeck and destined for Prairie Creek. At Prairie Creek, he hoped to sell the valuable animals to the Grand Trunk Pacific Survey team. The survey team pushing ever west had recently purchased the Prairie Creek trading post from two partners, Jack Gregg and H. N. Jock; Americans who had established the post several years before.

Hornbeck and his man reached the Big Eddy. The horses were exhausted as were the men. An early storm hit the area and the beasts floundered in snow. Hornbeck talked to the Frenchman who had established a small trading post high above the swirling waters of the

1

McLeod River on the bank of the Big Eddy. He was told of a flat along the Sundance Creek that provided good pasture for horses and had been used often by survey teams. He decided to rest, and as the weather grew more severe built a cabin not far from the post. One or two other cabins dotted the landscape. The weather worsened, feed grew scarce and Hornbeck watched as his animals starved. Watched and watched while his life's investment grew leaner and gaunt. Through the long days and nights he brooded, and then went berserk, as the first of his horses died. His partner fled to the safety of the post. Hornbeck followed and entering the post scattered a hail of bullets helter skelter. The men retreated to another shack and listened to the unmistakable sounds of wreckage within the post. A sackful of flour was thrown out the window and split when it hit the ground. The man was not only berserk he was ruining their winter's supply of food. One man was sent to get help and the three remaining men conferred. It might be weeks before help arrived. In the meantime their food would be gone. For days they watched and waited. Occasionally Hornbeck ventured to the door and shot at the cabin where the men huddled. They conferred and decided they could not wait for help. They would shoot him at the first opportunity. All three would shoot simultaneously so the blame would not rest on one.

The next time Hornbeck ventured out the door of the post, all three men raised their rifles and at a signal all three fired.

Whether the above events happened exactly or are garbled in the telling, the following is the report as contained in the Royal North West Mounted Police 1907 Annual Report.

APPENDIX U
REPORT OF CONST. H. SHAND OF TRIP FROM EDMONTON TO THE McLEOD RIVER IN SEARCH OF A MISSING RANCHER, WINTER 1906-7.

'G' DIVISION, Edmonton, January 26, 1907.

Sir — I have the honour to forward the following report re patrol to the McLeod River.

On December 20, 1906, I left Edmonton for Lac St. Anne, in company with Constables Stark and Worsley and S. Adams, hired as guide with team Reg. No. 2688 and 1928, arriving at Lac St. Anne on the 21st of that month. On arrival there I learnt from the Hudson's Bay Company the men who were going with us to bring out the horses of the deceased had not yet arrived. These men arrived the next day; Jock, C. Lowden and a half-breed with six head of horses for the trip. We left on two bob-sleighs hired to take us to the end of the sleigh trail on the morning of December 25, arriving at the Grand Trunk Pacific Railway survey camp on the 27th, which is the end of the sleigh trail. Here we sent back the bobsleighs, and loaded the flat sleighs and pack horses, and started across country to strike a pack trail which runs up

2

to the Macleod River. We had a distance of about 10 miles to make, but owing to the depth of the snow — which I should judge would be about three feet deep — and the nature of the country we had to cross, i.e. muskeg, which had apparently not frozen solid under the snow, as the horses were constantly breaking clean through, this short distance took us four and a half days.

On our arrival at the pack trail we found it covered with a foot to a foot and a half of snow, and very poor travelling with the loads which we had on the flat sleighs, so I had a cache built here, and left half our rations and oats, so that we could travel lighter. Const. Starke, who had been sick the day before, was quite unfit to travel the next day, so we waited over a day, and as he still was unable to travel I decided to go ahead and leave him 2 horses and a flat sleigh, and also the man S. Adams. I left next morning with the men, Jock, Lowden and the half breed, and four horses with two flat sleighs and after travelling over a very rough country for five days in very deep snow we made the McLeod River on January 9, at which place Const. Starke and S. Adams caught us up the former being in good health again. One of their horses had strayed away, and we did not see any sign of him on the return trip.

We made the Big Eddy on the Macleod River the next afternoon at 4 p.m., and I was there informed by three men, Noorgaard, Berthou and Mourrou, of the shooting of the deceased man, Hornback (sic). I took statements from these men, and measurements of the places where he fell, and where they stood when they shot him. I also drew a rough plan of the shacks and positions with measurements filled in of the scene of the shooting.

Next day I went to Hornback's shack, which was in a state of chaos, all sorts of tools having been thrown in the fire like cartridges, rifles, tools, pots and pans. I took list of all available property of the deceased, and took it up to the store of Berthou, and left instructions with a freighter who is going up there very shortly to bring these goods as far as Lac St. Anne.

For five days, I sent men out to collect all the horses they could find of the deceased, and at the end of that time, as our oats had run out, and 33 head of stock had been collected, decided to start back for Edmonton.

I started out with the three men concerned in the shooting of the deceased, Lowden and S. Adams, and 33 horses in a starving condition. Two or three of them dropped down every day and were unable to rise, so as our rations were short until we reached the cache, I had perforce to leave them where they fell.

I left two men at the Big Eddy with grub and a flat sleigh and two horses to try to collect another band of nine horses that were known to be roaming somewhere in the vicinity.

We made very slow time coming out owing to two heavy storms having completely blocked the trail, and also to the intense cold weather. After travelling for seven days we struck Lobstick Lake, where there are three stacks of hay. As our bunch of horses at this time only numbered 20, and were in a thoroughly exhausted condition, I decided to leave a man there in charge of them, with orders to bring them to Lac Ste. Anne as soon as they were able to travel. Every colt but one, out of sixteen head, died on the way or dropped exhausted. We left early the next day to try to make within 20 miles of Lac Ste. Anne if possible and met Corporal Munro and Constable Dowler with teams and a half-breed at the crossing of the Pembina river.

On the following day we made Lac Ste. Anne, and from there to Edmonton.

Owing to the immense size of the body of the deceased, I could not bring out the biggest part of his personal property. He was a man measuring six feet two inches, exceedingly well developed, and was too broad to lay on his back on a flat sleigh. I had also bedding and provisions for seven men to bring for a trip lasting anywhere from two to three weeks.

I have the honour to be sir,

Your obedient servant,
(Sd.) H. SHAND, Const.
Reg. No. 4069

CHAPTER ONE

The Discovery

The Alberta Coal Branch.

"Where the devil is that?" ask some. "Never heard of it," say others.

Then you come across another who once lived there.

"Ah, yes, the Coal Branch."

A pause. The conversation lapses momentarily while memories chase one upon another. A sigh, a shrug, "Ah, the Coal Branch, what a wonderful life was there."

If you'll look on a map of Alberta, you'll see a tiny line that winds southwest of Edson, Alberta, 130 miles due west of Alberta's capital, the City of Edmonton.

The Alberta Coal Branch, an inverted crooked Y with a spur on the left flank that is Luscar. The stem of the Y, upside down as was said, leads off from Bickerdike, to the McLeod River, Erith, Weald, Embarras, Robb and Coalspur. From Coalspur we head south-east to the Lovett Branch; first there was Diss, then Sterco, Foothills and Lovett — Coal Valley came later and Diss disappeared from memory. There was Shaw, which came after Mercoal on the left flank of the Y, followed by Leyland, with a spur jutting out to Luscar, then Cadomin and Mountain Park.

All were sites which became towns or villages, although none ever incorporated as such. They were mining camps called towns by some, that once bustled with life, and have since become overgrown, reclaimed by nature's beauty. A beauty relished by campers, hunters

5

and anglers and former residents returning 'home' to gaze at the foot-hills, the mountains . . . and remember.

It was an unusual life insomuch as being just a couple of hundred miles from the province's capital, the camps were for three decades as isolated as if located many times that distance. From this isolation an 'esprit de corp' grew and continues through a third generation of people now scattered throughout North America. The bond is strong, and only time will tell how long the feeling of closeness will endure. While emigrants of countries look back to their homelands with nostalgia, the immigrants to this area, from all nations feel the same pull to the Alberta Coal Branch. Leaving was not of their choice.

The camps existed because of coal.

Coal. Marco Polo was sneered at when he brought back stories of the Chinese, who used as fuel 'the black rock that burned'. History

A wood and coal burning stove. Reservoir at right kept water hot.   — Nielsen

6

tells us that the 'black rock' or 'coal' was used as fuel in the Roman occupation with evidence of its use recorded before 50 B.C.

There are primarily three kinds of coal, all of which stem from plant life. Ordinary coal as the mature adult knows it is called soft coal or bituminous coal. Mature adult is used because many of today's children in this year of 1974 have never seen coal used in daily life.

Children who have never known the heat emanating from a stolid iron kitchen stove or a pot bellied heater in the living room which was later thrown out for one modishly square. A fire coaxed and kindled with wood, surfeited with lumps of coal that burned slowly, flames dancing with vari-colored hues, the lump then dissolving into ashes.

They will never know and not miss the feeling of security felt by parents when the winter's supply of coal was paid for and safely in the wood-shed out back or perhaps in the large coal bin in the cellar.

The bickering that ensued when announcement was made by either parent; "The coal skuttle is empty," and brother and sisters argued as to whose turn it was to refill it. Periodically ashes must be emptied, and again the bickering. Whose turn to open the grate, newspapers aspread on the floor to catch glowing flyaway ash, to put on an old glove kept expressly for that purpose; to carefully pull out an elongated rectangular pan overflowing with ashes. Then gingerly, for the handle was hot, lift the ash pan, while others held the door wide, and carry it outside to spread along the alley road, or add to a steadily growing pile of ashes.

How will the homes of their children be heated in future decades? The coal waits — for man's need and decision.

Hard coal is called 'anthracite'. While 'as black as coal' is a common enough saying, not all coal is black. Lignite, softer than common coal is brownish in color. Then there is peat, which if left alone for a few thousand years would eventually turn into coal.

Coal for lack of a better classification is termed a mineral. We are not here concerned with technicalities. Because of this mineral this area of the Alberta Coal Branch, grew, flourished and died in the space of a few decades. Once again there is industrial life in the area, at Luscar, a stirring at Foothills, but we go back . . .

In 1909 F. B. Smith, B.Sc., E & M.E. and his party turned south after going west of Edmonton for some 130 miles. It was January and they followed the McLeod River using the ice as their road. They were looking to see the developing of a mine. A coal mine.

There had been prospectors in the area for some years. The Canadian Geological Survey staff had been in and around the foothills and the mountainous region mapping since 1884. Jasper Park boundaries had been marked in 1907.

A General Butler who visited the foothills area before the North-West Rebellion mentioned in his reports of hearing the tales of Indians of 'stones that burn'.

John James Greig, referred to in earliest reports as Jack Gregg and John Gregg was one of the earlier known prospectors in the area.

Man with pipe is John James Greig, known variously as John Gregg and Jack Gregg. Jack Gregg staked claims at Mountain Park in 1909 and later Luscar, in 1911, although Luscar was not developed till 1921.

— Mrs. Charlie Lee

Mr. Greig was born in 1840 in Iowa and travelled overland to Oregon with his parents in 1846 in a covered wagon. Mr. Greig's mother was killed in an Indian raid when hostile Indians attacked the homeseekers several times on that journey. He learned to trap and hunt at the age of twelve and several years later joined Custer's Scouts. He was in the famous battle with Geronimo, the outlaw Indian, and was wounded in that battle. During the now famed Custer's Last Stand he had been sent on a scouting expedition undoubtedly escaping annihilation for that reason. However, he lived, and came to prospect and trap in what was then known as the Northwest Territories in the latter part of the 19th century. He lived to be over 100 years and an interview with him was recorded in the Jasper-Edson Signal at the age of 101. He had retired some years previously to his homeland in the U.S.A.

During his travels he met up with a fellow American, N. H. Jock who had come to the mountain region in 1888. 'Jock' had taken part in the Civil War in the states, and was also an independent 'critter'. Jock helped blaze the trail from Lac Ste. Anne to the Yellowhead pass, and the road was known for decades as 'Jock's Trail'.

Jock and Gregg established a trading post on Prairie Creek and traded with Indians and trappers. They became friends with John Lewis Swift who settled in the Athabasca Valley in 1890. The trading post was sold in 1904 to an early Grand Trunk survey team.[1]

[1] David Lake

8

Between 1906 and 1909 several discoveries of coal were made by prospectors, among these, Donald McDonald, Bill Bailie and P. A. Robb.

Lakeside mine at Robb and the Bryan mine were discovered and prospected by Baillie, Gregory and Robb in 1908, but no claims were staked.

Because Peter Austin Robb had been in the area many residents assumed that the point had been named after Mr. Robb who was better known as 'Baldy'.

At Mile 6

Bear shot in Lovett — 1911 by Herman Thorin.

9

However, Len Stevens, who was a friend of Baldy's states in a taped interview, "I asked him if Robb was named after him and he said 'No, it was some fellow down East.'"

D. B. Dowling was considered one of the ablest members of the Canadian Geological Survey team. After a 1908 exploration he reported coal fields of large extent.

In his summary he states:

[2]*"One of these fields is situated on the headwaters of Embarras and Pembina rivers.*

Higher grade steam and coking coals may be obtained from more distant fields, to which approach is more difficult, since they are situated behind high, rocky ridges. The areas containing the best grade of coal extend in narrow strips from the Saskatchewan river to near the Athabasca, behind the Brazeau, Bighorn and Nikanassin ranges. On the McLeod the upper part of the coal-bearing horizon was observed to have about 20 feet of coal seams."

About this time too, coal was discovered in the Athabasca Valley near Brule and near Hinton.

Meanwhile further up the ramparts of the Nikanassin range at the base of a mountain later known as Mount Cheviot legend has it that John Gregg camped with his half-Indian wife, Mary, daughter of Chief Cardinal, a Stoney Indian. She was highly respected by both Indian and white. Seven sheets of typewritten paper, the writer unknown, have been mimeographed several times over and are treasured by former residents of Mountain Park. Mrs. S. Dagil, formerly of Mountain Park passed her copy on.

Mary Gregg Lake near Luscar, named after the daughter of the Stoney Chief Cardinal, who became the wife of John Gregg.

Charlie Lee photo

The paper reads that in the summer of 1909 "the two made camp where the Whitehorse river joined with the small creek to the left."

The papers state that John Gregg "thought he had made a good discovery and was now on his way to the small newly established mining camp of Yellowhead. Once there he would show his find to his good friend Harry King, who would give him advice as to its worth and value."

In 1909 John Gregg staked what became known as Mountain Park. However Gregg and his partner Jock had known of the coal's existence along the foothills for several years prior to 1909. Mary had mentioned the black rock but as there was no need for the substance no effort was made to stake it at that time. The coming of the railroad survey teams changed this. In an obituary memoriam in the August 9, 1928 issue of the Edson-Jasper Signal, a line reads:

"With his partner, Jack Griggs he located what is now Luscar and Mountain Park, and later he acted as guide and packed supplies for the Grand Trunk Pacific Railway."

The mimeographed papers read, "In the spring of 1910, John Gregg in the lead, followed by seven pack horses being herded by his wife, Mary, landed once again at the same camp-site. This time they were accompanied by three men.

One could tell that these three men were not used to this strenuous outdoor life. They were all Englishmen and had not been in this country long. In fact, the smaller of the three had hardly been in this new country for a month. His name was Robert Thornton, a mining engineer, and he had been sent over from England by a British company to investigate this coal discovery of John Gregg's. The names of the other two men were Ned Harrison and Bill Ashley, both miners from Newcastle and whom Thornton had hired to prospect and develop this discovery.

Thornton in awe, looked at tall straight spruce trees, wild mountain flowers and the whole basin surrounded by snow-capped mountains.

"If we do start a mine, I have chosen a name for the town that will be built. This is like a park in the old country. We will call it Mountain Park."

Thornton satisfied himself that this was indeed a find.

Towards the end of September Thornton had sufficient information and put the two men to the building of a permanent camp with John Gregg packing in supplies.

Having laid his plans, Thornton returned to England to make his report and secure the necessary capital for the new mine.

It was probably from Dowling's geological survey that the Grand Trunk Pacific Railway had already predetermined that when the railroad reached this far west, a spur line would be built south-west for

2 David Lake

fifty-eight miles off their main line plan. The Brazeau line which became known shortly as the Coal Branch line would be built under the guarantee given by the Provincial Legislature at the rate of twenty thousand dollars per mile.

For the Government of Alberta was very much interested in the rich deposits of coal mapped in the area.

CHAPTER TWO

Edson

The Grand Trunk Pacific pre-determined too, that a few miles west of the south-going spur would be the ideal point for a divisional point. It was strategically located. Directly north just 252 miles away was a rich agricultural area known as Grande Prairie. There were coalfields too further west and then the 5200 square miles of territory which comprised Jasper Park.

Why, with all this going for it, the divisional point would become a city in no time. The name of this unborn city would be Edson, named after the Vice-President and General Manager of the Grand Trunk Pacific, Edson J. Chamberlain. The fact that the area had a post-office name of Heatherwood was of no consequence. Post-offices shifted with the population and a few miles difference saw the opening of a new post-office with a new name.

And so the promotion began. Realtors encouraged by the GTP produced brochures painting a glowing picture of this thriving industrial and agricultural city that would emerge soon after the railroad reached Edson, 130 miles west of Edmonton. The hue and ballyhoo was taken up by realtors throughout Canada, overseas and in the United States.

A Seattle realtor carefully set out a replica of this Pittsburgh of the Canadian West. Edson! The display even featured miniature streetcars.

Speculators bought and bought, encouraged by promises conceived . . . in imagination.

Edson was very well known before it yet existed as a village. Anything connected with the place was widely publicized, which became a detriment . . . as did the absentee land owners.

In the spring of 1910 the railways raced each other across the nation. Two, the Grand Trunk Pacific and the Canadian Northern had closely allied lines.

May of 1910, J. H. Lloyd and his two sons arrived from England and having gone as far as possible by rail, had outfitted packhorses and came to the Edson area. Lloyd saw a party of surveyors busy at work laying out a townsite. The trio pitched a tent and talked to the surveyors. They learned that the coming of the Grand Trunk Pacific Railway would make this a town — once steel had arrived this site would become a divisional point of a great trans-continental railway system. It was destined to become the portal of the famous Grande Prairie and Peace River districts; eventually it would get its share of the trade that goes through the Yellowhead pass. Here was opportunity indeed.

The first newspaper of the area, The Edson Leader, notes that Lloyd bought as soon as the townsite was laid out — two lots. Twenty-five feet frontage each, located on the third avenue. Lloyd paid two hundred dollars each and on one built his first house — a tar paper affair.

Within a month he was offered three hundred dollars apiece for his lots and Mr. Lloyd sold. Six months later, the purchaser sold Lloyd's holdings for $1,100 each.

Steel arrived in August, 1910. Edson now had a permanent population of 15 persons.

This changed rapidly. Every train from the east brought its quota of red-blooded opportunity seekers. Business houses and tents began to go up on its main street. The town population rose and fell with each surge but by January 1911 had a permanent residency of four hundred and ninety persons. Real estate doubled and redoubled in value.

The advent of civilization into the virgin western territory was followed by the usual quota of bootleggers, gamblers and crooks of all kinds — and the ladies of ill repute.

A Royal North-West Police officer, Charles Cummings Raven was ordered to Edmonton for construction duty along the GTP and was promoted to inspector and assigned to Edson headquarters in 1911.

As noted in the columns of the Edmonton Daily Bulletin — Feb. 3, 1911 this was no easy task . . . 'the bulk of the police work is in enforcing the clause of the Dominion Criminal Code which prohibits the sale of giving away of intoxicating liquor or the having it in possession for that purpose, within a distance of ten miles on either side of the railway under construction.'

As an instance of the difficulty the police have in enforcing the law it might be mentioned that recently some twelve cases of whisky which were seized had been discovered concealed in boxes marked as merchandise. The twelve cases were packed in the centre of larger boxes and packed with straw and shavings. Suitcases and trunks are also sometimes found to contain the forbidden liquid. Cases of tomato cans also sometimes contain liquor. The police are armed with a long sharp iron rod which they prod into innocent looking sacks of oats and occasionally thus find a bottle which does not contain horse medicine.

Rightly or wrongly, it was believed that the enforcement of this law was the secret of preserving order in the camps.

There was a small army in the camps. At Wolf Creek, or Thornton, eight miles east of Edson a camp had been set up to see to the permanent building of two large bridges. West of Edson, in the construction camps there were over 2,000 men. First the surveyors, the station men who took small sub-contracts of short stretches of rock cuts; the gangs building bridges and culverts, and the men engaged in laying the steel rails, followed by the gangs for ballasting, surfacing and the section men, whose duty it was to keep the track in repair for the safe running of the trains.

It was the duty of Inspector Raven and his four constables to keep order in the settlements which sprang up. One constable was at Bickerdike, one at Jasper Park where Fitzhugh, the next divisional point was to be built. Two of the constables made their headquarters in Edson with the inspector. Their 'beat' was from Wolf Creek to the B.C. boundary.

Then there was the area to the south-west on the proposed coal branch line where coal mining companies had already begun development work in earnest, and were but waiting for the steel to come through to the Embarras and Brazeau rivers.

The Yellowhead Pass Coal and Coke company was waiting for the railroad. Development work was proceeding on their property on the south end of Last Chance Creek, about sixty-seven miles from Edson. Their mine was three miles off to the side from mile 58 on the branch line. Two tunnels had been opened for a total length of nearly 200 feet.

"They have a hoisting engine, cars and a pile of coal awaiting the arrival of railway transportation.

Mr. O'Brien, of Renfrew, Ont. and Messrs. Doheny & Richardson, of Montreal are interested in a coal mine to which a spur will be built this winter from mile 37 on the branch line of the GTP. There are three seams of a good grade of bituminous coal, one being 12 feet thick and another seven feet thick. Development work has been proceeding for two years. The tunnels extend in a 24 degree slope and the seams have a dip of fifty-two degrees.

The Bulletin notes — The Pacific Pass Coal Fields Limited is a strong company, as indicated by the names of the directorate which are said to include: E. G. Greenshields as president; Hon. Robert McKay, vice-president; W. Molson McPherson, H. A. Lovett, K.C., J. W. McConnell,

15

F. L. Wanklin, A. H. Cook, R. Brutinel and A. DeBernis, with G. A.
Cousins as secretary-treasurer; P. Christensen, Mine manager and
Chas. Fergie, chief engineer.

There are several seams of good bituminous coal, including one 15
feet and another, 17 feet thick. Men have been working there for a year
and about twenty men were employed in the early winter. Supplies have
been hauled over the trail from mile 16 on the main line. This company
has contracted with the Grand Trunk Pacific to supply 300 tons per day,
to be shipped within three months after steel reaches the mine. Thus the
G.T.P. will be able to secure fuel for its locomotives when building the
G.T.P. on westward to the coast.

At Brule Lake, in Jasper Park, at mile 76 on the main line of the
G.T.P. some coal is now being mined, and at mile 86 the Jasper Park Col-
lieries purpose to develop coal mining extensively."

There was coal everywhere, or appeared to be, and an army of amateur prospectors also set out to make their fortune. The Edson Leader
started to carry regularly the Canadian Synopsis of Canadian Northwest Mining Regulations which stated:

'Coal — Coal mining rights may be leased for twenty-one years, re-
newable at an annual rental of $1 an acre. Not more than 2,560 acres can
be leased to one applicant. Royalty five cents per ton. In unsurveyed terri-
tory the tract must be staked out by the applicant in person, and personal
application to the agent or sub-agent of Dominion Lands for the district
must in all cases be made, and the rental for the first year must be paid to
the agent within thirty days after filing application.'

W. W. Cory,
Deputy Minister of the Interior.

In March of 1911, Mr. Johnson, secretary of the Jasper Park Collieries visited Edson to purchase supplies for the mine. He stated that
although work had been held back because of non-delivery of machinery that coal had been sold to railway contractors, and after it had
been packed to the blacksmiths it cost them almost double the price.

"Mr. Johnson has his headquarters camp near the Sulphur springs
on Sulphur creek, and in order to reach the springs, which are twelve
miles from the railway bed, he cut a pack trail through the bush. He
says there are in all seven springs, six hot, and one cold. The temperature of the hot springs ranges from 111 to 126 degrees.

"He also states that the country has only been explored along the
rivers and pack trails, and he expects that valuable mineral deposits will
be discovered when prospectors can get supplies at points along the rail-
way. Hitherto prospecting has been almost impossible, owing to supplies
having to be packed in over the mountains with the expenditure of much
time and arduous labor."

In March of 1911, too the G.T.P. announced that the following
station names would replace the mileage designations being used
along the railroad bed.

The respective names of these station sites west of Edson would be
Ansell, Bickerdike, Dandurand, Galloway, Medicine Lodge, Harg-
win, Obed, Roundcroft, Pedley, Hinton, Dyke, Shackell, Fiddle Creek,

Jasper House, Moberly, Swift, Fitzhugh, Thomas, Mansur, Yellow-head Pass.

"Fitzhugh[1] will be a divisional point, but as it is in Jasper Park, a national domain, it will simply be a point for the exchange of engines and train crews, so that Edson will be the chief divisional point between Edmonton and Fort George,[2] the latter place being beyond the summit of the rockies."

Secure in the knowledge that all coal from the Brazeau mines had to be handled in Edson, residents of the town of Edson still believed that the prosperity of future growth depended on the road north to Grande Prairie, a rich agricultural region.

Agriculture, as anyone knew was really the backbone of a country. The fledgling Board of Trade at Edson prepared a circular with the following information:

"FREE HOMESTEADS are available in the Edson sub-land agency which comprises all the territory lying 25 miles to the east of Edson, 15 miles to the south, to the Rocky Mountains on the west and to the Athabasca river on the north (approximately 3,528 square miles). Five thousand homesteads are now open for entry and more will shortly be opened. There are many first class homesteads close to the town, chiefly lying north, northeast and northwest. Along the government road to Grande Prairie, which starts from Edson, there are some particularly fine tracts of land awaiting enterprising settlers. The best of timber for building, fencing and fuel can be obtained close at hand by every settler. Edson will afford a market for all produce raised. While it is possible to obtain homesteads with a considerable amount of land free from bush it must be distinctly understood that on most of the land clearing will have to be done before it can be tilled. Frank Fulmer is the local land agent."

J. R. Andrews, Editor and Manager of the Edson Leader ran a subhead on his masthead which read — The Edson Leader (Grande Prairie and Peace River News).

He notes that Premier Sifton promises immediate aide for the construction of the Edson-Grande Prairie wagon road and that the government will make it a summer as well as a winter road.

In March 1911, the Leader carried the following message: Mr. Sides, foreman of the Grande Prairie road cutting gang, who is now in town, received a letter informing him that open country had been reached by the axe men at the north end of the road, and teams could now go right through to Grande Prairie from Edson.

Mr. O. Hoff's bull train started north with 22,000 pounds of freight for the Grande Prairie road. In the outfit there were plows, scrapers etc. The balance of the iron work for the ferries and bridges was also taken out.

He made the distance between the Athabasca river and Edson coming out, in three days and reported the road 'good' and his bulls in fine condition.

---

[1] Fitzhugh is now Jasper, Alberta.
[2] Fort George is Prince George, B.C.

Fulmer & Covert ran an ad in the paper headed

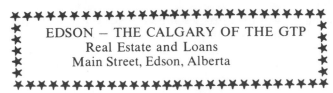
while Creighton & Son, Props. informed everyone that rates for the Boston Hotel on Second Avenue, Edson, Alta were $2.00 per day.

The immigration hall at Edson was nearing completion and track laying on the Coal Branch had started.

The Wolf Creek ferry was removed to the McLeod River southwest of the town where supplies could be carried to the workmen on the GTP Edson-Brazeau branch. The cable was taken to the point by team.

Charlie May was busy hauling supplies to the Bremner coal mine on the McLeod river west of Edson while the two coal mines in the Brazeau developed for a daily out-put of 2,500 tons each.

Early Edson

A test of the Brazeau coal was made on the G.T.P. Locomotive 507 despatched from Edmonton with a full tonnage and a heavy train. The coal was found to possess excellent free steam qualities, and the engineer stated in his report that he was well pleased with it.

A report states that Const. Holtby of the RNWMP made another large haul of contraband booze on the arrival of the train from Edmonton. "In spite of repeated seizures the illicit traffic up the line goes on merrily."

A week later it reads, "Some good old Scotch Whiskey was wasted when the baggage men in letting a trunk, which contained some of the

I walked from Mile 38 with all my belongings and it was sure cold.

— Roy Bromm

contraband, fall too heavily on the station platform. The police immediately cached that which remained unbroken."

By May, 1911 the paper reported the discovery of marl 18 miles west of Edson, "the marl is so situated that it can be handled with a steam shovel, which will be an important factor in the cost of manufacture". There would be a cement plant there!

This would allay in future the problem the GTP was having — "The work of completing the G.T.P. round house here is being delayed on account of the difficulty of getting cement for the concrete floors, the contractors having failed to secure a supply beforehand."

To the west a Winnipeg company is organized to develop and operate a coal mine at Fallis and is capitalized at $750,000.

A delegation of 80 businessmen from Edmonton headed by Hon. G. H. Bulyea, Lieutenant Governor visit the marl deposits. They lunch at the Capital Hotel in Bickerdike and have dinner at the Boston Hotel in Edson. Edson greets them with an arch across Main Street with a banner which reads "The Gateway to Grande Prairie and Peace River District."

By summer the fledgling town of Edson had 1,200 people with a number of stores and business concerns; some of which quietly catered to the influx of men coming in from the camps for a spree. Bootlegging flourished quietly as did the gambling dens, and always there were complaints of the lack of accommodation.

Men along the construction sites complained about the difficulty of cashing their time cheques, and everyone complained about the mail. The town was called Edson, but its post-office was Heatherwood. Mail for Edson and beyond travelled by train to Wolf Creek, where it was held until Saturday "when the mail carrier goes from Edson to Wolf Creek with outgoing mail and returns with the big week's mail to Edson. Answers to this mail, if posted in the government post-office or carried by a government mail carrier, cannot leave Edson till the next Saturday.

From Edson, or more properly speaking from Heatherwood P.O. mail is distributed to residents for 140 miles westward and to the Coal Spur. At one time there have been as many as ten full sacks."

So while Edson was Edson to all, the federal government continued the name Heatherwood on the objection that Edson was too similar to the name, Edison, a village north of Morinville; and the confusion mounted.

Finally the postal authorities decided to name the Edson post-office the same as the town and Edison would be renamed Clyde, Alberta.

In mid-summer another boost came to the area. The Canadian Northern Railway announced that it too would establish a divisional point for the CNR, just a few miles south on the McLeod River. Edson would have a twin city, which would be known as Tollerton, named after the native town in England, of Mr. Welby, the CNR's divisional engineer.

The Leader states that "Mr. Bickerton, a right of way agent for the company was here taking up options on the land which he recently obtained from local people who were in possession as homesteaders."

Profit came early to some homesteaders who were on the 1,500 acres of land secured by the Canadian Northern.

The article continues, "The Leader has authoritative information that the company's plan for this divisional point involve works and expenditures that will make it the greatest centre on their line between Winnipeg and the Pacific coast terminus at Port Mann.

The company have valuable coal properties six miles south of Edson which they intend to develop and work on an extensive scale. A spur line will be built to the mines from the main line south of the McLeod. Assays and tests have shown that the coal in this locality is superior in every essential point to that found on the Brazeau, where extensive mines are also being developed."

The thriving town of Edson, incorporated September 7, 1911 showed every sign of progress.

It was noted that nearly five hundred pack ponies are in commission in the Edson district with railway engineering parties, land surveyors, prospectors, coal mining companies, etc.

Tests on the marl west of Edmonton show that it is ideal for the manufacturing of cement. "It is almost pure carbonate of lime, averaging about 90% according to mechanical chemists in Toronto. The clay is also a very large deposit located in the same township. The deposit was quite unknown until the G.T.P. drained a muskeg lake by making a cutting through it for a right of way. The clay is of exceedingly fine and uniform quality and contains more than 60% silica."

The Edmonton Portland Cement Company was formed and advertised for laborers, teamsters and carpenters.

A small cloud on this rosy horizon occurred when a Winnipeg correspondent in a publication called 'Canada' stated that the adjoining lands to Edson were located on muskegs. This statement was hotly denied by the Edson Leader.

There had been a few problems with bears in the countryside with provisions being ransacked, and there was the incident on the coal spur where three men in a spirit of revenge had blown up a supply car of Phelan & Shirley over an imagined slight.

The injunction, issued at the instance of the Grand Trunk Pacific against the Canadian Northern restraining the latter from continuing construction work at Mile 44, west of Edson, was raised and the contractors who had been idle for two weeks resumed operations.

The G.T.P. complained that the C.N.R. were encroaching on their right-of-way and sought to restrain them. The two lines ran close together from a point a short distance west of Edson into the mountains.

The men idling in Edson went back to their camp and work.

Building the Railroad   — CNR Public Relations, Edmonton

North of the town, the Leader reports, "Nearly all the men employed on the Edson-Grande Prairie wagon road have quit work to seek employment in the harvest fields on the prairies, being tempted away by the prospect of higher wages, although their jobs would have been good until well into the winter.

All the men working under Foreman Johnson, 45 miles north, pulled out this week, and he was compelled to strike camp and return to town with his outfit.

"It is reported that men in the gangs further north are also arranging to quit. Mr. Johnson states that the road considering that it is a new one in a hill and bush country, is in good shape. He came in in two and a half days with an ox team drawing a 1,500 pound load and a team of ponies drawing 1,100 pounds."

These were but small setbacks and work steadily progressed.

In November, 1911, "The elevated coal chutes in the Grand Trunk Pacific yards were brought into commission. Engine 508 did the initial stunt, with engineer George Harrison and fireman J. W. Fraser at their posts, and looked as though she fully realized the importance of the event as she climbed the ascent and spotted the first cars of coal that marked the opening of a very important factor of railway improvements in Edson. The structure is situated about 150 yards east of the round house. It is elevated 37 feet above the tracks. Six engines can coal at the same time, and where it used to take three hours to shovel fourteen tons of coal into an engine, the work is now done in five minutes."

By December real progress was made on the Brazeau Branch. "The steel on this line is being laid by hand but the weather has been so favorable that a mile of track has been laid, and with a continuance of present conditions the head of steel will be in the vicinity of Mile 40 by Christmas Eve. From 42 on this line Phelan and Shirley will shortly start to build the branch that will connect with the main line at the Yellowhead pass.

In Edson, Col. Rambo prepared for the opening of his new Idyl Hour Theatre, delayed some weeks because the generator for the lighting system had gone to Edison instead of being shipped to Edson.

In Edmonton there was talk in some circles that a better route to Grande Prairie led off from that city. Edson residents shrugged that off and saw the year 1911 out with much hoopla and real optimism.
1912

The Edson Town Council with Gilbert Laurence as Mayor reviewed the record of accomplishment of the town and district. Over 231 homesteads had been filed at the Edson Sub Land Agency during the last twelve months; the G.T.P. monthly pay roll averaged $40,000.00 per month.

The Yellowhead Coke and Coal Company, Pacific Pass Coal Company and Mountain Park Coal Company development work was proceeding and would be ready to ship by summer.

Over 150 lots in the town had been sold. The town prepared to sell debentures for a $60,000.00 school.

Then in February the Edson Trail was knocked by H. B. Clifford in an Edmonton paper. Mr. Clifford said he had been told it would take seven days to reach Grande Prairie and it had taken twelve.

Steel laying delayed because of a shortage of steel was laid to 50 miles west of Fitzhugh.

There was grave concern in American commercial centres when it was announced that 75,000 American farmers emigrated to Western Canada between July 1910 and July 1911.

On March 14, 1912 the Leader carried a story titled, TOWN OF FRANK IN DANGER ZONE[1] — The Citizens of Frank were much perturbed last week when they became acquainted with the report of the commission that was appointed last fall to inquire into the condition of Turtle mountain. The commissioners were W. G. Miller, Ontario Government Geologist; Prof. R. A. Daly of Boston, and G. S. Rice, United States coal expert.

According to the report the mountain is unsafe, and the whole of the town is within the danger zone and will have to be moved. The report states that the mountain is rendered dangerous from natural causes, not from mining operations and that coal mining can be continued at certain specified points. There is no fear felt for the immediate future but it is understood that the town will take up the question at once with the provincial government and ascertain what it is going to do about the matter.

However Edson was not too concerned with problems that far away. Its immediate concern was for the slanderous articles that started to appear regularly in the Eastern papers and then spread to the West.

Canon Matheson when visiting Edson said that it would appear that according to Eastern newspapers and street talk not only is the condition of morals a blot on the town but Edson itself on this account a blot on Canada.

The town which had been so publicized was beginning to feel the effects of the overblown publicity in reverse.

Bob Edwards in the Calgary Eye Opener after a visit to the town describes it scathingly as "a little burg of one short straggling street, all a muskeg." Mr. Edwards advises his readers to go West "if only to have a hearty laugh at the Edson town lots." to which W. C. Garrioch, Editor of the Leader replies, "Well one can only surmise that he must have had a heavy jag if he couldn't tell the difference between a whiskey keg and muskeg."

By June the paper recalls,

"Edson for the past few months has been slandered, maligned and poked fun at more than any other town in the West. A story got about that Edson was nothing more than a muskeg town and the real estate was under water. Edson is on a gradual slope which drains the water down the

---

[1] An earlier slide had taken the lives of 66 people.

23

*road toward the G.T.P. tracks, consequently when one passes through
Edson on the train, the impression is gleaned that Edson is the same,
nothing more than a watery country. What a mistake, for it is some of the
finest land anywhere out West.".*

The population of the town rose and fell with each new surge of
workers for the Coal Branch and the west, and the paper laconically
notes "The train has discharged several hundred men and a solitary
negress."

Also in June retail and wholesale liquor licenses were granted —

*"After a delay — or hold-up — which probably has no parallel in the
West, liquor licenses have been granted to the town. It is probably really
not worthwhile recounting the various pretexts that have been given for
witholding the privilege from the town. While Edson with a population
of over one thousand was refused a license on the ground that it was in
the restricted territory, owing to railway construction, Entwistle with a
population of less than three hundred, and with railway construction
going on, was allowed a license.*

*The people of Edson would not, as a whole have objected to the
witholding of licenses had it simply meant that there was as much whiskey consumed here as there would have been with licensed houses. During the greater part of the winter there were between ten and fifteen
'blind pigs' some of which were run almost wide open. This was well
known to the department, and apparently was very satisfactory as the
revenue from fines exceeded many times the total annual revenue that
would accrue from two or three licensed houses.*

*These fines impoverished the town in more ways than one. The money
instead of staying here went to the Department, and in order to pay the
heavy and frequent fines, it was necessary to charge exorbitant prices for
liquor. The prices ranged from three to eight dollars a bottle, and twenty-
five cents a drink — straight — over the counter. It will be seen, therefore,
that the town was the victim of a double injustice; and it is not to be wondered at that strong temperance men supported the granting of licenses.*

*In future the sale of liquor will be in responsible hands, and it is not
too much to expect that the 'blind pigs' with their other sidelines will
vanish, and the town cease to suffer the ignominy of being styled a town
of 'red lights' and 'blind pigs'."*

It would seem that this would have calmed down the town, but
over the next few years licenses were granted and revoked, granted
and revoked with a far from monotonous regularity, and the 'blind
pigs' with sidelines continued to flourish.

While a core of solid citizens lived their established way, another
core of stolid citizens took care of the wants and needs of the tide of
workers who washed in and out of the town.

The Mines Become an Actuality

By 1912 the coal bearing area was aswarm with men; hundreds
continued to arrive weekly in Edson. There was work for all. Five
hundred men worked on the G.T.P. railroads on the branch spur;

hundreds packed supplies and equipment for the construction and development of the mines, and hundreds more worked at the sites.

By the fall, 1912 the Edson Leader reads:

> *Right in the heart of the Jasper National Park situated on a high plateau, commanding magnificent views of Mount Miette and the other stalwart peaks of the Canadian Rockies, is springing up a well-ordered and well-built mining village, having its own church and stores, school and hospital. About fifty houses have already been built, of which 40 are occupied by the men and the rest are adapted for offices, stores and for management purposes. Another 40 houses for the men will be erected almost at once.*

Trestle at Lovett — 1912.

Lovett — 1912.

25

South slope in Lovett – 1911.

A water plant, with reservoir on the mountain side above the village has been put in at a cost of $10,000. The machine shop, power house supply shops, etc. are nearly completed and it is expected that the mines will be in full operation by December 1st.

Last month the number of men on the payroll was 227 and when the mine is in full operation, producing its full output of 2,000 tons per day of ten hours, the number will be increased to 500. At present a number of men are employed on development work though the mine is producing about 10,000 tons of coal per month.

Practically every ton of coal that the company can produce is taken by the Grand Trunk railway, which is using the Jasper Park Collieries

Lovett – 1915. The first layoff.

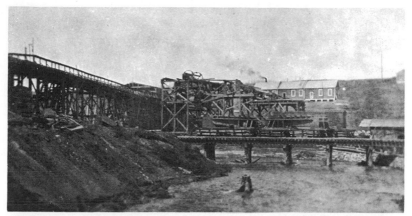

Building new tipple, Lovett — 1915.

Fire Brigade at Lovett — 1913.

Fishing in Fairflax Lake, Alberta.

coal on the service west of Edmonton and also on the main line east. The coal is a high grade bituminous coal, of a very fine coking quality, and it is able to take the place of the coal now being imported from the Crow's Nest and Pennsylvania.

Financed by English capital and owning some 12,000 acres of land near the point where the main line of the Grand Trunk Pacific railway crosses the Pembina river, the Pembina Coal Company, Ltd. will also go right ahead with the development of its property.

A number of British financiers who are now touring the west under the direction of A. M. Grenfell, chairman of the Canadian Agencies Ltd. went out to the company's property, being conveyed over the G.T.P. in a special train. The party included Sir Ronald Lane, president of the company; A. M. Grenfell, R. N. Grenfell, Capt. Newton, W. E. Stavert, Barrington, Kennet, Capt. Machell, W. J. Chalis and Forbes Sutherland. Already the mine at Yellowhead on the coalspur was showing signs of being a permanent hamlet. More and more this point on the coal spur was run together as one word and some mail addressed "Coalspur".

Einar & Dionna Lund. Mr. Lund was warden on the Lovett Branch in early days.

Mr. O'Donohue, purchasing agent for the Yellowhead Pass Coal and Coke Co. brought complaints from men working on the Brazeau branch railroad. Though charged twenty-five cents a month for bringing mail, the firm hiring the carriers would not allow the carriers to take in newspapers. The men regarded this as a hardship and were contemplating engaging a mail carrier of their own so they could get the news of the day.

The Coal Branch was a Leaky Roof line, a nickname that later became synonymous for the Grand Trunk Pacific. It was opened for traffic between Bickerdike and Coalspur, 37 miles, in October, 1912, and from Coalspur to Lovett, 20 miles, three months later.

Fergie, Lovett or Lovettville

From Coalspur the elevation climbed 800 feet midway to the mine site at Lovettville or Fergie as it was variously called to where the Pacific Pass Coal Fields Limited worked.

The company controlled 40,000 acres of coal land, which contained six seams giving a total thickness of 108 feet. The mine workings, some fifty-five miles south of Bickerdike were connected to the GTP line by a spur of three miles. In the summer of 1913 output was approximately 300 tons per day, the major portion supplied to the G.T.P. Eight miles of steel had been installed at the mine-yard for the accommodation of loaded and empty cars. New machinery was on the ground and mine officials were proud of the plant which would be capable of handling 4,000 tons per day.

Thirty new miners' cottages, a cottage hospital, office and residence for officials were erected.

Edmonton representative for the company was B. S. Scott, 636 First Street; President, E. B. Greenshields, managing director Chas. Fergie, Directors M. Curry, John T. Ross; H. A. Lovett. A. H. Cook; Wm. M. MacPherson, J. G. Scott; Hon. T. A. Choquette, Carl A. Norman and A. de Bernis.

McLeod Collieries Ltd.

This company was under the management of Jas. A. Collins with other directors being John A. Hamilton, George B. Henwood and S. B. Stowe.

Considerably smaller, it controlled 2,193 acres, but the installed plant would be capable of handling 1,000 tons a day. Located a short distance south of Mile 32 it was connected by a mile spur line. Coal here in common with the area was of a quality to be used for both steam and domestic use.

Yellowhead Pass Coal and Coke Company Ltd.

By the summer of 1913 this company had been in operation for some months, employing over seventy men.

G. H. Richardson was managing director with the Edmonton offices located in the Credit Foncier building. M. J. O'Brien and M. Doherty were president and vice-president respectively. Coal lands of the company comprise 8,515 acres, located about three miles south-west of Mile 37.

The plant installed was capable of producing 500 tons per day. Modern miners' cottages had been erected and steady work for underground development was being carried on.

The mine workings, situated on the south fork of the Last Chance Creek showed good bituminous coal on both sides of the narrow valley.

One winter's fur catch by Hanson, an early trapper on the Lovett Branch, consisted of 137 coyotes, 19 lynx, 2 timber wolves, 2 foxes, 10 skunk, 3 mink and 34 weasels.

CHAPTER THREE

Mountain Park

Thornton had done his work well. He came back from England to Mountain Park with financial backing to the tune of two and a half million.

He had apparently impressed on the overseas financiers that although the coal deposit was vastly richer than could be thought possible, the prime necessity was the building of a railroad to join the Coalspur line. This meant a tortuous climb through canyons, rivers and grades from Coalspur to where the Mountain Park mine was located 5,800 feet above sea level. The higher ridges surrounding the site reached more than 7,000 feet above sea level. Thus Mountain Park shortly became known as the highest civilized point in Canada at 6,200 feet.

John Gregg in the meantime had quietly staked another claim in the summer of 1911. This claim would not be worked for another decade and eventually became known as Luscar.

H. M. Thornton, consulting engineer had been named general manager of this fledgling company known as the Mountain Park Coal Company, Ltd. Headquarters of this company was located in the Tegler building in Edmonton. Officers included H. M. Thornton, Pres., C. J. Heyland, I. W. Jones, J. C. C. Bremner.

Not only had he the new mining venture to develop but see to the building of the company's own 31 mile rail line which would cost $750,000. Miners came and found themselves employed at multiple

Mountain Park — year unknown.

Wild Flowers at Mountain Park.

tasks. Men with names like John Baruzzini, Primo Piccoli, Frank Livero, Jim Bello, Louis Dominic, Pete and Joe Chiesa and many more; their personalities as varied as their surnames, but each ruggedly individual, searching for a new life in this new land. Men came little knowing they would spend the bulk of their lifetime in this raw, magnetically beautiful setting.

The development continued on the company's holdings comprising 6,000 acres.

The Edmonton Daily Bulletin notes that:

"There are eleven workable seams on the company's property. Two of them have been opened up with five mines, the output of which is

*handled by a common tipple. The present temporary tipple, which re-
sembles more than anything else a railway trestle, spans a valley 800
feet wide.*

*The five mines are located on both sides of this valley, all within a
radius of 1,300 feet of the centre of the tipple, thus making a decidedly
compact and economical layout. A tipple is the arrangement required for
loading coal from mine cars into railway cars. This tipple is of special design, built to meet the requirements of the undertaking. It is provided
with large storage bins. It is constructed so as to feed four loading tracks
which will accommodate both gondola and boxcars. The railway sidings
are laid out in a manner calculated to handle most effectively and economically the largest output.*

*The output of the five mines, which constitute the first colliery,
averages 500 tons per day. These five mines are being developed to produce 500 tons each per day, a total of 2,500 tons for the first colliery. The
eleven seams on the company's holdings will admit of the opening of two
additional collieries when the market demands.*

*The construction of the company's connecting line of railway with
the coal branch was commenced in January 1912, and was completed to
the mines on July 16, 1913. In the meantime, the mines had been opened
up and immediately upon the steel reaching the temporary tipple the
company commenced shipping.*

*The construction of this line of railway is held to be a piece of the
finest engineering work and was engineered by R. W. Jones of Edmonton,
passing as it does through the first range of the Rockies, with a maximum
grade towards the mines of 2.4 percent, or 126 feet in the mile.*

Years later his son Bob, Brig. J. R. B. Jones, of the University Commission relates that his father worked alongside Jack Gregg, working
the survey to Mountain Park . They lived in tents and it was tough
sledding for the hardiest. Bob Jones says Gregg chided his father for
picking pieces of fat out of the stew. The older man said the only time
he ever did that was when he spotted the jack rabbit's eyes peering
out at him from his own bowl.

*The elevation of the colliery is 6,000 feet above sea level which makes
this the highest railway in Canada. The colliery is 2,300 feet above the
level of the coal branch at Coalspur and 3,300 feet above the mainline of
the Grand Trunk Pacific.*

Thornton named the largest mountain towering above the townsite Mount Cheviot. Although it was many times larger its shape re-
minded him of the Cheviot Hills near his former home on the other
side of the Atlantic.

Transversing this natural amphitheater were two small creeks, the
headwaters of the McLeod and a small creek that joined the McLeod
about a mile lower down. One of the new miners had jokingly called
this Thornton Creek and the name became synonymous.

So on this site which compared more than favorably with the
beauty spots of the world two rows of houses swept the basin. More
than 80 dwellings in all, painted white with green facings to harmon-
ize with snowcapped mountains and green spruce and jack pine trees.
The workmen's houses were 28 feet by 28 feet, some with cottage

roofs and the other with gable roofs. Gable roofed houses had large second floor rooms with access gained by an outside staircase. These were designed in such a way that families could take in boarders and still attain complete privacy. The chief officials were provided with handsomely designed six-room bungalows.

In rapid succession a hotel named the Cheviot was built, a large poolroom, a bakery, ice cream parlour and Chinese laundry, and a large general store.

The company although Canadian incorporated, Mountain Park Collieries, Ltd., was financed by mainly British capital. The company controlled the village.

So began an era that was repeated up and down the Coal Branch. As new mines opened, the companies virtually controlled the lives of their workers. They controlled the rents and lives of the citizenry. One former resident looking back says. 'In many cases they were little dictators, but on the whole they ran things well. The men were happy'."

A far more romantic version of this time is contained in the mimeographed sheets.

"Roy and Cam Matthews took a contract to pack in supplies from the end of the steel to the new mine. Miners were driving entries and rooms in what was called the East Side Mine. A tipple was being built in readiness for the coming of the railroad. Thornton knew he could not start the new town until the railroad came so more bunkhouses were erected to house the growing number of employees. Finally the new railroad reached the mine. A small steam plant had been erected with two boilers and a small generator plant. Thornton's plan was to get the mine into production first then expand the development later.

The first shipment of coal was sent to the outside. The coal was taken straight from the mine, dumped down chutes on the tipple into boxcars. These were loaded by hand and although the production was slow, around four to five boxcars a day, it was at least a start and could pay some of the overhead expense of the new mine.

When construction had to be stopped in mid-November, due to cold weather, four houses had been completed. It was a joyous occasion when the first woman stepped off the train to take residence in one of the new houses. She was the wife of Jimmy Graham, a fireman in the boiler house.

Thornton was proud of what had been accomplished in the last two years. On a small rise of ground overlooking the creek that bore his name, he planned to build a house. At night in his small office he drafted plans for the new structure for house. He knew, his wife, being of good birth, would take harshly to this new land and so decided to make his new home an exact replica of the one he had in the old country. He even had a name chosen for it: when it was completed he would call it 'Doves Cottage'."

As more married men were employed with the company, the problem of what to do for a school for the increasing number of children arose. *"So it was decided to use one of the new houses for the time being. The first enrolment consisted of five children, but as more new families*

The tin roofed cabin from which the area gained its name.

— Mrs. Charlie Lee

Near Tin Roof, eight miles south of Mountain Park. Often miners only worked a two or three day work week. Favorite recreation was riding, fishing and hunting.

— Mrs. Charlie Lee photo

arrived each day, the school attendance gradually increased. Two of the larger houses were used as a store and general office. After a larger store was built, this house became the residence of John Price for over twenty years.

The new store was built and run as a co-operative. The miners bought shares for $25. each and elected a board of trustees, who in turn hired a manager to operate the new store. The basement was turned into a beverage room, where the miners could slake their thirst after a hard day in the mine.

35

Plans were drafted for a new hotel and on its completion Harry King became the new manager.

The Big Fire

Two miles from Mountain Park, a timber camp had been started, to supply mine props for the mine. This was owned and operated by Frank Seabolt. On securing a contract from the Mountain Park Collieries, as the new mine was now named, he had sent to Georgia for some of his friends to help him run his new business. On the arrival of Bright Rhodes, Bumpus Woody and Howard Scott, everything had been running smoothly and large piles of cut props were being stacked in the mine yard.

The summer of 1913 had been very dry. The needles of the spruce trees were turning brown from lack of moisture. The water in the muskegs had dried up and all vegetation seemed to have died. To the experienced lumber man this was a very dangerous situation and one to cause alarm. It was on such a morning as this that one of Frank Seabolt's men decided that he would burn some tree cuttings lying around in the bush. The flames ate their way into the dry vegetation and soon the whole forest seemed ablaze. Men were called out of the mine and from the town. They immediately started back fires to try and stop the fierce progress of the fire towards Mountain Park. They fought for two days and nights but it was a losing battle. Some of the men buried a few of their treasured possessions in the ground. Thornton was like a man possessed. All they had worked for was now going to go up in smoke.

When word came that the fire had jumped the railway tracks, Thornton knew that it would only be a matter of hours till they were trapped. He issued orders for everyone to abandon the town and gather at the station where a train would be waiting to take them to safety.

It was a grim-faced group of people who made their way to the station; some were openly crying at having been forced to give up their homes in this way. Suddenly there was a glad cry. "It's raining," and indeed it was. The fire didn't and couldn't fight against driving sheets of rain. Mountain Park was saved."

By now Doves Cottage had been completed but Thornton used it only on his frequent trips to Mountain Park from the head office in Edmonton. As yet his wife had not decided to leave her beloved England and move to this new land."

* * *

Early in 1913, a second paper, The Western Star made its appearance in Edson, and an expected rivalry between its editor, O. Queeber and the Leader sprang up.

The Star notes that Mountain Park mines has erected residences for workmen aggregating a total of over $40,000 and that the coal there has beaten the famous Pittsburgh steam coal in several tests.

Over 500 men were still hard at work making permanent structures of temporary trestles and battening down the railroad bed.

Prospectors swarmed the entire Edson and foothills area and the Feb. 6th issue of the Leader carries notice of 15 different mineral claims in one week!

A sleeping car service between Edson and Edmonton is instituted with "brand new fourteen section tourist cars with large smoking room. Cars are ready for occupancy at 10:00 p.m. at Edson."

The first reading of the new Mines Act is read in the Legislature and after August 13, 1913 it will be illegal to employ women in or about a mine, except in such employment as office work, charring, etc. No boy under the age of sixteen is to be employed underground and the age at which a boy can be employed above the ground has been raised from 12 to 14.

It is also required that the manager of a mine shall visit it in person once in ten days.

At Marlboro, the three quarter million plant for cement gets ready to open, while at Edson, the mayor hires the Alert Detective Agency of Edmonton to 'make a clean-up.' As a result the Edson police chief is placed under arrest and taken to Edmonton for trial.

The entire business block between third and fourth avenue at Edson is consumed by fire, fanned by high wind. Dynamite is used to control its spread and three Edson men are injured in the blast and wind up in the General Hospital in Edmonton.

The mining camps along the Coal Branch have grown in size but in the spring of 1913 there is still no government post offices and mail is delivered by private arrangement. The camps start agitating for better postal service.

At Coalspur N. K. Wade returns to Edson from Mile 37 where he had the contract for painting several houses.

Steel has reached Tollerton and there is already a lively population. The Bulletin notes that Tollerton lies just west of the McLeod River where the big bridge over the river has just been completed. The officials of the Canadian Northern state that steel will be laid as far as the summit this fall and it is expected that the two ends of the steel will be linked up some time next year.

The provincial election is over and the Star says: Only one class of voters were disappointing in their verdict, and they were the miners. In the provincial parliament they have had to date two avowed champions — Chas. O'Brien and the Hon. C. W. Cross. In the Rocky Mountain constituency Mr. O'Brien, the lone socialist in the Alberta legislature was defeated by a Conservative and in the Edson constituency Mr. Cross would have had the same experience if he should have been obliged to rely on the miners for his support. It is a thing that seems incredible; but still the mine workers may not be to blame. It appears that at the mines in the Edson constituency the mine owners had sounded their men and arranged the shifts so that those intending to vote Liberal should be kept from the polls. In the Jasper Collieries at Pocohontas they were hoisted up just at 5 o'clock, with the result that they arrived at the polls five minutes too late to vote."

After 13 issues the Western Star changes its name to The Edson Critic. The Edson Leader when speaking of his contemporary writes, "As a master of repartee he is alone in his class. The fact that nobody can see the point of his wit, wisdom or satire is ample proof that he is mighty deep."

The Edson Grande Prairie Stage Line with Church & Weatherly, prop. announces that it carries mail and passengers to and from Grande Prairie twice per week with a round trip ticket $50.00.

At Mountain Park the excitement of the rails reaching the hamlet was marred by the first death; a 25-year-old Austrian named Joseph Scarritch on July 29, 1913.

Dr. A. B. Wickware testified that he saw the body inside half an hour after the accident and that it had been taken to the hospital tent. He declared death was instantaneous. Bill Grant, miner and Bill Eccleston, fireboss had been working with the deceased in No. 111 Mine East and testified Monobel had been used to fire rocks and Scarritch met his death through a fragment of rock hitting him on the head. Constable Wilson of the RNWMP at Coalspur was required to call six witnesses for the inquest which was held July 31st in the hospital tent. C. W. Watson coroner from Edson attended the inquest and duly presented his bills for the rental of the speeder at $10.00 a trip, both coming and going to the Park. He had ridden the freight to Coalspur and the speeder to the Park. Jury members of this first inquest included Samuel Cain, foreman, John Hallas, John Kelley, Daniel McSherry, Samuel Preston and Walter Young.

In August, Mr. Thornton, the mine manager visited Edson on his way to Edmonton. Among other things he had to hunt up 50 miners

Recent picture of graveyard at Mountain Park.

— Smilanich

Funeral procession at Mountain Park.

to bring with him out to the mines, which owing to the increasing demand for coal are extending operations almost daily.

In August of 1913 Phelan and Shirley complete their work on the coal branch saying it took much longer than expected. They are "pulling out, taking with them the army of men they employed."

The train on the Mountain Park Line was christened the Blue Flea and had from its inception been leased to the GTP.

In September The Tollerton Board of Trade hold a successful dance and "a jolly bunch of Edsonites braved the bumpy corduroy road in order to attend."

At Mountain Park, "seven cars at the Mountain Park Coal mines commenced leaving the mine on their own accord, after going about a half mile down grade they struck Engine 22 and Engine 30 which were more or less damaged also two of the box cars were derailed."

Edmonton papers become more vocal about a road to Grande Prairie and the Edson Critic notes, "for a big brother, Edmonton certainly is some sorehead."

The big GTP station at Edson is built and the Edson Critic notes that "the silly cry of muskeg which was all you could get from many people in the early days might have been avoided by a little more discretion in locating the station."

The Pacific Pass Coal company erects thirty workmen's cottages at Mile 57. There still remains to build the $3,500. residence for the superintendent.

In the fall of 1913 Grande Prairie farmers by the hundreds take advantage of snowfall to do brisk business in Edson.

But the injurious effects of the bad publicity Edson receives begins to take its toll.

The town receives the following letter:

G. M. Phillips, Esq.
Sec-Treas. of the Town of Edson,
Edson, Alberta.

Dear Sir:

We regret we are unable to place your municipal debentures although we have made every endeavor to do so. We have taken the matter up with three of our special clients, and had all arrangments made for the bonds, when they received an adverse report regarding the general conduct of affairs in your Town. It seems there has been considerable publicity given to the municipality, and these reports are copied in a great majority of the Eastern Publications. To show what we refer to we enclose a clipping which speaks for itself.

Regretting the unfortunate circumstances, we are
Yours very truly
The Alberta School Supply Company
per A. F. Carrothers

The Critic indignantly comments:

Here is one visible result of this infamous slander. A debenture issue of $135,000 knocked in the head through the systematic if not organized campaign carried on against Edson.

* * *

1914

Edmonton and district experienced an exceptionally mild January, 1914, with stacks of coal lasting far longer than usual for heating. Many of the mines out of Edmonton operated at fifty per cent production but this was felt little by the Coal Branch mines whose primary customer was the G.T.P.

At Lethbridge miners held their annual convention. Work on Sundays and holidays was condemned and a resolution passed fining an individual $10 and a local $100 for Sunday work. A motion to reduce the salary of the officers was turned down, and an amendment to restrict them to strike benefits only during strike periods met with the same fate.

Statistics for 1913 were published.

The output of the 289 Alberta Coal mines in Alberta during the preceding year, 1913 was 4,306,346 tons with 8,063 employed in production.

28 men had died in mine accidents and 72 mines had been abandoned. Most of these had been opened up for prospecting purposes and closed for a variety of reasons; finances, lack of railway transport, etc., or just temporarily.

By Dec. 31st of 1913, the bulk of the town of Frank had been moved from the danger zone under Turtle Mountain where the disastrous slide had occurred some years earlier.

Twenty-nine of the 289 mines had electricity and there were 4,132 lamps of the Wolf pattern in the province. 836,563 pounds of explosives had been used in the coal mines in 1913 in the province.

The province was divided into six districts for the purpose of holding examinations. First, second and third class certificates were granted to mine managers, overmen and examiners respectively. A board was appointed for each district consisting of a manager and working miner appointed by the Lieutenant-Governor in council and a district inspector appointed by the chief inspector.

The boards in the northern parts of the province were composed as follows: Edmonton: Alex C. Dunn (manager) David Astley (miner); Jasper Park: Edwin Sparrow (manager) David Stone (miner) Elijah Heathcotes district inspector was also a member of each of these boards. Edson Chamberlain stated in January, 1914 that the Edson-Grande Prairie Railway would be commenced in the following year, with the application to be presented to the next sitting of the house and voted on in the fall of 1914.

The Edson Board of Trade took up the cudgel for fair freight rates stating that 'they feel that the G.T.P. in placing the divisional point for computing freight rates at Thornton (eight miles east) places a hardship upon local merchants who have to pay high freight rates from that point. Prairie rates cease at Thornton and mountain rates begin at that point.'

Edson citizens decide to call in an expert to look over the field for oil. Chits were signed by citizens to defray the expenses of said expert and negotiations made for W. H. Williams a well known expert at Coalspur to do the initial prospecting.

Then came June 19, 1914 when a fire damp explosion crushed out the lives of 195 Alberta miners; practically all the male population of Hillcrest was dead. The victims of the mine disaster were laid to rest in the shadow of Turtle Mountain. The mines on the Coal Branch closed down in sympathy and many mourned the death of relatives and friends.

The advent of war put oil development in the area temporarily in the background. The Editor of the Western Leader, L. J. Siljan writes, "Edson has already been hit and hit hard by the war, distant as it may seem. The laying off of men and cancelling of all construction operations by the G.T.P. has come suddenly and proved itself severe. But the coal mines are still working to full capacity and are likely to do so."

Under 'Marlboro Notes' in October, 1914 the correspondent writes, There is a regular famine for houses and several families have to reside in tents. The cement works are now very busy and several large consignments have already been shipped. The works are busy both day and night and the town seems to be in a lively state.' By December, 'The cement plant is about to close down for the winter months. The majority of the workers are married men with families who remain here until the plant reopens.'

1915 and the shadow of war hung over the world. Methodist Minister Rev. Dr. Chown superintendent of Methodist churches urged his ministers to secure the bride's consent to enlistment before performing wedding ceremonies.

The recruiting for the 49th battallion was carried out at various points one of these being Edson.

The new acting editor of the Western Leader wisely editorialized, "Let us not regard the road to Grande Prairie as the predominant feature of our existence."

Shortly after Postmaster Garrioch received official notice that the last mail to be despatched from Edson to Grande Prairie via the Edson Trail would be ended. The mail was to be rerouted from Edmonton through High Prairie.

The Edson Board of Trade asked for the establishment of a permanent Land Office but were told that in view of financial conditions throughout the country this could not be granted. They also urged that the coal from the Pacific Pass and Mountain Park mines be used beyond Rivers as American coal was used past that point, and resolutions were sent to this effect. A further resolution was passed to communicate with Winnipeg and Prince Rupert Boards of Trade urging the extended use of Alberta Coal instead of American coal as this was good for the whole of Canada and especially the west.

The Edmonton Daily Bulletin wrote that there were now 264 mines in operation in the province, with new mines being opened and 45 abandoned the previous year.

Spring winds playfully sent coal cars moving down the coal chute at Edson. The impetus carried the cars three miles along the track and section men out of Yates gave chase in a handcar until they could catch up, climb on and apply the brakes.

Manager M. H. McLeod returned to Winnipeg after a trip by 'gasoline jigger' to Vancouver over the Canadian Northern track. He stated, "I have been over all railway systems that cross the Rocky Mountains in North America and I know what I am talking about when I say that we are going over the lowest grade through the mountains of any of them. In order to bring this about it has been necessary to construct forty tunnels at various points and our bridges are all of massive steel with concrete masonry."

The Editor of the Western Leader laments,

"Edson began with notions of expenditure which were too high for the time and place. The property owners away from Edson were very largely responsible for this inflated view."

"The removal of the Superintendents office to Jasper during this fall is only one more, though a very palpable withdrawal of support to this town.

So far as the Grand Trunk are concerned there seems to be a perpetual tendancy to fall away from what they were already doing and supposed to be doing to make a town here."

. . . and Peter Addison Robb, familiarly known as Baldy, who seemed to have a finger in everything from prospecting to stage coach lines to mining ventures made a bid for the Edson Municipal Council and lost out completely. Vocal Baldy was not popular with his political views, the Conservative party being a minority.

W. P. Hinton became Western Traffic Manager of the G.T.P. with headquarters at Winnipeg. The positions of passenger traffic manager and commissioner of colonization and industries were abolished at time of promotion.

To round out the year of 1915 Ottawa sent Captain Palmer to Jasper to complete arrangements for the erection of buildings to accommodate prisoners presently in the internment camp at Brandon.

"The houses will be of log and there will be a sufficient number to accommodate 200 prisoners as well as quarters for a military guard of 75 with officers quarters, etc.

As soon as these are erected the prisoners will be transferred to their new quarters, where they will be put to work making roads, etc."

Certainly, roads were a prime requisite for the ever increasing population of the west.

1916

1916 was not an auspicious year. By summer a considerable area of land within the Edson town limits had been forfeited for non-payment of taxes.

Gloom further descended on the country when under The Liquor Act of the Province of Alberta Prohibition became law, July 1, 1916. The act stated

WHO CAN ADMINISTER PROFESSIONALLY OR GIVE LIQUOR IN ALBERTA

1. Registered Dentist
2. Registered Veterinary Surgeon (to animals only)
3. Hospital official, hospital nurse, matron or manager (to hospital patients only on physician's prescription).

4. Attendant of a sick person (on prescription from registered physician.)
5. Registered physician in regular practice.
6. Minister of the Gospel (for sacramental purposes only)
7. Occupant in dwelling house only (except to a person under 21 years of age. Liquor can only be administered to a person under 21 years of age on prescription, and by the father, mother, guardian or physician of such person.)

Thus began the era of the ailing animals and the upsurge of the bootlegger, who found himself sought by persons of all station. However the limits of those who could professionally administer liquor were stringent, one pint to dentists, two quarts to physicians, and one gallon to veterinary surgeons.

It was up to the police to enforce the act.

By the summer of 1916 the train was running daily between Mountain Park and Coalspur. The train from Edson to the Branch was on a three day schedule. This greatly expedited the problem of stocking the Co-operative Society at Mountain Park. The Leader notes that "Much interest is being taken in the Co-operative Society and treasurer Henry reports the issue of stock as now rapidly approaching the $5,000 mark. The interest among the foreign speaking population is keen and they are digging up well. Shares were $25. each. The new co-operative store is in full swing under the management of Mr. Bateman. A visit to the store one Saturday night counted five clerks doing their best to wait on twenty customers. Fresh meat, oysters, poultry, green vegetables and fruit were among the attractive dainties in evidence. A visit to the warehouse revealed great piles of Royal Household flour which was selling at $5.00 per cwt, granulated sugar at

Old power house at Mountain Park.

44

First Mountain Park annex.

$9.75 per cwt, potatoes at $1.20 per one and one half bushel sack, all of which speaks well for the co-op movement as a solution of the problem of the high cost of living even in isolated places.

It is also noted that Dr. Wickware was fortunate enough to land a good healthy young sheep within four miles of the camp one day this week. "He is having its handsome head mounted by Mr. Letcher as a souvenir."

Work at Mountain Park was progressing well. In October of 1916 Mountain Park had a snow depth of 18" and the picture theatre was nearing completion. Records show that on Tuesday, October 24th, nineteen cars of coal were loaded.

Another mining venture started in the fall of 1916 when Olliphant-Munson Collieries opened in the East Arm at Mile 40, with the first two cars loaded the last part of October. The mine was incorporated with a capital of $500,000 with offices in Edmonton. Stock was not on the open market. This mine would produce about 100,000 tons of coal in its four-year life span.

At Mountain Park, Mr. Rogers the new hotel manager invited the Library Committee to fit up the library and reading room at the hotel. He proposed to fit up the 'bar' as a gymnasium and make the place a popular rendezvous for the men.

Such were the days of prohibition.

A Mr. McGillis assumed duties as GTP coal inspector residing at house No. 132, while it is noted that Mrs. E. Watson is keeping house for her sons in No. 153 on the hill.

Harry King and John Benson.

General satisfaction was felt by the single men of the camp in the hotel accommodation with a popular comment being said of Mr. Rogers, "He feeds 'em."

Early in 1917 Mrs. George Pike of Mountain Park died. The Western Leader marked the death. "With the exception of a man killed in the early stages of opening the mine this is the first death of an adult that has occurred at Mountain Park since the place was established though two or three children have died there. Mrs. Pike was 67 years of age. Rev. W. H. Irwin of Edson was telephoned for and went up on Friday to conduct the service returning on Saturday after the funeral.

March 10, 1917, Fred Dolenski was killed in a mine accident. Father Louis was telegraphed for and conducted the interment ceremony on Tuesday the 13 March at 4:30 p.m. That afternoon the mines lay idle giving an opportunity to the men to pay their last respects to their fellow miner. Mr. Dolenski left a widow and two little children with a third child born the following month.

CHAPTER FOUR

Father Louis

As the Coal Branch grew the dioceses of Edson and Edmonton expanded to include the growing camps. Perhaps the best known of these wonderful and forbearing ministers and priests was Father Louis and a tribute written many years later explains in part their work.

'A Tribute to Father Louis'

HE HAS PREACHED HIS LAST SERMON

by J. W. Horan (A Non-Catholic)

The beloved Father Louis Culerier, O.M.I., has preached his last sermon. Never again will we see him picking his way across the railroad ties of the Coal Branch. Never again will we send for him in our hour of need.

It is doubtful if any other individual missionary was held in such high esteem as this "modern day Saint." Someday, his name will rank with those of Father Lacombe, Father Leduc and Bishop Grandin. I have known hundreds of priests in my time. Some were pious, some were generous and others were lovable. But Father Louis was everything a human being could possibly be. It is small wonder then that he will be missed and mourned by every christian from Edmonton to Prince George, B.C.

Anyone who was in that vicinity between the years 1914–1931 will remember seeing Father Louis trudging along the railway tracks with his heavy pack strapped to his back. His tired, kindly face was always wreathed in smiles. He never enquired of a man "to which church do you belong?" He never asked for alms. He didn't have to. When he built his churches at Cadomin, Luscar, Mountain Park, Brule, Poco-

47

"Father Louis" picks up a ride from one mining camp to another on the Alberta Coal Branch. Although it was technically against railroad rules, the railway speeders and their operators often served as unofficial "bus drivers" on the tracks.

(Giovinazzo)

hontas and Jasper, the citizens of those towns came forth and helped without being solicited. They would do anything for the "Old Priest" as they affectionately called him. In return, he would do anything for them. When the Coal Branch was reeling under the effects of the flu epidemic in 1918, Father Louis walked all the way from Mountain Park to Mile 33, carrying a bottle of rum for the stricken men at the sawmill. He said that hot rum was the only medicine he knew of that would break the flu. It was a very cold night, but the old priest didn't mind. He had a job to do, and he did it. Three days later Bill Simmonds and his partners were back on the job.

Another time Harry King of the Mountain Park Hotel gave Father Louis a Christmas cake, beautifully iced and decorated. As he handed the cake to the priest, he said, "Now, Father Louis, this cake is for you. If you give it away to anybody I'll never let you come inside this hotel again." Of course Harry King was joking, but Father Louis didn't know it. A few hours later, Father Louis walked slowly up the steps of the hotel. Harry King was waiting for him.

"Well, Father Louis, how did you like the cake?" he asked.

Father Louis held his head in shame. "Mr. King," he said, "I have a confession to make. Mrs. So-and-so, whose husband is in the hospital needed that cake far more than I did. She has five little children to feed. Those children are hungry and this is Christmas Eve."

Tears filled the eyes of Harry King. Placing his hand on Father Louis shoulder, he said, "Father Louis, I'm not a Catholic and I don't believe in saints, but, if there is such a thing, you're it." The good deed soon became a topic of the little mining settlement, and an hour afterwards, the family of the sick miner was deluged with Christmas gifts.

Whenever a man was injured in the mines, Father Louis was notified. No matter where he was, he hastened to the scene of the accident.

Rev. Louis Culerier, O.M.I. who was known as the "patron saint" of the mining villages. In 1910 he visited mines to McBride, B.C. and from 1913 to 1931 he was a constant visitor to the Alberta Coal Branch and walked the railroad ties to reach the mining camps. Pictured with him are Violonda and Victoria Giovinazzo.

If the man was still in the mine, Father Louis descended into the workings in the bowels of the earth. Often he was never told who the unfortunate victim was. It didn't matter to Father Louis. They needed him, and he administered to them.

In 1914, Father Louis shared the Edson directorate with Father Beaudry, O.M.I. Father Beaudry looked after the district between Edson and Lac Ste. Anne, and Father Louis travelled as far west as Prince George, B.C., stopping at any section house or trapper's cabin whenever he thought or knew that a family wished to see him. He walked all the way. Willow River and McBride had Sunday services, McBride once a month, and Willow River, once in three months. Jasper was a Hudson's Bay Co. post in those days. The Coal Branch was being prospected and explored. Lovett was a leading mining community. Luscar was hardly thought of at the time by the people although Gregg had a stubborn desire to put it on the map. There was no Cadomin, but Mountain Park was a growing mining village. Yellowhead Mine was a busy place, served out of Coalspur by a spurline.

There were no missionaries along the "Branch" and Father Louis decided to visit the miners and their families. He was welcomed with open arms by everyone. Children were baptized, the dead were buried, and the Word of God was preached in tents, houses and bunkhouses by the obliging Oblate Father. However, the strain of such an enormous obligation began to tell on the priest, and in 1916 he paid a farewell visit to McBride. He had made his last 600 mile round trip to that little mountain divisional point.

Yes, there are many who will remember these things about Father Louis and when they read this, they will say as I do:

Kindly old preacher, the friend of mankind
You're the saint of the Coal Branch, 'tis true,
Be it rich man or poor man, to you they're the same,
Father Louis, many blessings to you.

In the heat of the summer, or amid winter snow
Never once did you refust to call,
Be it Luscar or Lovett, you'd get there somehow;
Father Louis, you're king of them all.

From the Park down to Edmonton, any place on the Branch,
Ne'er a bad word is spoken of you,
You are loved by them all, man woman and child,
Father Louis, you're one of the few.

With the Host and the wine you would run till you dropped,
When wanted in one of the towns;
For someone is dying they are needing your help,
Father Louis, you'll wear a Saint's crown.

But it's lonely without you, you counsel no more,
Though your memory forever will stay,
There are glories in Heaven for you and your kind
Father Louis, the Saint of the Branch.

Father Louis was born at Soulitre in the diocese of Le Mans in France, Sept. 22, 1873. After preliminary studies in his home land, he came to Canada in 1893 and entered the Oblate novitiate at Lachine, Que. He made his theological studies at Ottawa and was ordained to the priesthood there on June 12, 1897.

* * *

More and more, the country began to feel the pinch of war, in the year of 1917. Mines were opened, went bankrupt and closed, or sold out to larger concerns.

Mountain Park steadily producing, erected a new mine managers office near the lamp house. Along with a new hoist tracks were extended to make room for eight or ten additional cars of coal.

Mark Rogers of the Cheviot Hotel provided his own bulwark against rising costs and went off to buy a carload of stock which would include dairy cows, swine and chickens and ponies for the use of summer tourists.

The spring of 1917 saw the reopening of the Yellowhead Mine.

The Leader writes: Sixty men engaged on development and opening up the burned workings at the Yellowhead Mine on the Coal

Branch now have the property in No. 1 condition, and the outlook for a heavy production is very bright. A fire in the mine two years ago wrecked it pretty badly, and although it was the oldest mine in the camp it lay idle until a few months ago when the present management, undertook to put it on a shipping basis.

At Port Mann an experimental plant was built to determine whether the coal at Brule was suitable for coke making.

In April the mineworkers organized the first local of mineworkers on the Coal Branch. Steve Begilie international organizer of the United Mineworkers visited the camp, and the paper reports:

The Mountain Park local starts with a membership of 262 which includes almost all the working miners in the camp. A large percentage of these, however, were already members of the organization holding cards in locals in the south country of the lignite fields.

There is no question of scale involved at Mountain Park, as the scale there is approximately the same at all times as in the south country and whatever settlement is reached in the Crow will undoubtedly be construed to apply in the organized camps of Brule and Mountain Park. The men and the management have always gotten along remarkably well at Mountain Park, and the outlook is for a very strong union and a permanent harmonious understanding.

Pocohontas, Lovett and the other camps along the Coal Branch will be organized in the near future.

* * *

The Yellowhead mine was not to operate long before disaster struck. The mine manager, Donald McKay, 41, was killed by a fall of coal, April 11, 1917. Peter Raimondo testified that a piece of coal weighing about one and a half tons hit the manager while the manager had been in a crouching position.

* * *

The Coal Branch and Edson's politics were largely Liberal with P. A. Baldy Robb heading the Conservative opposition. At a rally in Mountain Park in April Hon. O. C. W. Cross was the foremost speaker. Mr. Cross, J. W. Adair, J. A. MacKinnon and S. G. Bawden were conducted to Mountain Park from Edson by speeder driven by the Chief Mechanic, of the G.T.P. there, A. Mahon.

The Western Leader says of the trip: To reach there a little ahead of the appointed hour the party left Edson on the speeder at 2:00 p.m. and covered the 76 miles in three hours and 28 minutes, which, while not a record on the Coal Branch, was some speed considering the meterological conditions of snow and wind which constituted almost a blizzard.

Over 300 people attended the rally with Joseph Ciciarelli interpreting the remarks of the speakers into Italian.

The 1917 Cross Club of Mountain Park had the following executive: President: James Darbyshire; Vice-President: P. A. McNaughton, Secretary: Alberta Bastion, Treasurer: Mrs. A. Bastion. Executive: M. Brobosky; W. Ashton; A. Longhurst; J. Mossotti; M. C. Robers; T. Fishwick; J. Price; T. C. Pridmore; Joe Berland; A. Soderlind; Wong Hughes; J. S. Thompson; D. S. Macdonald; L. Laboir, J. Fanscescutti, W. Boise, Mike Vitaly; Mike Furnich; P. Barruzini; J. Porwock, E. Atherton; H. Crowder; L. Chase; W. Morgan; H. Arnell; W. Thick; B. Ingman; Kit Byers; W. Kehoe; Sid Berth; W. Maddison; M. Brown; J. Bulo; H. Natta; P. Preame, Ed Woods, Dr. Wickshire.

The Ladies Cross Club were active also headed by their president Mrs. Crowder. The executive included: Mrs. Maddison; Mrs. Mossottic; Mrs. Ciciarelli; Mrs. Cutti; Mrs. Longhurst; Mrs. Atherton; Mrs. Mullen; Mrs. Rogers; Mrs. Price; Mrs. Francis; Mrs. Falkner; Mrs. Morgan, Miss Walsh and Mrs. Vojtechuck.

* * *

Politicking of another nature spread when southern mines throughout Alberta went out on strike. Mountain Park Local, No. 18, United Mine Workers of America met to discuss the situation.

"The trouble arises over the wage scale. When, some four months ago, the miners of District 18 went out for an advance an increase of 15 per cent was granted them in the form of a war bonus. This increase was made to the employees of the southern mines having agreements, but automatically extended to the northern field. At the expiration of the agreement in April, officers of the union and representatives of the coal mine operators association went into conference with the purpose of making a new agreement. After six weeks, in which very little was accomplished, the same scale, approximately as that in force before was submitted with the difference that the 15 per cent, which had heretofore been war bonus was put in the form of regular wages. The agreement, upon being submitted to the men, was almost unanimously turned down and the southern miners went out. Nordegg, on the CN Branch quickly followed and at the latter end of last week, Brule on the main line, went out.

The southern demand is for a 30 per cent increase over the old scale, which the men contend, in view of the present high cost of living, and the recent advances in coal prices is by no means an unreasonable demand."

Mountain Park struck in sympathy.

A peculiar side-light of the strike, (the beginning of many disputes) was the displacement of the miners from the company's quarters to tents. Alex Valla, a miner who had come from Poland to Mountain Park in 1913 commented on the situation in a tape recorded by Andy den Otter. Mr. Valla said the single men moved to tents by Miner's Head and lived in the tents for the duration of the strike. The company continued to supply the men with groceries and $5 a week was charged against each man. This sum would be taken off the cheques when the dispute was settled and the men returned to work and their regular living quarters.

* * *

CHAPTER FIVE

The Railroads Become Bankrupt

Citizens of Edson were outraged. With all the promises that had been made and broken since the town's inception, this latest event had to be a disaster. The Federal government wanted to tear up the railroad track!

From Ottawa there arrived an engineer named Ferguson sent out by the Railway Commission.

He was met at the Edson station by a delegation headed by Mayor H. A. Switzer, Ex-Mayor Hope, Councillors Laycock, Jellis and Fyfe, and Ex councillor Fulmer. Secretary of the Municipality Morgan and Treasurer Tucker were there armed with facts and figures comparing settlement and values of the G.T.P. and the C.N.R.

Mr. Ferguson made it plain that his instructions were to find three hundred miles of steel for the western front.

The representatives of Edson made it plain that the people of this country were prepared to make any sacrifice necessary in behalf of the empire, but contended that where two roads lay so closely parallel, both running from the same point to the same point, a choice should be made in such manner as to be least harmful to the country, pointing out that the settlement lay almost exclusively along the G.T.P. and that the G.T.P. had the necessary facilities at Edson for handling the divisional work whereas the C.N.R. at Tollerton was very poorly equipped.

Mr. Ferguson spoke of the steel of the two lines stating:

That there is a difference in the 'section' of the Grand Trunk Pacific and the Canadian Northern steel, that the particular character of steel used on the Grand Trunk Pacific is the character of steel being used on the western front, in the battle area much of the steel laying must be done in the dark where a mix-up about the steel might precipitate a disaster, and that, therefore, it is the Grand Trunk steel rather than the Canadian Northern that must come up if the Dominion is to furnish the Imperial authorities with the three hundred miles required at once in France.

Local railroaders stated that the contention that there is a difference in steel is absolutely without foundation; that the steel is identically the same — 80 pound Algoma — and interchangeable.

A rather strange side-light upon the thing was the admission by Mr. Ferguson, that up until the time of his arrival in Edmonton he had no knowledge of the extent of the coal mining industry in the Edson district, and that the Railway Commission had, as far as he knew, no data upon this industry. From his admission it appeared the Railway Commission was totally unaware that two trainloads of coal a day, about fifty cars was being shipped over the G.T.P.

The matter was taken up by the Edson Board of Trade who appealed to merchants and settlers along the line, from whom a flood of telegrams was sent to Ottawa.

Deluged with figures, Engineer Ferguson promised after he had come to understand the figures that he would recommend the commission to move the C.N.R. steel from the C.N.R. to the G.T.P. roadbed on that section between Chip Lake and the intersection of the two roads just west of Ansell, thereby leaving Edson and the population section along the G.T.P. still on a railway line, and that for the rest of it the C.N.R. would be used by both roads all the way from Entwistle to Resplendent.

Mr. Ferguson visited Tollerton and looking at the roundhouse facilities there realized that Edson certainly did have the better facility.

He made the recommendation and reported he was prepared to go ahead immediately on receipt of orders ripping up the steel from the G.T.P. Roadbed.

By telegram on May 19, 1917, Ottawa contacted the Edson Town Secretary.

MILITARY NECESSITY COMPELS US TO TAKE TWO HUNDRED MILES OF GRAND TRUNK PACIFIC RAIL IN YELLOWHEAD PASS. WE ARE ARRANGING NEW LINE, USING CANADIAN NORTHERN RAILS, LAYING PARTLY ON ONE ROADBED PARTLY ON THE OTHER SO AS TO LINK UP ALL TOWNS COAL BRANCHES AND INDUSTRIES. YOU SHOULD NOT, THEREFORE BE SERIOUSLY INCONVENIENCED.

F. COCHRANE

The Town of Edson, still puzzled about the alleged difference in steel let out a collective sigh of relief.

* * *

The format of the newspaper was changed and July 6, 1917 a new masthead read The Edson Herald.

W. J. Keith McKay, General Superintendent of the Yellowhead Coal Co. at Coalspur decided to enlist in the overseas force and the whole community turned out to say good-bye.

While prohibition was in force the Herald duly ran a headline which read 'Lots of Liquor on the Branch'.

The article notes that "Corporal McLean of the Provincial Police stationed at Edson, accompanied by Inspector McBrayne, Chief Detective of the Alberta Police left for points on the Coal Branch on Sunday last, and on the afternoon took possession of seven barrels of bottled whisky at the station of Mountain Park consigned to Mark Rogers and which had been reshipped from Yellowhead."

We can surmise that the so-called gymnasium in the revamped bar of the hotel was not entirely used for gymnastics.

The two proceeded to Lovett on the following day and seized two boxes of liquor, one containing one dozen bottles of brandy and the other five gallons of rye whiskey. Then it was back to Coalspur and then Edson.

Whether the police ever realized that on the very train in which they travelled, sympathetic engineers signalled the countryside with their whistles which served a warning that a liquor search was on, is a point much debated.

The above two cases were heard before Mr. Henderson, Justice of the Peace on the following day at Mile 40 where each was fined $10 and $20 respectively.

Such was prohibiton.

* * *

The unknown author winds up his short history of Mountain Park with:

"If a dance was not in progress for a Saturday night, house parties were usually arranged. No invitations were necessary; a person could just walk in and make himself at home. An accordian player was nearly always in attendance. These impromptu house parties used to last all week-end, usually till Monday morning when the miners would have to call a halt to these activities and ready themselves for another week of work.

In the year 1917, Thornton committed suicide in a hotel room in Edmonton. This came as a shock to the many people who liked and respected him; no one seemed to know why he had done such a thing. Dove's Cottage, the home he had worked so hard on, was now used as a school for the ever increasing number of children.

A happier event to the people of Mountain Park was the beginning of a new mine, eight miles lower down the valley. This new town would be called Cadomin. From all reports this was to be a large mine, with many employees. The residents of Mountain Park knew that with the building of the new town they would not seem so far from civilization and friendly activities between the two places would surely come."

The Edson-Jasper Signal[1] states that the Cadomin mine was located by an Englishman by the name of Cause. The name came about through a contraction of the developing company, Canadian Dominion Mine and was named Cadomin by the Cadomin Coal Company's first president, F. L. Hammond.

This centre was destined to become the largest camp on the Alberta Coal Branch and was to be its commercial centre.

1918 is probably best remembered on the Coal Branch for the flu epidemic which raged throughout each camp leaving its mark on the populace. Fr. Louis tirelessly plodded the track, sharing his lunch with other walkers he met enroute. Alex Valla in his taped interview said he remembered the epidemic well and suffered with it himself but would not trust himself to be ministered by others. He stayed in the house he shared with three other miners. Other patients were carried to the 'picture show hall' where beds had been made up. Dr. Wickware and his voluntary staff strove to make them as comfortable as possible. Liquor was by prescription only. The man who ran the drugstore, name of Richards, had little on his shelves besides the gum for the children and a few patent medicines, but always carried an ample supply of liquor, some of it bona fide, some of it moonshine.

Miners relax under the stairs of the Mountain Park Hotel annex.

"Sometimes when Richard had imbibed in his own cures superfluously he would retreat to his hotel bedroom and amuse himself by taking potshots at the passing populace with an air rifle."

In 1918 the Pacific Pass Colliery at Lovett employed 90 miners and produced 700 tons daily.

Closer down the line this was the year that Herman Tunke brought his bride of a year to the Yellowhead Mine at Coalspur. His father, also named Herman came too as did his mother, and Fred Tunke and

---

[1] See Chapter on 'Cadomin' where original discovery is disputed.

Harry Kramer. The young Tunkes lived in "a lovely log house" that cost them $1 a month, the more expensive lumber houses renting at $5.00 a month. Here her daughter Ella was born with Dr. McDonald in attendance at the log house.

Mrs. Tunke remembers that Mr. Maxwell had the General Store, and that a Mr. Chestick was the water man who delivered water twice a week.

A Mr. Fahlbacker worked in the mine and trapped on the side, she says. This man was one of several on the Coal Branch who disappeared and whose bodies were never identified.

The whole clan decided to move to the Olliphant mine at Mile 40 and settled in tents until houses could be built.

They were not there long when one day, the young blacksmith came shouting down the track shouting a warning, "Run, the powder house is going to blow. Take your baby and go."

Mrs. Tunke says "I run with my baby, you bet I did. Everybody ran." We were all running down the track. Suddenly the blacksmith stopped and said he had left his bankbook. He was European and had been saving to bring his family over. He ran back to get his bankbook and was killed, as was the general manager. I often think of that. The poor blacksmith could have got his money, he didn't need his bankbook." Although the powder house blew up the men working in the mine were unaffected.

After this the group moved back to Coalspur. "My mother-in-law never got over that explosion. She nagged at the men until they finally quit and we all went farming at Three Hills. Now a resident of Edson Mrs. Tunke talks of the Coal Branch and says, "We just spent a year there, but I really loved the life there."

On the main line to Jasper, the Jasper Park Collieries had increased production from 361,000 tons in 1916 to 550,000 tons in 1917 and 611,000 in 1918. The Edmonton Daily Bulletin notes optimistically that 'The Jasper Park coal field is large enough and has enough coal in sight to itself supply the Prairie West for all time'.

The paper also notes that by the Mine Owner's Act a tax of five cents a ton would be levied 'upon each ton of coal removed from his mine premises, the tax to be payable the first day of each month'.

While Cadomin flourished, smaller mine enterprises that had started faltered. In 1918 an operation at Foothills started with a modest initial capital investment of $300,000 and forged ahead steadily.

The effects of the war were fully felt in Edson. The Edson newspaper says it was 'an unmixed blessing because it put a stop to real estate wild-catting — a catastrophe because it tied up capital and prevented development. All public improvements that were not absolutely necessary were stopped, and many people lost faith and moved on'.

The close of the war found two great Canadian railway systems bankrupt, The Canadian Northern and the Grand Trunk Pacific. The

Canadian Government had guaranteed their bonds and in order to keep Canada's credit good was compelled to take over the roads. This necessitated the formation of one great government owned railway system. Wherever these two lines were in competition the equipment that was not needed was moved and the material used to extend the system in other parts. And so the Canadian National Railway came to be.

More directly, the CNR had its origin in the Canadian National Railways Act of 1919. This Act created the Canadian National Railway Company and became the original source of the company's powers. In due course, there were brought under unified management and operation five major railway enterprises, private and public which had commenced operation in this order: the Grand Trunk, the Intercolonial, the Canadian Northern, The National Transcontinental and the Grand Trunk Pacific.

The Department of Education encouraged adult education in the mining centres by giving financial assistance to local school boards. Lovett opened a night-school in 1915 and taught mining technology, English and Mathematics. In 1920 the program moved to Mountain Park where twenty miners enrolled in the English classes and nine in the mining course.[1]

At first the Pacific Pass Company exploited coal from the Silkstone seam on the southwest side of the valley of the Lovett River. Tunnels were driven in both directions along the strike of the anticline. To the southeast a rock wall was encountered, and to the northwest fire started in the mine workings. The only alternative was to try working the Mynheer seam on the northeast side of the River. This proved to be unsatisfactory, and operations ceased in 1920.[2]

Mercoal Mine

58

But as Lovett closed, Mercoal opened. The mine at Mile 5 was opened by Nick Gurvich of Prince Rupert; a shaft was sunk and the hard coal put on the market. Mr. Gurvich associated himself with Mr. J. G. Scott of Prince Rupert, and a number of other businessmen of that City. They incorporated as the McLeod River Hard Coal Company and for the next four years struggled along with a high quality coal but very inadequate resources. Finally in 1924 the mine was sold to the Saunders Ridge Coal Company, Limited which installed a complete power plant and modern machinery and began to develop a real mark for the Coal which had by this time attained a splendid reputation.

R. W. Jones was chief engineer of the spur into Luscar. He knew and worked with the original Luscar owner, the father of Col. Sir Harold Mitchell, the President of Luscar Ltd. as did another member of Bob Jones survey party, Bruce Purdy who retired in Edmonton.

Mr. Purdy, an instrument man on the survey, says he just remembers how tough it was laying out a railway the five miles from Leyland up to Luscar on a three percent grade.

In 1921 an important spur line was built from Leyland station near Cadomin to Luscar a distance of five miles. Staked by Gregg many years before this mine operated under the name of Luscar Collieries Ltd. Legend has it that Gregg received $3,000 for this stake which he had sold many years before development began.

The mining camp of Cadomin in the early twenties. This camp became the largest on the Alberta Coal Branch and was the commercial centre. It was also the only camp that had a government liquor vendor.   — Mrs. Charlie Lee

At Luscar the mine was pinched into a narrow valley formed by Luscar Creek, and the houses stood close by perched on the surrounding uplands. In and around Mercoal there was much swampy land

[1]The Social Life of a Mining Community — The Coal Branch, Andy A. den Otter.

[2]The Historical Geography of the Coal Branch by David Lake.

Luscar

Foothills store and Station.

near the creeks which was not drained because of the cost involved. Instead settlement tended to locate on the more rolling uplands. At Mile 33, the Lakeside Coal Company built most of its company town along the tortuous course of the Embarras River in its narrow valley. At Sterco, Coal Valley and Foothills there was also much undulating terrain. Mountain Park nestled at 5825 feet above sea level in a picturesque basin, had the most scenic site of any settlement in the region.[3]

Cadomin was located beside the McLeod River on a fairly broad, gravel-covered floodplain.

In the spring of 1923 the McLeod River went on a rampage. Mrs. Edward McAdams woke at 3:00 a.m. to find water swirling round her bed. The house was only saved from floating away by being anchored to some nearby trees until the waters abated when it was moved

[3] David Lake

Foothills

to a safer location. Coalspur was an important railroad centre and was the headquarters of the Brazeau Forest Reserve. Its location at the junction of the Lovett and Mountain Park branch lines of the CNR well suited the town for serving these functions. A roundhouse and railroad sheds were used to repair railroad cars and engines. Because trains bound for the East Arm, West Arm or Bickerdike always stopped at Coalspur, the hotel and pool hall were busy places. This business was not profoundly affected by the closure of the Yellowhead mine in 1922 since the mine had been idle much of the time during its existence.

Catholic Church — Mountain Park.

The mine had a fire which they had been unsuccessfully trying to combat. An explosion in which three men met their deaths — ended its production days.

File No. 1705 of The Alberta Provincial Police reads:

On Monday, November 27, 1922, William Shaw, E. Irvor Roberts and Hiram Davies met their death in the Yellowhead Mine at Coalspur. The trio were inspecting the mine to ascertain if it was safe for men to carry on their fire fighting operations. A fire had been in progress for some time in No. 3 and help from other points on the Branch had been solicited to fight the fire.

July 20, 1920. On top of Mt. Cheviot. Harry Hilton, Jake Lee, Cam Matthews.
— Photo by Charlie Lee

Dr. P. A. MacDonald and Dr. G. Minorgan examined the men in the boiler room and spent several hours applying the Pulmotor. The men were also given strychnine. The medical report of Dr. Minorgan stated, "In my opinion death in all cases was the result of gas poisoning, probably carbon monoxide. The faces kept their colour which is the chief sign of carbon monoxide poisoning. Carbon monoxide as far as I understand stops the circulation immediately and kills almost instantly. I believe all the deceased were dead when brought out of the mine."

Const. C. A. McElroy of the Alberta Provincial Police arranged for an inquest to be held in the hospital and schoolroom on Nov. 28, 1922.

Twenty-one men took part in the inquest heard by jurymen Herbert Harper, Mike Ferguson, James Smith, George Mills and McDermid Byrrell.

Allen and Elsie Godby, Tex and Janie Byers, 1924.

The Alberta Provincial Police served the province from 1917 to 1932 but throughout the province the RCMP also governed and an early posting was made by the RCMP at Cadomin.

By the middle twenties Cadomin was such a flourishing point it threatened to exceed Edson. Men worked steadily there, while at Mountain Park Vic Riendeau (who died in retirement at Edson, July 1970) in his taped interview says, "Between 1920 and 1925 you could count the men on our fingers that would make $2,000 per year." At Cadomin where they worked on contract Alex Valla says "they made 56¢ a ton and many men made up to $4,000 per year." They both agreed that for a long time Luscar was one of the worst mines in Canada for lack of work.

Mac's chickens and Mike Vukelich in Mountain Park.

Sports day at Mountain Park in the twenties.

— Mrs. Charlie Lee

By this time a small hospital had been built at Mountain Park, one room for women, one room for men, with a dispensary and living quarters for the nurse. The nurse owned one of the two pianos in the Park, the other was in the community hall which doubled as the picture theatre. The hall had been built by the company. Rent was $2.00 and it was open for the use of all community functions, union and church meetings.

Ball team at Mountain Park. Included in line-up are Tiny Turner, Don McKinnon, Supt. Scott, Tex Byers.

By the middle twenties Cadomin had established itself as the leading centre of the Coal Branch. It's population exceeded that of Mountain Park.

Residents of the three camps saved their money and made periodic trips back to the 'old country'.

This decade saw the beginning of a fierce sports rivalry between Luscar, Mountain Park and Cadomin.

The Lovett Branch served many mines, Bryan, Lakeside, Coalspur, Coal Valley, Foothills, Melrose, Confederation and Superba. Although these two branches were not that far apart geographically they had quite separate identities. Coalspur and Mercoal were again set into a different niche. This difference only became 'togetherness' when residents were 'out' of the Coal Branch altogether.

Cadomin prided itself on having one of the most modern camps in the province.

Ball field — Mountain Park.

The twenties was an era when picnics drew entire camps. The picnics invariably had one or two kegs of beer and Alex Valla says, "The women drank as much as the men." Everyone chipped in $1.25 for the beer.

At Mountain Park, Harry King, manager of the Cheviot Hotel supplied two kegs of beer and the entire population turned out to clear a baseball field. Vic Riendeau said that Billy Owen made a rig with four horses that chewed up brush, men banded together rolling the big rocks and the women and kids picked up the little rocks. "We had a baseball field in one day, a Sunday."

Vic said he remembered a game when the superintendents of two mines, McMillan at Cadomin and Scott at Luscar "started a game at 3:00 and called it because of darkness at 10:00 p.m."

Each camp had a community hall and a dance drew participants from every camp. Vic talks of the young men who used to run down the tracks to Cadomin for a dance and dance all night, then return to Mountain Park. "It would take us an hour and a half to run down — it was a long way coming back. Eight miles."

The dances were many times formal affairs, "Lots of the men would buy their wives dresses that would be fit for affairs at the Macdonald Hotel."[4]

Because of the non-existence of roads, horses were the mode of transportation, and almost every family owned at least one horse. Most families owned more than one.

Situated in an area that boasted some of the finest big game hunting in the country, big game hunters came from all over the continent and were outfitted by one of the outfitters that settled on each point on the Coal Branch.

Tex Byers of Mountain Park periodically left his barber's chair and headed out with a party of hunters.

Mountain Park on train day, 1925.

Futher down the line Baldy Robb took groups out too. Baldy, an intrepid adventurer had his hand in a dozen enterprises. Cam Matthews, another guide and outfitter says of Mr. Robb, "Baldy used to

[4] A leading Edmonton hotel.

be a great friend of Gentleman Jim who prospected out of Mercoal for tén or twelve years all along the base of the Mountains. There's a falls higher than Niagara south of this branch."

Len Stevens roomed with Baldy for a period of time and maintained that Baldy was a delightful chap to talk to, but you had to be very careful when doing business with him. 'Money didn't mean a thing to him. Baldy was a curious fellow and said there were only two books worth reading, Hansard and the Bible!' Baldy was always active politically and "did some time for padding the voter's lists." Baldy always made sure that everyone in his party got their quota of big game. He would stand back of them and fire precisely at the same time to ensure it. "He was a good companion."

Horses would be set free to forage for themselves but hay would be imported and much of this hay came from Roy Bromm's Lone Star Ranch just out of Bickerdike. Roy sold hay to the mines too and 'got paid 6 or 8¢ a bundle, which wasn't bad pay. The biggest problem was getting it there.'

Roy had his origin in Ohio and left home when he followed the harvest north through the states ending at Provost, Alta. He continued on to Lac Ste. Anne, a thriving trading settlement, then onto Edson and '35 on the Grande Prairie Trail. "We spent the winter without a stove and baked our bannock on a makeshift fireplace."

Roy worked in Edson and on the B & B, finally purchasing the farm, "two quarters, 80 acres cleared when I bought it. Then our troubles began. There were no roads, just a trail to Bickerdike. We would haul hay to Bickerdike for transport to the mines. A trail angling across country, across muskeg, and upset, upset, and upset again. The mosquitos were so thick you'd swipe at your face and there would be blood all over. You couldn't get a rack through the trail from our house to the railroad at first, so we would float it down the river. Later we did more than our share digging ditches, putting in culverts. We finally got paid for a quarter of mile road we'd put in from the Department of Highways."

* * *

Prohibition[5] was a belt blow to the miners who sweated in the coal seams below ground.

The railroaders didn't like it either for that matter and the most popular figure on the branch was the bootlegger. In fact his stuff was so good it even went for export down the main line.

As long as there was no highway he was never caught. If the 'law' was on the 'mixed' a signal went out and a fire got damped out somewhere in the bush. Some say it was a train whistle that sounded a warning but it was never proven. Others said the law was tolerant in the circumstances peculiar to the Coal Branch.

If the law was tolerant, not so the magistrate at Edson. He was wise to railroad ways. The magistrate was also the locomotive foreman —

[5] CNR Public Relations – Edmonton

Jock Thompson. His favorite verdict was "thir-r-r-ty dollars or thir-r-r-ty days."[6]

The magistrate would travel often to various points on the Branch listening to cases in school rooms, halls or even in hotel lobbies.[6] Always the difficulty was in arranging to get there at a given time, for court hearings or for accidents. Later many cases were heard in Edson.

An instance of the difficulty of travelling is made in a report of Coronor F. A. Laycock listed in the A.P.P. files:

"Some time after I sent in an account in respect of Ilke Semkovich deceased on which there was a charge of $4.50 for use of speeder by way of mileage, I received the enclosed account from the Collieries Company, I wrote in reply saying that I paid $4.50 to the men asking if the $5.50 was additional. When I was at Luscar last week they gave me the account again and said that it was additional; the men who took me claiming that staying all night at Mountain Park took practically all the $4.50 I paid them. I am therefore adding this expense to the above case though it should really have gone on the Semkovich case at Luscar. $10.00 may seem a good deal for travelling sixteen miles but one could not have travelled with horses for $20.00 and I was glad there were two men there because it took them both to keep the speeder going. I might otherwise have been in the wilderness until morning.

Signed F. U. Laycock.

One of the banes of police work, and accident coverage was collecting transportation fees and the endless correspondence that went into same. Many of the A.P.P. reports start off similar to the one below of T. A. Lees, Constable, A.P.P. Coalspur Detachment, Dec. 16, 1925.

At 3:30 p.m. on Tuesday, December 15, 1925 I left Coalspur by speeder escorting the above named for Preliminary Hearing . . . . .

Much of the police work entailed the pursuit of bootleggers and in this respect only, the majority of residents conspired against the law as it stood. Prohibition was not a successful affair anywhere, and certainly not on the Coal Branch. The King of the Bootleggers was a man named Jack L'Heureux better known as Jack the Frog.[7] Jack the Frog did his share of hunting and trapping but his main source of income was his moonshine, and long after prohibition was repealed his wares were still a highly sought commodity.[8]

Len Stevens says of Jack the Frog, "He was a Californian of French extraction. I believe he was up there in the early days of railroad construction. The police came down to Embarras, the station before you get to Robb and pinched him. The trainmen put the still off the train about a mile away so he could get it".

Whether that particular charge could be carried through without the 'evidence' cannot be ascertained.

[6] See John Kapteyn's biography.
[7] See Mike Lukach biography.
[8] My husband James C. Ross, a CNR fireman on the Coal Branch brought a bottle of Jack the Frog's moonshine home in Dec. '49. I remember it being as clear as water and although I have never tasted diesel fuel, I would imagine it similar.

Cam Matthews who years later owned the store in Coalspur says in his taped interview, "Jack the Frog was a gentleman moonshiner. Many a time he'd sell $5 worth of moonshine and give $5 worth of groceries to the poor."

* * *

A pack train near the Southesk.

— Mrs. Charlie Lee

One of, if not the first radios in Mountain Park was owned by Charlie Lee and Allan Godby. Here Mountain Park residents gather to listen to the latest news.

— Mrs. Charlie Lee

Three female residents of Mountain Park on "train day" at Mountain Park. The arrival of the train Monday, Wednesday and Friday became a social event. Travelling salesmen would set up at the store with the latest fashions, the store drawing a commission for their share. The clothiers visited the camps several times a year.

CHAPTER SIX

Cadomin

'Old-Timer' in the columns of the Edmonton Journal under the 'Story of Cadomin Mine' states:

The Cadomin coal vein was discovered in 1912 by the late Frederick L. Hammond who became president and chairman of the Cadomin Coal Company, formed to develop the vast deposit. Mr. Hammond was a political economist whose first connections with the Canadian West were in colonization schemes.

However, his interest soon turned to coal mining.

Development at Cadomin was on a small scale for five years after the deposit was discovered. A temporary tipple and plant were built, and production was on the order of a few hundred tons per day. In 1917 the Cadomin Coal Company began operations, and within a year the company's potential output was estimated in the seventy-five million-ton range.

First year production alone amounted to 153,000 tons. Disaster struck the company operation in 1920; fire closed the mine.

The coal company, with hardly a loss in pace, moved its operation to the other side of the river valley. It was believed that sealing the original mine was the best way of extinguishing the fire.

For two years at the new location, production totals were huge. Then schedules were upset again, for the second time by fire.

Following the 1920 fire, the company had developed what was called the rock-tunnel mining system. With this procedure, a main tunnel was driven through the rock formation adjoining the coal seam. At intervals, cross-tunnels tapped the coal deposits.

This permitted production to continue even while the second fire was burning; and despite the loss suffered in man-hours diverted to fire control efforts, production totals in 1923 actually increased. The rock-tunnel system also provided a wider margin of safety for the miners, and allowed more uniformity of production.

* * *

A teacher recalled the days before ATA and the UMWA reached the camp. 'I got off the train in Leyland in September, 1924. My grey suede sandals and long tight skirted navy tailored suit were not appropriate for the sloppy roads.

It was a depressing sight, four inches of snow, I saw a narrow valley, the east side bleak with charred upright reminders of what had been trees, evidence of fire that had swept the hillside and razed some houses a few months previously. The west side, a contrast of green and gold rolling up the gaunt grey rocks of the mountains. The railroad snaked its way south and west to Mountain Park and there seemed scarce enough room between the McLeod River and the eastern mountain cliffs.

Dominating the valley, Mount Cheviot was strangely reminiscent of a Japanese print. The camp was a spread of log houses, frame houses, a general store, a community hall, a three-room school, two cookhouses, two beer parlours, a dairy and a post-office, later a pool-hall.

Regulating the working hours of miners was the mine whistle, its shrill prolonged keening heard throughout the valley. This emanated from the powerhouse — a vital centre of the whole mining operation. When for some reason, there was no work, the number of blasts informed the camp. When disaster struck the whistle also alerted the community. All who had men on shift froze, waiting for whatever fate had in store.

Cadomin was noted for having the only symphony orchestra between Edmonton and Vancouver. Quite excellent musicians were encouraged by the offer of good jobs around the mine. There were good crowds at the concerts as the ticket money was collected through the payroll.

The Superintendent was musical, poetical, a very idealistic person, whose ideals were thrown to the winds in moments of stress. Many are the tales told and in retrospect they are humorous, but at the time they caused worry and a real fear of perhaps losing one's job. To be fair, this seldom happened, although no one was immune from the threat, real or imagined.

I can remember Dorothy and Frances Foster, two teachers who skated from Mountain Park to Cadomin and arrived with black and blue knees.

The face of the camp has changed, even the silhouette of the mountain ridge where the mining of limestone is going on. The river has meandered in small streams over the valley, not nearly as attractive as in the early days; but the trees again clothe the eastern hillslope. Unchanged are the great grey masses of rock to the west and south and the eternal wind that howls its way down through the townsite.'

* * *

Cadomin progressed steadily and much of the lifestyle of that period is written in the biographies and autobiographies in the second part of this book. The Edson-Jasper Signal in a flowery summation of the town in 1928 carried an article entitled

'CADOMIN'

A Steam Coal Mine and Modern Camp Second to None in Alberta.

The mines of the Cadomin Coal Co., Ltd. at Cadomin are modern in every respect, and are managed by an organization, the members of which are the youngest and most progressive in Western Canada.

The general manager, Mr. W. J. Dick, of Edmonton, Alta. is as yet a comparatively young man, and is full to the brim with progressiveness and initiative. Mr. Dick is a graduate of McGill University.

The Superintendent, Mr. J. H. McMillan is also a comparatively young man, but notwithstanding this he is recognized as one of the foremost mining authorities in Western Canada. One has only to visit Cadomin and view the magnitude of the operations at the mines, the general activities and progress that is going on to appreciate the ability of Mr. McMillan. As the name would indicate, Mr. McMillan is a Scotsman.

The mine manager, Mr. E. Couplan, has risen from the ranks of labour, and it is to his credit that during the last five years he has not had one single fatal accident. His mine holds the record for the Province of Alberta for the absence of accidents. Mr. Coupland is from the North of England.

The master mechanic, Mr. Robert Brown is another son of Scotland. The underground pit bosses are Mr. George Nicol, a native of Scotland, and Mr. John Roberts, a native of Wales.

The method of mining followed at Cadomin is entirely new and unique, and is recognized as being the last word in safety. (A far cry from Mountain Park where Vic Riendeau said you could almost count on one fatal accident a year.)

The idea was worked out on the ground by the President, Mr. F. L. Hammond, Mr. Dick and Mr. McMillan. The system is known as the isolated panel rock tunnel method, which divides the mine up into separate districts, each being absolutely independent of the other. In this way, should an accident occur in any one district or panel the others are not affected.

The panels are opened up from the solid rock tunnels, one of which forms the main haulage away from the mine to the tipple, and the other the intake airway from the ventilator to all districts of the mine. As soon as a panel in a district is worked out, the openings from the rock tunnel to the coal in the panels are filled out with concrete, and the old working hermetically sealed off from the live workings of the mine.

The main rock tunnel is now under the mountain for a distance of nearly two miles. The coal is brought out from the mine by what is termed Main and Tail Rope Haulage System. The speed of the trips going into and coming out of the mine is around fifteen miles per hour, twenty-four three-ton capacity cars making the trip.

The tipple, where the coal is dumped, cleaned and loaded is electrically operated throughout and embraces the most up-to-date methods known.

The Cadomin Coal Company in 1928 commenced the sinking of two 1,000 foot shafts to tap the coal at lower levels. When these are completed the Company will be in a position to produce up to 5,000 tons per day, which will give employment to an increased number of men.

At Cadomin one can see clearly what can be accomplished through co-operation between the employer and employees. The fact that the employees are happy and contented, and that not one single day has been lost in five years through labor troubles, is a compliment to the sound judgment of Mr. McMillan and his splendid organization.

The town is modern in every respect, and there is a fine community spirit. There are three hotels and rooming houses, three churches and a large community hall, where concerts and dances are held. Mr. Fred Falkner, the genial tipple boss, operates the community hall, and gives first class moving picture shows twice weekly.

The business section of the town includes two large departmental stores, an up-to-date drug store and lunch counter, a fine butcher shop, a splendid dairy and the Bank of Nova Scotia also have a branch here, which is under the management of Mr. R. Hickson.

The service at the hotels is excellent, and Mr. P. McKenna is the genial host of both the Cadomin Hotels.

The education of the children is taken care of in modern well-managed schools. A large modern school is now under construction, and when this is completed the old building will be used as a library and recreation centre for the employees.

"The law required every child to attend school and the government made sure that facilities were available. In 1924 six schools served the children on the Branch; the seventeen children of the Blackstone, Balkan and Lovett camps shared a one-room school and an enrollment of thirty-one pupils; a one-room building in Coalspur served the thirty-two children from Mercoal and Coalspur; the Luscar school had two rooms and fifty-four pupils; and both Cadomin and Mountain Park had three-room schools with attendance of 117 and eight-four respectively. After

1924 two more schools were built, one at Robb (1925) and one at Foothills (1928)." [9]

Cadomin is rich in other things besides coal. Nicol's orchestra supplies up to the minute music for all concerts, banquets and dances, and Sandy Nicol is solo violinist and leader of this orchestra. In passing it might be stated that Sandy has won every medal at the Alberta Musical Festivals from Junior to the Senior Open Class. The Superintendent, Mr. McMillan is also an accomplished musician and solo violinist, and we understand that it was Mr. McMillan that started Sandy on his way as a violinist some eight years ago.

The town has four fine tennis courts and some very fine tennis may be seen here during the summer evenings.

* * *

Tennis was a game much enjoyed on the Branch during the twenties with courts maintained at Mountain Park, Luscar and at Coalspur.

Charlie Lee and Allan Godby on the tennis court in Mountain Park.

— Mrs. Charlie Lee

An item in the Signal notes that the Cadomin Annual Tennis Tournament, emblematic of the Western Alberta Championship was completed in August, 1928 with Coalspur, Luscar, Mountain Park, Edson and Jasper competing.

Cadomin wins.

While the late twenties saw Cadomin forging ahead all was not so rosy in the other camps. As Vic Riendeau put it, "There were people on the Branch who didn't even know there was a depression."

[9] Social Life of a Mining Community: the Coal Branch by Andy A. den Otter.

This applied particularly to Cadomin, next, to Mountain Park where both camps' output was regularly swallowed by the railroad. Luscar's output was irregular but it was as nothing compared to the problems that faced Mercoal, the mines of the Lovett Branch and those on the main line to Jasper.

* * *

1928

A weekly newspaper the Jasper Signal was started by J. L. Hollinshead in Jasper early in 1928, but after only seven issues was moved to Edson. After ten issues the name was changed to the Edson-Jasper Signal. Much of the events of this and following years are gleaned from its pages.

Perhaps here too, mention should be made of the wide ethnic personalities on the Coal Branch.

> *"A survey made in 1918 ascertained that men of twenty different nationalities were employed in the mines of the Coal Branch; and a later census which counted the whole community in 1925 confirmed this plurality of the population. Both surveys agree that those of British origin formed the largest group (41.5 percent in 1925) and that the Italians, Serbians and Ukrainians were also substantial groups while smaller clusters consisted of Poles, Americans, Rumanians and Swedes. The miners did have a tendency to congregate according to nationality but almost every ethnic group was represented in each camp. One notable exception to this was Coal Valley where the directorship successfully maintained a stable ethnic composition by ordering that 75 percent of the miners be French-Canadian or Roman Catholic. The ethnic ratios varied as miners moved from camp to camp seeking better wages and living conditions. While wanderers drifted along the Coal Branch for many reasons, a phenomenon especially true in its early history, yet in each town a fairly large solid core of permanent settlers remained which gave continuity to community life and modelled its social structure."*[10]

* * *

Alex Murray says, "the only danger was man-made. Each of us had to depend on each other. Miners went out of their way to depend on each other."

Because of this absolute life sustaining dependence a deep kinship developed between the miners of whatever nationality. The isolation of the camps led to constant social intercourse, too, in sports, music and dancing, but racism reared its ugly head occasionally. Perhaps it was most pronounced when the tentacles of the depression began reaching out to touch the country. It was to be felt again in the Second World War.

---

[10] Andy A. den Otter: Social Life of a Mining Community; the Coal Branch.

Len Murray in his taped interview says, "The only people I've never worked with in the mine were Chinamen. They were prohibited by the Alberta Government."

W. L. Hammett was employed by the Foothills Collieries as an accountant from 1922 to 1952 and by the Canadian Collieries (Dunsmuir) Ltd. to 1959. He was ordained as a minister in 1960.

Of this period he says "We had no other influx till 1927–28 when there was apparently an easing of the European immigration law."

Bias was very apparent in a letter written to the Asst. Deputy Attorney General of the Province by the Justice of the Peace, G. D. Strong in his letter of February 7th, 1928, and contained in A.P.P. files.

Referring to a disturbance in the Coalspur bar part of his letter reads:

"It is most important for the prestige of the Constable at Coalspur, myself and the Constitution that this appeal should not be allowed to be won by the accused.

It should be pointed out to the Judge that from Embarras to Mountain Park and Coalspur to Lovett, a territory of 75 miles or so with no roads and in a forest reserve where there are nothing but mining camps and ONLY ONE CONSTABLE and a MAJORITY OF FOREIGNERS that law and order must be kept and an example must be made of these Foreigners who are getting so that they will soon rule the country with the Red Flag. We who live amongst them know and realize this far more than those living in a CITY.

This man is not a BRITISH SUBJECT.

What protection has the Hotel Keeper or Bar Tender at a small place like Coalspur when a disturbance occurs in his place. If the Constable is up at Mountain Park 40 miles away and as a preventitive method of repetitions of this kind.

If it is necessary the Hotel keeper at Coalspur and Bartender are willing to engage Counsel on their behalf to fight this appeal as well. There is far too much breaking of the Law on these Branches mostly all by foreigners and it is impossible to cope with same due to the nature of the Country, the train service and no Highways.

If this man wins this appeal it will just strengthen these foreigners hands and there will be no ending to these kinds of disturbances.

If he does not win the appeal you can feel that we shall have far less trouble up these branches and it will teach these foreigners to respect this Country's laws instead of running things as they do in Central Europe and Russia."

Yours truly,
(Sgd.) G. D. Strong."

* * *

Spring of 1928 found Tex Byers, the Big Horn Guide of Luscar and oft-time barber of Mountain Park out on the winter range looking over his horses. He reported them all fat and healthy after the winter. Tex already had some very interesting parties booked for fall hunting. Forty horses coming across country from Nordegg were all purchased, most of them by Tex.

In April the coal miners of the branch took a referendum to see whether they would cease work or not, but this concern wasn't shared by the Coalspur Collieries. A brief item reads:

The Coalspur Collieries at Mile 40 on the Coal Branch was ordered placed in the hands of the receiver last week. Sheriff Rae was given charge of the receivership.

By May differences in attitude had been settled and both the Mine Workers Union of Canada and the United Mine Workers of America had announced there would be no cessation of work.

Both mines at Robb were running steadily. Mercoal was having difficulty financially and the mine was shortly to be sold. By midsummer owners of the Brule mine gave up. An announcement was made:

"The Blue Diamond Coal Co. have decided to discontinue operations at Brule from July 20th, according to the announcement of Manager O. N. Brown. The mine closed at 4:00 p.m. on Friday afternoon, and nearly all the miners turned in their tools at that hour. A few men are being kept a short time for underground and surface work, but already many have left, and it is expected that Brule will be practically deserted within a month.

The Brule mines have been operated continuously since 1917, with the exception of a six month shut down in 1924.

The present population of the town is about 500, and it is claimed by many to be the most comfortable and pleasant mining camp in Alberta. It is unusually well laid out and equipped with large public buildings, golf course, tennis courts, athletic ground and other improvements."

Many of these miners moved their families to the Coal Branch. It was a bad summer too for Jack the Frog. An item notes that:

"J. L'Heureux of Weald was found guilty of illegal possession of liquor, and fined $350 and costs when he appeared before Co. Geo. Mc-Leod at Edson, on Friday the 24th. He was also found guilty to the charge of ownership of a still and fined $300 and costs or twelve months; the conviction in this case is being appealed."

Fred Estabrooks of Mercoal got the contract for the erection of a lookout cabin to be built at Grave Flats and known by this name. The cabin would be situated 19 miles south-west of Mountain Park at an altitude of 6,804 feet and have telephone connection.

This was the summer that A. N. Jock died leaving his wife impoverished. Mr. Jock left his old six shooter and gold pan to an old friend P. A. Robb. Pall bearers were four of his old time prospector friends Messrs. Frohers, Groat, Robb and Peel.

* * *

E. D. Conger purchased the business known as the Mercoal Store from J. G. Paulson. Mr. Fitzhugh Burns of St. Paul, Minnesota, President of the Saunder Ridge Coal Company visited the mine briefly and work commenced on the restaurant building which was owned by J. Paulson but recently purchased by a co-operative society.

Many mine owners visited their interests this summer including Jesse Young, President of the Superior Coal Co. at Lovett.

An item notes that Lieutenant-Colonel Lindsay of Scotland, Mr. Jones and Mr. Drinnan of Edmonton, directors of Luscar-Mountain Park Collieries together with H. Mitchell of Scotland, son of President Mitchell of Luscar arrived to spend a few days looking after their interests.

At Cadomin P. Burns & Co. purchased the butcher shop from T. G. Shaw with a Mr. Gillespie to manage the business.

R. A. Craig, local timber contractor purchased a new tractor. Fred Faulker purchased a Ford 'bug' thus giving the town of Cadomin a total of one car and three tractors. J. Matthews of Mountain Park also became a coal branch auto owner, and Baldy Robb bought a new one-ton Chev truck to haul mine props to Coalspur.

A large petition was signed by residents of Cadomin, Luscar and Mountain Park asking the provincial government to connect the three camps by road.

Representatives from throughout the Branch met at Coalspur with the Edson Board of Trade to discuss a Branch Highway. Full of enthusiasm the group would have been disheartened if able to look into the future to learn that this was to be one of the longest fights for a road in the Province of Alberta

George Johnson of Edmonton riding a Harley Davidson motor cycle made the trip from Edmonton to Jasper in 13 hours and 45 minutes actual riding time. Loose gravel and deep ruts gave him and his companion A. E. Strange several spills.

A Californian visiting the province managed to drive to Avola B.C., ship his Lincoln car to Jasper, drive to Hinton, ship his car to Obed and finally slither in on muddy roads to Edson.

So while the residents of the Coal Branch agitated for a road, other areas were somewhat less than happy with the roads they already had.

At Marlboro the Signal reports 'a very important and busy industry where the Edmonton Cement Co. have their plant. During the season over 100 men are employed at this plant, and operations are carried on 24 hours a day. During July, 1928, 150 cars of cement were shipped from this plant, and whilst this was perhaps a peak shipment, the shipments are very heavy all through the building season. The cement is handled by all leading builders' supplies houses, and some very important buildings erected recently have used Marlboro cement. These include the new CNR station at Edmonton, the new Edmonton City Dairy, St. John's College at the University, Imperial Oil Building and a new Edmonton Public School.

On December 1, 1928 the Cadomin Coal Co. began actual sinking of two huge vertical shafts to mine their seams at depth but the year ended on a sombre note.

"A fatal accident occurred in the Cadomin Coal Company's No. 1 Mine on Dec. 24th when Mr. Matt Hall, Timber Boss, lost his life by being jammed between some timber and a hoist that was being moved down a steep grade.

Mr. McMillan cancelled all public dances and entertainment while the body was at Cadomin. The mine was also closed for the day."

This was the first fatal accident to have occurred at the Cadomin mine in five years.

* * *

1929

This year was to be an auspicious year for the bustling camp of Cadomin. On January 5th a spanking new Recreation Centre provided by the Cadomin Coal Company was opened for employees. A bowling alley, indoor curling rink, and recreation area that boasted English billiard and pool tables was put into use.

Almost at the same time a full sized outdoor skating rink was completed under the auspices of the Cadomin Sport & Amusement Association.

Wages were good and a special rate of $6.75 per ton to all Ontario points was to be in effect from January 15th for all the mines on the Coal Branch. In 1928, 46,000 tons had been moved to Eastern markets and although this was disappointingly small, none of this effected Cadomin very much anyway. Their market was assured in the railroad itself.

Choice leg pork was advertised as 23¢ per pound, homemade pure pork sausage at two pounds for 35¢, homemade pork and beef sausage at 15¢ per pound, choice fresh pork tenderloin at 55¢ a pound, mild cured cooked ham at 50¢ a pound and dill pickles at 35¢ a dozen.

Sidney H. Cliffe arrived in Edson from England and took over as Editor of the Signal. Sidney had been taken aback when docking at Halifax to notice a sign "No Englishmen or Dogs Allowed," on a restaurant door. When asked years later what his thoughts had been at the time he replied "I thought, 'You son-of-a-bitches lured me into coming here, and I'm staying.' He was to become a staunch Liberal, a persistent ever-plugging advocate of the Alberta Coal Branch Highway, and a good friend of J. H. McMillan.

Miss Sadie Cuming of Trapp & Cuming Ladieswear in Edson announced she would visit Cadomin regularly with a full range of dresses, and Mr. A. S. Paterson, storekeeper for the Cadomin Coal Co. went to Edmonton to buy furnishings for the new reading room and library. Unfortunately before January was out the Cadomin Theatre was completely gutted by fire.

Peter McKenna became the agent for the Chevrolet line and residents although admiring his foresight joshed him about an agency in an area where there was no road.

The challenge hockey game between Luscar Tigers and Cadomin Wild Cats for a side bet of $50. put up by General Superintendent J. H. McMillan was postponed because so many of the Cadomin men were down with the mumps.

The Cadomin Symphony Orchestra fostered by Superintendent McMillan presented a sophisticated program for Robbie Burn's Day followed by dancing to the 'wee hours of the morning.'

By July a new community hall at Cadomin opened boasting a grand dancing area of 40 × 100 feet and a stage that measured 10 × 40 feet. Fred Faulkner re-opened his Picture Theatre with the movie 'Wings' and under the direction of Supt. McMillan the Cadomin Symphony Orchestra played the original score prior to its showing.

The Symphony practiced hard and later in the summer an entire program was presented with attendants from Luscar and Mountain Park. All proceeds were put towards the purchase of a grand piano. Supt. McMillan presented young Helena Hudyma with a wrist watch on behalf of the townspeople when she saved Marguerite Moldowan from drowning when Marguerite slipped off a narrow bridge crossing the McLeod River.

However, a fatal accident marred these happy events when Thos. W. Milligan, age 62, was killed at the company's No. 2 new mine shaft, which was being readied for use.[11] The body was found on the buttment 200 feet below the pump landing.

* * *

Elsewhere on the Coal Branch trouble was brewing at the mines in Robb and Mercoal.[12] And in July a fire broke out on the Lovett Branch. Men who were laid off at the Mercoal and Lovett Branch mines spent weeks fighting the danger.

'The heavy forest fire which commenced on the watershed of the Pembina River on July 23rd, and raged with great intensity before finally being brought under control, is still burning in numerous places within the fire guards that surround the burned-over area. Men are still employed in extinguishing the fire, which is well embedded in deep moss and litter beneath the heavy spruce and along the border of the muskeg area. The fire swept over an area of more than forty square miles of timber, destroying many stands of young growth of great potential value. Some 260 men fought valiantly to save stands of valuable mercantile timber, and were successful in saving one block of thirty million feet, located between the Pembina and Cardinal rivers.

[11] See Joe Henderson's biography
[12] See Mike Krypan & Al Foster's biography

Men and equipment were furnished by all mining companies, more particularly by the Foothills Collieries Ltd., who closed their mine and sent 120 men to combat the fire.'[13]

The Luscar Collieries Silver Band returned from the Edmonton Exhibition well satisfied with their performance. For the second year in a row they had topped all provincial bands. B. Roberts of Luscar also carried off the solo saxophone honors.

The Oddfellow Lodges of Luscar, Cadomin and Mountain Park met at Mountain Park at a special memorial service, a special train bringing the participants. Arthur J. Bishop, assistant to the Rector of St. Catherine's Edson was in charge of the service.

Royalty came to Edson when Prince Leo Galitzine purchased 160 acres four and a half miles south-east of Edson with the intention of specializing in fur farming.

In mid August an explosion occurred at the Cadomin No. 1 Mine when several miners were burned. Commendation was given Messrs. Terry McGuire, Alfred McPhail, John Hydma, Bill Boyd, Charlie McAdam, Jack O'Connel, Sandy Thomson, Con Doherty and J. D. Carson "for the unselfish and heroic work they did in remaining in the face of danger and rescuing their comrades".

The accident was used as an example by the Cadomin Local Union to point up to the Provincial Government that

"something be done immediately towards linking up Cadomin, Luscar and Mountain Park mines by a highway so that help may be available at once at any of the mines in case of such an emergency as occurred at Cadomin. They must see to it at once that these mines are connected by a highway so that 'experienced First Aid and Mine Rescue men from adjacent mines can rush by car to the seat of the explosion and render all assistance'."

The accident interrupted Dr. McKenzie's planned holiday to the Coast, (the resident physician at Cadomin.)

Labor Day was celebrated throughout the Branch. At Mercoal a capacity crowd filled the hall with Thos. Hallet, M. Milo and W. Mills acting as M.C.'s. The orchestra was happy to welcome back Jim Herman who had spent the slack summer months working at Coleman. Jim was their trombone player. After supper cigars and cigarettes supplied by the community were passed around, and much enjoyed by attending Robb and Coalspur residents, as well as 'members of the telephone gang stationed at Mile 8'.

Fishing was exceptionally good in the fall of '29 with one Mercoal lady reporting a catch of forty-two grayling and trout secured in less than two hours.

At Mile 5, a lump of coal weighing one and three-quarter tons was mined at Mercoal to advertise the McLeod River Coal in Winnipeg. 'It is the largest piece of coal to be taken from this mine, and there was practically no loss in taking it from the mine to the car'.

---

[13] Edson-Jasper Signal.

J. H. B. Smith, a farmer at Wolf Creek outside Edson, won the World's Wheat Championship at the World Show in Chicago with a new strain named 'Reward Wheat'. The winning wheat weighed 66.03 pounds to the bushel.

At Mercoal the community bid farewell to the Misses Borden who left to take up the barbering business in Edson. Mercoal would miss the two sisters mostly for their catering efforts in the town's social functions. "The best caterers on the Coal Branch" was their well-deserved reputation.

The Jasper Coal Co. who had purchased equipment of the Blue Diamond Collieries at Brule prepared to open up their newly formed company leases of which M. A. C. Dunn, M.E.; W. S. Cupple and R. G. Drinnan, M.E., were directors.

At Foothills the newly completed Community Hall was opened November 9th. The hall 'is being financed entirely by the subscriptions of residents and funds are now in sight to cover the total cost'.

Hon. O. L. McPherson, Minister of Highways met a delegation of the Edson Coal Branch Highway Committee. It was headed by Mr. C. E. Barry of the Coal Valley Coal Co.; Mr. Chris Pattinson, M.L.A., Mr. R. E. Thurber, secretary of the Edson Board of Trade; and Mr. S. H. Cliffe, secretary of the Coal Branch Highway Committee.

Mr. McPherson said that he could not take any other attitude than he had adopted towards other delegations that had been in to see him. He said the road through this territory could not be considered as part of the provincial road system, but he would be willing to help on the basis that had been suggested, that is, on a fifty-fifty basis with the industry. He said that as far as he was concerned he would be willing to go into any part of the system without considering the whole, if necessary, providing the road built served the communities.

Mercoal miners met regularly at their favorite spot, the pool room. The affairs of the day were discussed and much interest shown in the snooker tournament run by A. E. Owens.

Cadomin people mourned the death of three residents in November; Peggy, a 9-year-old favorite, daughter of Mr. and Mrs. J. Roberts and two miners.

The whole village of Cadomin was deeply stricken with the triple tragedy which occurred at Cadomin on the 13th, when two men were killed and three others badly burned from an explosion which occurred in the new shaft, and in addition·the sudden death of little Peggy.

"Rev. Fr. Louis said Mass at the Roman Catholic Church, Cadomin on the 16th for R. McGrath and Peggy Roberts, and at the same time Rev. Mr. Wright held service in the Community Hall for Mr. J. W. Stewart, where a joint service of the I.O.O.F. and ex-servicemen was held for Stewart and McGrath, the whole village turning out in procession headed by the school children, who were led by Mr. H. O. Harper, school principal, followed by members of the I.O.O.F., Rebekahs,

Elks, ex-servicemen and the residents of Cadomin. The procession walking four deep was over a mile long, stretching from the Community Hall to Leyland Bridge."

CHAPTER SEVEN

The Railroaders

"Railroading[14] on the Alberta Coal Branch was always unique because of its isolation. It was a frustrating line to operate because of curves and grades and F. H. Keefe, CN's assistant superintendent at Edson found the area in his territory.

Fifteen miles an hour was the permissive speed for freight trains. Not until 1927 did the Santa Fe's arrive to replace the Grand Trunk 400's. Trains were short but frequent. Train crews rarely lacked work in the days when coal was king, but the work wasn't easy. They were railroading in high country.

Trains "froze-up" frequently. Cars waiting in sidings had to be "warmed up" in small cuts before they could be moved. Train inspection when the winter winds swept down from the mountains was an invitation to frozen fingers, feet and noses.

Equipment maintenance for the Coal Branch was a special chore. Every car that left Edson for the branch was fully inspected, brake piston travel adjusted and handbrakes put in good working order. There were no facilities on the branch itself except for a small roundhouse at Coalspur.

Operating instructions call for use of retaining valves when descending grades of one per cent or greater. As far as the Coal Branch was concerned it was a standing order.

---

[14] CNR Public Relations Edmonton

Early twenties — A Canadian National Railway freight wreck near Mercoal on the Alberta Coal Branch.

Crews not only set the spring-loaded brake valves on every car but also travelled the catwalk for the length of the train to wind on the hand brakes.

Not all the hazards of setting brakes topside on a moving train were those inherent in railroading.

Going through Mercoal one New Years Eve, a trainman found himself the target for the bullets of a celebrating marksman. No harm was done but the descent from the catwalk is said to be the fastest on record. Such playful antics were regarded as foolish, maybe, but not hostile in the tolerant Coal Branch atmosphere.

Isolation breeds independence. Coal Branch crews were rugged individuals as their nicknames testify: Popeye Allen, Grey Owl McKenzie, Grizzly Bear Atkins, Snakey Rutter, No Clothes Jones, Trapper Davis were a few.

Despatchers and supervisory personnel respected them for what they were and the work got done. On the Lovett Sub for instance, the 'mixed' had a number known only in the timecard. It was "Sam's Train" after Sam Sutherland, the conductor, and that was the way the orders read.

Best loved on the Coal Branch were the kids. Train crews always had goodies for them and would shop for the parents on their return to Edson. Mrs. W. H. Hills, the former Edna Matheson remembers some of the Blue Flea conductors who were so good to the young people; Tony Oakes, Pop Conrad, Dinny Flaherty and Arnold McKeever came to mind.

Miners await the train on the platform of the station at Mountain Park (early twenties). Sitting on barrel is Ray Jones, Station agent. Extreme right, Jim Price. Others un-identified.

— Mrs. Charlie Lee

At Coalspur Trueman Williamson's caboose burns.

Proximity to the mountains bore in more heavily on the agents who had to remain among them day in and day out. At Mountain Park, however, Ray Jones turned isolation to advantage. Ray was the originator of the one-man business band. He was also the only agent Mountain Park ever had in its 34 years existence. Not only did he handle the Mountain Park Coal Company's business but also arranged passage for the miners returning home to Europe.

In his off-duty hours Ray sold insurance and later had an automobile agency. If you wanted to make a pack trip into the mountains, Ray could oblige.

Then there was Boomer Harry, the hogger who fought in the Spanish-American War, moved north to hire on at Melville and then drifted west with the tide of traffic.

Harry had the Midas touch and also a keen appreciation of card values. In time he came to own an interest in hotels, a coal mine and a fine dude ranch near Hinton.

He and his wife were generous to a fault. It is said she served more meals in the kitchen than in the dining room of their first hotel on the Coal Branch. Harry had a fondness for the section forces in their lonely outposts along the line and his wife, a Melville girl, shared his regard.

On his last trip before Christmas it was Harry's custom to drop off candies that his wife had packaged for the sectionmen's children. Harry was said to supplement the candies with something more potable for the men in the section house. He was a big man with many friends.

While train crews did their best, there was not much they could do to avoid hitting the many horses who wandered onto the track. There were no roads and the horse and the railway were the only means of transportation. Almost every family either owned a horse or had access to one. The horses were set free to forage among the mountains. Even after the roads came in horses were still a constant hazard to railmen.

Ken McEvoy, a CNR employee now employed out of Edmonton talks of one trip when three horses were hit near Robb. The train drew to a stop.

Ken says, "One of the horses was suffering at the side of the track. Charlie Marshall got out with an axe. Charlie really liked animals. Just as he swung the axe the animal turned its head so the blade just glanced off the eye. Charlie contritely apologized, "Oh, Gawd, I'm sorry, horse. I'm sorry."

Then he raised the axe again and bashed the horse out of suffering into oblivion.

"I'll never forget that trip," says Ken. "I can still see Charlie standing there apologizing to that damned horse."

* * *

CHAPTER EIGHT

1930 — A Black Year for Some Mines

Cadomin started off the year by making plans for a community hospital. Dr. D. C. McKenzie, local physician and surgeon addressed the meeting. The Cadomin Medical Board was formed with Mr. P. McKenna as president and Barney Fairclough, secretary. A Box Social held almost immediately realized $300.

Supervisor White and Ranger Neilsen of the Forestry Department found themselves riding a cold speeder at 2:00 a.m. one early February Monday morning heading for Leyland. A disastrous fire burned down Clyburn's store, threatened the CNR buildings and spread into the adjoining bush where it consumed a few acres. In addition, a wind of hurricane proportions handicapped the work of fire-fighting, ashes and debris being blown around and obstructing the efforts of the men. The winds in this area were unbelievably fierce.[15] A boxcar standing on a siding had been left with door open and by morning the boxcar had been turned over on its side. Crews were instructed to close all doors henceforth.

And again a delegation from Edson and the Coal Branch met with the Hon. Mr. Brownlee and the Hon. Mr. MacPherson to present the case of the Coal Branch Highway.

---

[15] See Dr. Begg's and Paullsen stories

Mr. C. Pattinson and Mr. J. H. McMillan interviewed the Cabinet Ministers and presented a written statement of which excerpts follow:

To date, delegations have not accomplished very much, due to the fact heretofore very little direct revenue has been obtained from the district by the Alberta Government. who quite properly stated on previous occasions that on this account they could not commit themselves to proceed with the work in whole or part.

The district under review has a population of approximately 7,000 souls, all of whom are isolated in the various mining camps, which are situated from three to twelve miles apart, with no outlet by highway to the outside world.

The residents of this district have accepted the viewpoint of the Government up to the present time, and have patiently waited for the past fifteen years for some means of communication whereby they might be able to reach outside points by a road, and also a means of inter-communication with the people of the adjoining mining towns within the district.

The delegation have met with sympathetic consideration from the Government who promised to supplement an amount equal to that which could be raised by the coal operators voluntarily agreeing to a tax on the production of coal within the district of One Cent (1¢) per ton, the said tax to be maintained until the highway was completed. It was impossible for the Edson Coal Branch Highway association to get the coal operators to agree to this proposal, and the matter now stands in this position.

In the meantime, as a result of the Natural Resources being transferred to the Province by the Federal Government, the Provincial Government will derive directly from the mining industry of this district approximately $136,000 per annum on the present basis of taxation, and as paid the Federal Government for the year 1929, and made up as follows:

Coal tax of 5¢ per ton	$ 88,400.00
Coal Land Leases (estimated)	$ 20,000.00
Oil Land Leases	$ 5,000.00
Timber Logging and Stumpage (estimated)	$ 8,000.00
Local Improvement District Tax	$ 5,000.00
	$136,400.00

Mr. Brownlee promised he would bring the matter before the Executive Committee for consideration.

* * *

Seven mines were represented at a meeting of Miner's representatives held in Edson when matters pertaining to general conditions were discussed. Those present were J. Childerstone, Luscar; Sub-Dist. Board Member M. W. C. Huges, Luscar; N. Scofosen, Mile 32 and 33; R. Sweegel, Hinton; G. Macleod, Cadomin and J. McDonald, Mountain Park.

An editorial in the Winnipeg Tribune stated: The Alberta operator contends that American steam coal is sold here at no apparent charge for the coal itself, but only for the cost of moving it from American mines to Winnipeg consumers; and they ask for fair treatment by "preventing this dumping of surplus American production", so that Alberta coal can compete in its natural market upon an even basis.

With respect to the suggestion that the price of Alberta coal to the consumer be reduced, the operators reply that it costs considerably more to lay Western coal down in Winnipeg than the coal itself costs at the mine, and that the dealer who nets 40 cents a ton on domestic fuels considers himself fortunate.

The price at which United States steam coals are sold in Winnipeg today puts Alberta bituminous coals out of the running. So much so, states the Western Canada Fuel Association, that Alberta producers no longer tender on the larger contracts, knowing that even at a cost-at-mine basis, they are undersold before they start.

Here is a legitimate field for investigation."

* * *

In late April an accident cost the life of Terry McGuire, one of Cadomin's most popular citizens. It occurred in the South Working, and according to reports an explosion of gas blew out a facing of coal, a large piece pinning Terry's foot and making it impossible for him to escape. Although help was rushed to him at once the escape of gas was so strong that he died before he could be released. 'Practically every person in Cadomin attended the service in the Roman Catholic Church conducted by Father Louis.'

* * *

On the political front Chris Pattinson, Labor and Mr. Charles Ewan Payne, Liberal and Geo. Maclean, Conservative, were nominated candidates for M.L.A.

Charlie, Ontario born, was active in labor activities, and soon after settling in Mountain Park became Secretary Treasurer of the Local Union of the United Mine Workers of America. A popular man he was nevertheless to be defeated, with Edsonite Chris Pattinson elected by a big majority. The United Farmers of Alberta had been in power for nine years.

Meanwhile extensive improvements were being carried out at Robb and Coal Valley. At Lakeside Collieries Ltd. a new tipple was being built and new machinery installed. The coal being mined at Robb would be placed on the fall market under a new trade name, Minehead-Inferno and would be trademarked by a special process, an attractive blue color having been adopted for the purpose.

At Coal Valley, "the cableway excavator which is an entirely new feature in the coal mining industry is making splendid progress. When the engineers become thoroughly acquainted with this new style of machine, a large tonnage will be handled daily, cutting overhead costs down to a minimum."

At Coal Valley too, employees carried out an extensive trail making and bridge building project to make fishing trips and picnics a little easier. However the spring was not a pleasant one with snow and rain disrupting activities until well into June. Baseball, tennis and football addicts on both branches chafed at each cancellation.

At Luscar mine workers were 'out' on a dispute. A story datelined Ottawa, July 15th reads — "An increase in daily wages for several classes of workmen at the Luscar Collieries, Alta. is recommended in the majority report of the board of conciliation which investigated the dispute between the company and the men, and whose report was issued by the Department of Labor here today. The increases follow: Mine drivers to be raised from $4.90 to $5.10; Roperiders to be raised from $4.90 to $5.10; Railway car handlers to be raised from $4.45 to $4.70; Firemen to be raised by $4.45 to $4.75; Engineers (second class license) to be raised from $5.70 to $6.90.

The increases recommended would average about one cent per ton on an average production between 246,472 and 291,859 tons in 1928 and 1929 respectively.

The majority report urges a rate of 25 cents a ton for pillar coal on No. 3 level should apply, with 56 cents on all other coal. The rate for angles, driven eight feet by eight is urged to be $8.26 per lineal yard."

* * *

For the third year in succession the Luscar Collieries Silver Band carried off the premier honour at the Edmonton Exhibition. They stopped enroute home for a triumphant appearance in Edson.

Trouble at Mercoal

July brought to a head a dispute that had been fermenting in Mercoal, throughout June.[16] A story datelined July 3, 1930 states:

"The first serious development in the quarrel between the members of the United Mine Workers of America and the members of the Mine Workers Union of Canada occurred at Coalspur last Saturday night, when an assault took place on Capt. L. J. Maine, J.P., and John Kapteyn, special constable, by pickets who were at Coalspur for the purpose of preventing men from going to Mercoal.

Pickets of the Mine Workers' Union of Canada have for some time been meeting trains at Coalspur and turning back miners bound for Mercoal, and it was one of these pickets, consisting of between forty and fifty men that started the fracas on Saturday night last. Capt. Maine and Special Constable Kapteyn were roughly used by the men, and the interference of townspeople saved a more serious riot. Const. Banks has requested that aid be sent to him, and it is rumored

---

[16] Read Mike Krypan story.

Tim Buck heads a parade in Cadomin — 1936.　　　　　　　　(A. MacKinnon)

that the Canadian National Railway will also have a constable on the job to prevent interference with train crews and the train schedules.

At Mercoal picketing developed into a riot when an over-exuberant miner wearing a brown leather jacket jumped one of four RCMP constables guarding the workers at the mine. This gesture prompted a demonstration that included rock throwing and fist-fighting by hundreds of miners at the scene. It also prompted sending a bevy of Alberta Provincial Police and special police to the scene. The editor of the Edson-Jasper Signal, S. H. Cliffe, writes:

"Certainly the introduction of over one hundred and twenty policemen with automatic guns is not common sense, not only will such actions not end trouble, but it is a gesture on the part of the authorities of their inability to handle the situation and only excites the workers in other places to pass resolutions such as was passed by the Cadomin Local. Arresting a few individuals will not settle the dispute either, for the simple reason that there is in the minds of those concerned a fundamental reason for the strike. Whether it is a just reason or not is beside the point. The point is that some of the men are not satisfied with certain leaders and they are not satisfied with the working conditions arranged by those leaders on their behalf. They have no quarrel with the company operating the mine, but they wish to have a voice in the terms of agreement. They may be wrong in this. They may be worse off if they break away from one union and join another. That is their business and policemen and guns will not settle that business.

The quarrel seems to be between leaders of rival unions, and if that is so the sooner they get together the better it will be for all concerned.

We cannot see how anything more reasonable or sensible can be offered than that proposal that was put forward by Mr. Chris Pattinson recently, when he visited Mercoal and suggested to the rival leaders that a vote be taken from all the men who were on the pay roll at the time of the strike, and that they should be allowed to say to which union they wished to belong. This proposal was accepted by the Canadian Union leaders and rejected by the American Union Leaders, in the meantime the strike goes merrily on, one class of workers are seeking protection from another class of workers, the men are losing time and wages and the company, who have nothing to do with it are losing production."

* * *

Cadomin Mine Workers Pass Strike Resolution

Whereas the Mine Workers of Mercoal, Alberta by a big majority decided to quit the United Mine Workers of America and join the Canadian Mine Workers.

Whereas the officials of the American Union secretly and without knowledge of the workers of Mercoal signed the agreement with the Saunders Ridge Coal Co. Ltd.

Whereas the unjustly treated employees came out on strike and the Coal Company with the help of the United Mine Workers of America began to bring in strike breakers and whereas the Provincial Government immediately permitted its police with Machine Guns to come to the aid of this unholy combination, and whereas that we as the mine workers did think that a change from the old time political parties to a Farmer Government in this Province was for the better and now to our sorrow we are to be clubbed into a foreign organization under the direction of the Provincial Government.

Therefore be it resolved that we the Cadomin Mine Workers of Cadomin, Alberta, protest most bitterly against POLICE and MACHINE GUN interference in our choice of Home Union and be it further resolved that we demand immediate withdrawal of the Police and Machine Guns and that this resolution be sent to the Hon. J. E. Brownlee, Premier, Attorney General Lymburn, and our local representative, Mr. C. Pattinson.

Passed unanimously by the Mine Workers of Cadomin, Alta. July 27th, 1930.

WM. MOLDOWAN,
Secretary

The mines at Cadomin were working every day, but not to capacity.

On the main CNR line Jasper Coal Co. Ltd. commenced shipping coal on August 1st. Equipment recently installed included two 15 h.p. boilers, a turbine driven generator and a Sullivan C.L.U. undercutting and shearing machine.

Owing to the fact that no arrangements could be made with the railway company to take the Edson and Marlboro ball teams to Cadomin, outside of a special train at a cost of $420.00 the visit had to be postponed. The need for a highway was aggravating.

At Coal Valley the correspondent facetiously writes:

"Coal Valley is going modern. All the houses have had running water throughout the summer, and arrangements are now being made to supply six of these houses with water during the winter. Due to this great advantage two of the householders are installing water closets and at a later date may possibly step out and install baths.

Mr. Ralph Blanchard, the timekeeper recently purchased a new Norman radio. Radio poles in the townsite are now becoming so numerous that when a person takes his evening stroll one is inclined to believe that he is walking through a dead forest.

Mrs. Dussault and Mrs. Dutton are more than pleased to see that their husbands can now stand on their hind legs and walk around unaided. Art Dussault was giving an exhibition of trick riding on a bucking horse, and being much heavier than when he last rode a horse, he sat down a little too soon on the saddle. Jack Dutton suffered in the cause of athletics when he was giving an exhibition of high diving in a trout hole in the Beaverdam Creek.

An Ottumwa Box Car loader arrived but is not yet in operation as several alterations have to be made to the tipple before it can be operated satisfactorily.

Stripping operations are now progressing very favourably. This work is being carried on during the night so as not to conflict with the loading. Mr. E. Cochrane is the steam shovel engineer and Mr. Flynn the craneman."

* * *

Up to July no light had been thrown on the mysterious disappearance of Pierre (Pete) Roberge who was last seen on the night of May 24th when he left the dance at the Foothills mine to walk home alone to Coal Valley. A public subscription was raised and reward for information amounted to $500; $100 given by the proprietors of the Coal Valley Hotel, $100 by Mr. Bernard Brady and the balance by the employees of the Coal Valley Mining Co.

Coal Valley men were busy taking correspondence courses. Steam Engineering seems to be the favorite followed by Bookkeeping 1, Salesmanship, Math, Electricity and Surveying.

* * *

At Cadomin the new United Church was becoming an actuality.

Labor Day saw Mountain Park acting as host for a Sports Day. A special train from Edson picked up hundreds of participants and spectators, while large numbers from neighboring towns arrived by horseback.

The Mount Harris Peak race offered the biggest excitement and was watched by a crowd estimated at a thousand. The Course, a mile and a half long and a climb almost perpendicular of a thousand feet drew nine entries with only three finishing. The race was won by N. Cinnamon, time 25 minutes, with a prize of $50.; F. Cinnamon 2nd, $35.; and M. Lozinsky, 3rd, $25.

J. H. McMillan took advantage of the large audience to urge the people of the district through the Unions and other organizations to keep up the agitation for roads. As one former resident put it, "McMillan seemed to be a moving force on almost every committee".

At Mercoal and mines of the Lovett Branch radio dances became popular, and F. L. Dunphy who operated a portable talking picture show visited Mercoal and camps on the Lovett Branch.

In September the hunting season opened and the Haggblad Bros. of Luscar; D. C. Matthews of Mountain Park and W. Mustard of Jasper all prepared to guide their parties within the boundaries of the Brazeau National Forest. The bulk of the hunting parties were Americans.

At Coal Valley the Slack-line Cableway Excavator was now firmly established and tonnage allotted by the CNR could be handled comfortably by this new method of open-pit mining.

By the fall of 1930 many miners were working but a few days a month, with every mine feeling the pinch of a tight economic system. The Cadomin Coal Company closed down one of the shafts and laid off sixty men. A movement began to take advantage of the Federal Unemployment Relief Program, and agitation to have unemployed men put to work on road building increased.

P. Rocchio of Cadomin died at Rochester, and a Galician miner at Reco attempted to stab his wife as she boarded the train. T. Oke, conductor, interfered and the man took off up the track with the train crew in pursuit. However he swallowed poison "and this together with self-inflicted stabs caused death almost immediately".

The CNR cut their train schedules between Edmonton and Jasper for the winter, running back and forth alternate days.

The long cold winter had settled in earnest and in October the Coal Valley correspondent wrote:

> "A strange feathered visitor appeared in camp on Friday last and great speculation was rife as to its identity. The town sages and backwoodsmen together with the homesteaders were called out to give it a name. After long and serious discussion and two or three near fights, it was finally said to be a Hell-Diver. It was given a chance for freedom on the creek but could not make the grade, so after a couple of days it was dispatched in no half-hearted manner. A post-mortem was held over the body and Dr. Gus, the assistant-bull-cook proclaimed inability to fly on account of a broken wing and leg. Such is the excitement we get in camp."

The Lakeside Collieries at Robb was now in readiness to handle heavy production of the 'Minehead Inferno Coal'. C. L. Stevens of Edmonton had designed the new plant with an investment expenditure of $150,000. W. Foster was mine manager.

As the year ended Wm. Muldowan, Secretary of the Cadomin Miners' Union asked if roadwork promised by Premier Brownlee on the Coal Branch had been purely an election dodge.

* * *

1931 - Roadwork Begins Through Relief Camps

In January, the big covered skating and curling rink was officially opened at Cadomin. Over five hundred people witnessed the opening game between Luscar and Cadomin, and Superintendent H. A. Scott of Luscar made a big production of collecting 'a few Kopeks' bet on the game from the Cadomin Superintendent, J. H. McMillan.

It is interesting to surmise just how many miners were hired at Mountain Park, Cadomin and Luscar on the basis of their ability to play (a) hockey, (b) a musical instrument (c) baseball, and other sports in lesser degree. Certainly no secret was made of the fact that these attributes could result in a hiring, as any number of former residents testify.

The Canadian National Railways advertised for tenders for the construction of a line of railway from a point on the Alberta Coal Branch at Luscar, Alta. to serve the Gebo coal mine. "The new line will be approximately 3.8 miles in length and will be completed before Sept. 15, 1931."

At Luscar the Band presented a concert with selections from the Messiah, overture to 'Oberon' and 'No, No, Nanette' by the orchestra section, while at Sterco the newly organized Sterco Dramatic Society presented a sketch 'Indian Love'.

Cadomin put in electric light meters and an article states, "In pre-meter days, our local merchant claims his customers scorned anything less than 100 watt bulbs. In some cases the poor chickens were foiled into believing the sun shone 24 hours a day, and on chilly days toasted their beaks by electric heater. Since February 1st, it's quite different. One customer said, "Aye, Barney, can you no gie us a socket tae fit a flashlight bulb?"

A rush of accidents took place in the mines. "Three men were badly burned in the mine at Mercoal when gas ignition took place causing serious injuries to John McLennan, pit boss; Otto Sando and A. Kurtz. The injured men are receiving every care in the hands of Dr. Begg."

Nick Pleskan, a miner of Cadomin, was the victim of gas asphyxiation on March 11th. The Miners Union Ritual was read at the graveside in Edson by Union secretary W. Muldowan.

Down in Peers the McLeod River Gold Dredging Co. prepared to unload fifteen cars of equipment shipped from Colorado. Mr. R. Thompson supervised the unloading. Fifteen cars were needed for one dredge only, this all iron work, as timber was to be brought in separately from British Columbia. The work was to have been undertaken the preceding year, but the stock market crash tied up operations.

While there was talk of gold, there was also talk of oil. Alberta Pacific Consolidated, Hudson's Bay Oil and Gas and the Nordon Cor-

The band at Cadomin — late thirties.
Back Row standing: Art Clark, Joe Dombroski, Harry Lane, Bill Owens, Jason Thomas, John Ferguson, Spud Dombroski, Steve Trestenski, Henry Dumbroski, Al Wilkie, T. Owens, W. Shearer.
Bottom Row: John Stromek, J. MacKinnon, Tal Davies, Joe Ferguson, bandmaster, Dixon MacKinnon, J. Chesney, Ruben Baker.

poration had taken up leases within seven miles of the Lovett Station. the A.P. Annual report read, "At present it looks as if various interests in the Brazeau area, in which we have a considerable acreage might form a pool and drill a community well."

At Cadomin F. Faulkner installed sound at the Cadomin Theatre and residents flocked to see and hear 'the Talkies'.

And at Cadomin, Enrico Carretti died through accidental suffocation at the mine on June 11th.

The July 1st sports day was to be held at Cadomin this year and arrangements were made for a special train to pick up residents of the Park and Luscar. Edson which now boasted a population of 1,543 sent up a ball team.

The Cadomin mines went on short time beginning August 1st, 1931, and something like 80 men were temporarily laid off until conditions could improve. The hard times didn't seem to effect the starlit eyes of the young. Six weddings were performed in Cadomin in August.

However, all were gratified to learn that at last work on roads would be started. A wire from Chris Pattinson, M.L.A. informed residents that "The amount set aside for the first expenditure is $60,000." This was half of what it was expected to be but nevertheless it was a start. This beginning called for a celebration and one was duly organized at Cadomin when both Mr. Pattinson and Mr. Cliffe, Editor of the Edson-Jasper Signal, received gold wrist watches and Parker pen and pencil sets for their efforts toward this end.

The Idyl Hour Theatre in Edson opened with sound pictures for the first time featuring Buster Keaton in a comedy, and townspeople gathered to watch as official opening ceremonies for the 32-bed St. John's Hospital were held.

On the Lovett Branch, Nick Silivonchuk was taken for a moose by a hunter and shot in the right hip. He was to spend eleven months in St. John's Hospital in Edson and close to two years in the University and St. Joseph's Hospital in Edmonton. Rumor had it that the bachelor had had his leg amputated and died in the operation. Upon his return to the mining camp he found his meagre house and possessions had been dispensed with. With a shrug of his shoulders he went to Edson, bought a small acreage and took up dog breeding.

By November road work was proceeding well with a gang of men clearing brush from Mercoal to Coalspur. One group was directed by Mr. McLennan of Lovett while the other gang working near Shaw, Mile 12, was under the direction of Mr. Carl Carlson.

On November 11th the men in the Mercoal road tent-camp woke expecting to smell the usual aroma of coffee and breakfast in the making. Nothing. On investigation they found Thomas Lornoda, camp cook, laying with his ear frozen to the wall of the tent. It was not until help arrived with hot water and coal oil that he was released.

On November 12th Cadomin miners complied with a call of a 24 hour strike of all miners in Alberta to protest against the personnel of the Workmen's Compensation Board for the "inconsiderate, inhuman treatment accorded some of our members by that Board".

The new cottage hospital at Robb contained an office, women's ward, men's ward, dining room, bedroom and kitchen and would accommodate a resident doctor. Dr. N. Begg of Mercoal was expected to move in shortly. The labor had been donated by the men as had the proceeds of a dance which drew so many people most had to be content to merely listen to the five piece orchestra as the floor was too crowded for dancing.

Christmas Day, a hockey game was enjoyed by all at Coal Valley on the new rink when Sterco and Coal Valley met with lineups as follows: Sterco: J. Stringer, F. Martin, B. Henderson, A. Martin, A. Holmes, E. Jones.

Coal Valley: J. Lanouette, L. Armstrong, J. Letendre, H. Gariepy, P. Phillips, T. Devaney, D. Bernard, F. Lanouette, R. Lanouette.

* * *

Cadomin Loses out in Provincial Baseball Championship

Hockey was the main interest the winter of 1931-32 with as much money bet on the outcome of the games as there was in the frequently held poker games.

Early in February, 1932 Dmytro Vakulch, age 38 was accidentally killed by a fall of coal and stone at the Foothills mine.

At Edson the Idyl Hour Theatre which seemed to have had bad luck dogging it since it opened was destroyed by fire.

At Cadomin J. H. McMillan, the versatile mine superintendent and Wildred Edwards combined their talents to produce a pageant 'Canada and Her Daughters', with dialogue written by J. H. McMillan and music composed and arranged by Mr. Edwards. The new anthem 'Stand Canadians' written and composed by Mr. McMillan and Mr. Edwards was also sung. This song was highly spoken of by Mr. C. Holden Rushworth, conductor of the Edmonton Symphony Orchestra and would be on sale ·throughout Canada in due course along with other classic and popular songs written by the two men.

Remodelling started on the skating and hockey rink which had an ice surface of 75 × 185 feet, with an additional ice sheet for the use of small children. Its features included a 1200 gallon hot water tank for flooding, room for 1,200 visitors and gallery to seat 400, public waiting room, lunch counter and room, ladies' powder room, electric loud speakers, phonograph, hockey boys' room with showers and lockers and living quarters for the manager Charlie Lawson. Mr. Lawson, well-known to northern Alberta sports had been handling rinks for several decades. Full of enthusiasm he would be assisted by Jack Richmond, one of the best curling instructors in the West.

Both rinks were operated by the Cadomin Sports and Amusement Association of which J. Hutchison McMillan was president.

Mr. McMillan was a busy man indeed. A Collection of his poems had been published in a small volume and some of them broadcast from CJCA Edmonton. In the realm of music Mr. McMillan was considered one of the outstanding violinists of Western Canada.

Working conditions at the Cadomin mine at this time were probably the most advanced in Western Canada and it is doubtful if the rates of wages earned could be duplicated at any other mine in the dominion.

The population of Cadomin in this year of 1933 was 1,700 permanent residents.

* * *

The Relief Road Building camp opened for work on the highway. Camps would be operated on the relief basis of $17.50 per month.

"Mr. C. Pattinson M.L.A., states that the government is opening another relief camp of fifty men at Leyland for work on the Coal Branch Highway.

The greatest difficulty now seems to be to get men to go to work in these camps at the rate of pay offered by the government; if this could be overcome there seems to be no reason why the work should not progress at a good pace.[17]

[17] See Pete Romaniuks story

After delivering a passenger at Robb, Grant MacConachie of the Independent Airways, operating between Edson and Edmonton made a forced landing. Just as he took off from Robb his engine cut out for some reason not determined.[18] He had to decide whether to put the Puss-Moth which he was flying into the trees or try for smaller ones across a ravine. Choosing the latter course he managed to put the machine down with nothing much more than a broken propeller, spar and under-carriage strut.

His friends in Edson were much relieved to find that the first reports of near death were unfounded. Mr. MacConachie was able to take the train into Edmonton and fly out to Edson in 'G-D' on Monday as usual. The Puss-Moth will be shipped back to Edmonton for repairs.

The following week, Mrs. James Rupert of Coal Valley was taken by train to Edson and flown from Edson to Edmonton by Mr. MacConachie.

An announcement was made in the Edson paper which read: There is a rumor current on the Lovett Branch to the effect that I am responsible for the burning of a Fiery Cross at Coal Valley on the night of July 19th last. I desire it to be distinctly understood that I had no connection with this incident whatever. I was on the train that day in the usual course of my own business, and I will at once take action against anyone circulating these rumors after this date.

The notice was signed by a trainman. The Ku Klux Klan flared briefly at Edson, too, but the incidents petered out with very little attention.

The Cadomin Miners, baseball team entered the contest for the provincial baseball championship that summer, and after winning three games out of five from the Edmonton Arctics, lost to the Nacmine Miners in three successive games, thus losing the provincial title.

Lineup included: Con Docherty, pitcher and third base, Johnny Gerlitz, pitcher and centre field; W. Docherty, pitcher; Nick Melnyk, pitcher and first base; W. Steen, second base; E. Clyburn, utility; M. Deitz, centre field; M. Susnar, utility; F. Braden, right field; Frank Lewis, captain, manager and shortstop; J. James, trainer; W. Pryde, left field; W. Zazulak, utility and T. Jones, batboy.

J. H. MacMillan was the honorary vice-president; W. J. Dick the honorary president and P. McKenna the president.

Five miles up the McLeod River on Moose Jaw Creek, M. Talpash found a large quantity of clay, and on having it analyzed found the same type used in the making of toilet preparations. Claynett Limited, Edmonton indicated that there was the possibility of establishing a plant in Edson for the milling, grinding and processing of the product.

The year 1933 saw Mercoal opening their new skating rink. Thanks were extended to the mine management for the support they gave to

[18] See Dr. Begg story

the undertaking, supplying teams for the excavation work as well as pipes and electrical fittings.

Down the river at Peers, the McLeod River Mining Corp., who, ever since their incorporation in 1926, faced one misfortune after another finally had started operations. Their September effort the previous year had come to a stop in a few days when an accident occurred which made necessary the manufacture and importation of a new part. Initial operations recovered some $400 in gold from the gravel of the McLeod river where the company had leases extending 117 miles on the river.

"The company had an authorized capitalization of 5,000,000 shares of no par value, of which at last report, 1,669,024 shares were outstanding. Officials state that the company has sufficient cash arranged to meet the cost of the repairs, and put the dredge into operation. The debts outstanding total about $200,000. made up largely by advances from Stobie Forlong Assets Ltd. and secured by a mortgage."

By early spring more than fifty non-paying travellers had been tagged by Edson and Jasper police as they passed through on trains on the main line and the Coal Branch.

The largest snow on record had fallen on the Lovett Branch the spring of 1933, '72; and reports of animal starvation were received regularly by Fish and Game officials.

Reports were received from Coalspur that deer in the district were dying for want of food and were coming round the station yards in search of food. From Weald came the report that "the deer and elk were in critical condition and animals are too weak to recover even after being fed". Mercoal reported deer and moose in poor condition and Lovett Train crews brought in dire reports of the condition of game in the district. The Edson Fish and Game Protective League sent an urgent message to the provincial government to send out carloads of hay, and wired S. J. Hungerford, acting president CNR asking for free transportation of the feed to points on the branch. Packers and forestry men had volunteered to take the hay to where the animals would have a chance to get it.

Hockey still much in the forefront of activities, saw the Luscar Girls hockey team travelling to Edson to play a two game series against the Edson girls. The Luscar girls in snappy yellow and black uniforms won both games. Line-up included: Annie Baker, Mary Davis, Frances Foster, Annie Kulyk, Rosie Onychuk, Julie Onychuk, Mary Small, Bertha LiBotte and Bert Domenchelli. Edson's lineup included: Mary Blasius, Jessie Hardacre, Millie Dutka, Helen McKeever, Annie Bridges, Mary Zelinski, Margaret Dobson, Dorothy Parnall, Edith Fowler and Alex Fyfe.

The Cadomin Colts pressing for the Class B title won and took off for Camrose, while Luscar Tigers met Blairmore in another forward step to the Intermediate competition.

* * *

In June announcement was made by Carbon By-Products Co. Ltd. Edmonton that it would build its first plant at the Sterling Collieries, Sterco, for low temperature carbonization of coal. A new process invented by Evan Lucas, of London Ontario would be used in a single unit plant having a minimum capacity of 50 tons per day.

Officers and directors of the closed corporation were: R. M. Halpenny, Sterling Collieries, president; Vice-president Abe Cristall, owner of the Royal George Hotel; secretary-treasurer O. G. Kelly; director, P. E. Pinsonneault, engineer William McKenzie; solicitor E. T. Bishop.

* * *

Mr. B. Higgins, B. Anderson, H. A. Higgins and a Mr. Rideout spent July recovering what was left of the Lovett mine.

* * *

A party of sixty left the Coal Branch for a two week excursion to the Pacific coast taking advantage of the 'cent-a-mile' rate offered by the railroad. A second group was to leave before school started.

Simon McIntosh built a new garage with two gasoline tanks. Cadomin now boasted twenty-nine automobiles and numerous motor cycles. The road from Cadomin to Luscar was at least negotiable and cars made frequent trips back and forth.

The non-working miners eyed with trepedition the striking miners at East Coulee in Drumheller who were cut off relief according to a new ruling issued the last half of August by the provincial relief department. Each applicant for relief would be required to produce a certificate from the mine where he was last employed declaring that no work is available for him before the government would sanction relief. The new order affected 300 families immediately.

Residents of the Coal Branch angrily expressed dissatisfaction with the Department of Education who decreed that Coal Branch High School students would have to go to Jasper to write final examinations. This meant a day in Edson going and returning, and students would be put to unnecessary expense. They asked to have the exams written in Edson.

L. G. Chavignaud, resident engineer of Cadomin Coal Co. was given a party before leaving to take over management of the King Mine at Hinton.

It was necessary to add another room to the Cadomin school which now consisted of five rooms.

C. A. Davidson, Provincial Works Commissioner and Major Harcourt, of the Dominion Relief Branch visited the Coal Branch for two days with Major Harcourt approving the placing of 500 men in camps for winter works on the Coal Branch Road. A few weeks later after the recommendation was sent to Ottawa, word was received that no provision would be made by Dominion Relief funds for the project. Some provincial funds would be available for work on the road between Cadomin and Mountain Park.

At Coal Valley a new recreation hall was opened with a small sacristy which could be shut off from the main portion of the hall by folding doors.

Mr. and Mrs. Boyd and their son Howard arrived to take charge of the Coal Valley Hotel.

At Cadomin 450 attended the Christmas Party for the children when $100 worth of gifts from the Cadomin Coal Co. and businessmen were distributed.

* * *

1934

January 1934 saw Claynett Ltd. Commercial Clay Products and Toiletries open up in Edson. The entire plant and office equipment were moved from Edmonton and the first carload of clay received from the deposit on the McLeod River, five miles up the Coal Branch.

The intrepid general superintendent of the Cadomin Coal Co., J. H. McMillan, was accorded membership in the American Author's Association.

Luscar Indians 'drove' to Cadomin for a hockey game, January 7th but found that an overnight thaw had forced cancellation. The team manager had tried to phone Luscar but the telephone line had been blown down in the storm.

The Burns concert at Cadomin was followed by a Ball which ended at 5:00 a.m.

In February, 1934, the government announced that 300 men would be employed on the Coal Branch in four different camps. The road connecting Cadomin and Luscar had been completed last fall. Citizens of Luscar were highly indignant at the government taking credit for building the road when Luscar residents had spent many volunteer hours with equipment donated by Luscar Coals towards this very same project.

An article in the Edmonton Journal, June 30, 1934, stated:

MOUNTAIN PARK, June 30. — After an isolated existence of 21 years in regard to highway communication with neighboring towns, the highest village in Canada, having an altitude of 6,200 feet above sea level, has just been connected by auto road with Cadomin and Luscar. No longer restricted to using the railway, residents are now enjoying the novelty of autos.

The completion of the road marks another step forward in communication on the coal branch. Already half a dozen new cars are enroute to Mountain Park and will no doubt be followed by more in the near future.

The establishment of this communication was made possible through the energy, determination and generosity of one man, A. N. Scott, general superintendent of Mountain Park Coal company and Luscar Collieries Limited. After futile efforts to obtain the co-operation, Mr. Scott decided to do the work on his own initiative and the result can now be seen in a good motor car road to Mountain Park.

> Last year Mr. Scott and his loyal supporters at Luscar built a road
> between Luscar and Cadomin which is much used and formed the chief
> means of communication between these two towns. This year, by im-
> proving part of an existing trail, using part of the government road built
> under relief measures and building four miles of new road, he has opened
> up the country so that some of the amenities of present day life can be
> enjoyed not only by residents but also by friends at Cadomin, who are
> already showing their appreciation by using the road to the fullest extent.
>
> Although the three Coal branch towns are now connected by an auto
> road, the dream of an outlet to the Jasper highway is still unrealized and
> it is hoped that some co-operative movement can be organized soon to
> attain this objective.

On June 15, 1934 Cadomin Coal Co. Ltd. began erection of a new
air cleaning plant at a cost of $55,000 and it was expected to be in oper-
ation August 1st.

W. J. Dick, president, said the plant was being built for the purpose
of supplying a low content ash coal for industrial purposes, smelters
and similar consumers. The annual meeting was held recently in Winnipeg with Mr. Dick re-elected president, W. H. Parmeice again
named vice-president and Miss E. M. Powley as secretary-treasurer.

It was in June too that Cadomin Sports & Amusement Association
sponsored a two day sports event. "Something to remember will be the
fact that this will be the first time that automobile road connections
between the various camps of Mountain Park, Luscar and Cadomin
can be used to bring visitors to the event." The fact that the visitors
had to travel in small caravans to push and pull each other out of
muddy portions was not stressed.

Some residents of Mountain Park started to make their yearly
periodic treks to the Miette Hot Springs by horseback. The Europeans
particularly appreciated the steaming hot mineral waters that sprang
out from the limestone walls, believing it cured rheumatism. A mud
and moss chinked log pool had been built by earlier miners in the
area. In 1934 a dirt motor road had been built to within a few hundred
feet of the first pool but it was not shown in the 1934 edition of the
provincial road map. Coal Branchers preferred the horseback trail
over the mountain.

In June, Harry King, president of the Hinton Collieries started to
build a new hotel at Hinton Station.

A Branch of the Canadian Legion, B.E.S.L. was formed at Mercoal.
Acting officials were J. Denholm, president and J. G. Davies, Secretary. Returned men in Coalspur and Robb joined the branch.

At Mountain Park Superintendent Pasco decided the soccer team
who had bested Cadomin, Camp 67 and Camp 57 were ready to go to
Edmonton to take on the city's crack teams.

And in September the Cheviot Hotel burned at Mountain Park.
The fire which broke out on a Saturday afternoon drew a large crowd
of onlookers. There was no use letting the beer burn so soon there was
a scene of much merriment with kegs of beer rolling down the hill and
miners running in hot pursuit. More than one head ached the next

day. The loss estimated at $40,000 was covered by insurance and a new hotel would be erected.

* * *

The Cheviot Hotel burns at Mountain Park, September 1934.

At Coalspur a business exchange of much interest occurred when Messrs. C. Matthews and Thos. B. Cuthbertson of Mountain Park purchased the general store and Yellowhead Hotel at Coalspur.

The store and hotel had been under the management of H. Neilsen for many years and had become well known to the travelling public. Cam Matthews was one of the better known guides and outfitters of the district and intended to combine these interests at Coalspur.

Mr. Neilsen moved to Edmonton and purchased an interest in a radio broadcasting station.

Cam in his taped interview said: "I owned the Coalspur townsite, the whole thing, dance hall, school, store ... I should never have let it go." He was not to sell till 1945.

The Coal Branch held a joint Miner's Conference early in 1935 at the Memorial Hall in Edson, with C. Pattinson M.L.A. attending as a fraternal delegate.

The conference lasted three days. Among the many resolutions passed was the following — Whereas: That owing to unemployment being so prevalent, we ask the Government to lower the age limit under the Old Age Pensions Act to sixty years of age so that younger men who are unemployed may be given a chance in industry.

Whereas — There is such a large amount of unemployment in Alberta, we urge upon the Government the vital need of developing an

106

adequate relief work programme of their own, independent of the Federal Government, and that men employed in this work shall be paid Trade Union rates of wages, also we further urge that the Edson Coal Branch shall be included in this project. And that we protest against the system of relief camps as at present organized on the basis of twenty cents per day plus board. Believing the work is necessary work, we affirm the principle of instituting Trade Union rates of wages for employees working in relief camps.

Whereas: We appreciate the work that has been done between Luscar, Cadomin and Mountain Park on the road connecting these camps, yet we must point out that this method is too slow to carry out the object of linking up all the camps and in providing an outlet to the main highway.

Whereas: There is no other such condition existing in Canada where so many people are isolated without an outlet by road, and the Edson Coal Branch is a large revenue producing district.

It is resolved: That this be placed under the Dept. of Public Works and that firstly the Government shall make a substantial appropriation to immediately connect all camps, and secondly, that there be an immediate survey to determine the best possible outlet to the main highway.

It is resolved: That we request the Railway Commissioner the need of a daily train service, reduced rates and modern coaches for the Edson Coal Branch.

It is resolved: That we request the Government to amend the Mines Act whereby there shall be a weekly wage instead of bi-monthly.

It is resolved: That this Conference go on record protesting against the action of the Cadomin Coal Company in charging $2.00 ground rent for residences at Cadomin, and that they should be brought in line with other coal camps in the Province to a charge of $1.00 per month.

The officers of the Conference appointed for 1935 were as follows: President, W. Moldowan of Cadomin; Vice-president, T. Foley of Mountain Park; Secretary-Treasurer, T. B. Rees of Luscar.

* * *

Robert Nicholl was the first casulty of 1935 when he was caught in a coal slide in the pit at Sterco. In March W. Kowalchuk, age 30 was killed when pinned between a car of coal and the roof of the entry in No. 1 slope of Mountain Park Collieries.

This was the year of the money chain letters in the U.S. and Canada, and the younger generation particularly spent hours writing letters.

The Canadian Legion, Cadomin Branch were busy building new quarters.

* * *

In April the Cadomin Miners organized once more: Protests that blankets allegedly unwashed for a year or more are in use at relief work camps 57 and 59 on the Alberta Coal Branch have been sent to the agricultural committee of the legislature by the Cadomin Miner's Union.

The complaint of the committee which is investigating camp conditions also states that two men have to sleep in each bunk which allows each man about 22 inches space. It is also stated that there are no recreation facilities whatever in these two work camps. The union requests that these conditions be investigated and rectified at once.

In April, sponsored by the Italian employees, miners tendered a complimentary banquet to Mr. and Mrs. J. H. McMillan who were to leave Cadomin in early May for a trip to Honolulu, later to settle at the Pacific coast. During the evening Mr. McMillan was presented with a set of mother-of-pearl cuff links and buttons set in platinum and gold. Mr. McMillan suffered from ill health.

Cadomin was to miss this Scotsman with the Jekyl and Hyde temperament. His patronage of the arts and sports and facets of his 'little Ceasar' personality would be a topic of conversation for decades to come.

One story recalls the white horse that McMillan would ride to the west workings in the early Cadomin days. The horse was of balky character and one day when McMillan tried to mount, the horse turned. Each time he tried to mount, the horse turned again. In one of his surges of temper McMillan pinned a note to the horse reading "Shoot this SOB when he gets back". He hit him with a riding crop and sent the horse galloping back to his quarters. The poor employee in charge of the animals was in a quandary when he read the note. He would be damned if he did, and damned if he didn't. Prudently he hid the animal.

In May two feet of snow covered the Mountain Park area, which was considered a record for May even in this altitude. Curlers and skaters enjoyed the novelty of May winter sports.

In May too, the new Hinton Hotel was opened and several Coal Branch residents went to Hinton to wish Harry King well.

Al B. Kluck became the new proprietor of the Valley Drug & Confectionery, and twenty new private homes were built in Cadomin.

The Oddfellows Lodges of District 34, comprising Luscar, Cadomin and Mountain Park sponsored a community picnic and it was held close to relief camp 59. Over 500 children and 600 adults attended. Men from the relief camp with J. D. Gillis in charge had built a track, swings and even a type of merry-go-round. The Cadomin Brass Band put zippy selections into the day's event.

And in July, falling from a speeder he was using to go to Sterco to Mile 54 to attend a patient, Dr. Ivar Lefsrud of Edson was accidentally killed when the speeder left the track and threw him to the ground.

May 24, 1944. Our car in front of the hardware store after a five foot fall of snow.
— Vivian Melnyk

Dr. Lefsrud was associated with Dr. R. E. Johnston of Edson, and at the time of the accident was relieving Dr. P. A. Macdonald of Sterco.

According to evidence he was being taken from Sterco to Mile 54 on a speeder owned and used by Dr. Macdonald in his medical calls to other camps. Raymond Edward Hickman of Sterco was in charge of the speeder and warned the doctor to hang on. During the run one side of the speeder left the track and according to the witness, the deceased either tried to jump or was thrown heavily from the speeder.

He was taken to Mile 54 and Dr. Long of Robb was summoned. The Signal notes: 'The intolerable condition which makes it necessary for doctors to travel to their patients on railway speeders and patients to be taken to the doctors by similar conveyances owing to the fact that there is not highway connection has been the subject of protest for some years, and the sad death of Dr. Lefsrud is another piece of undeniable evidence that a road between the coal mining camps is an absolutely necessary public service.

J. H. Unwin, the Social Credit candidate was elected in the provincial election. Chris Pattinson after nine years in the office of the Canadian Labour Party stepped aside.

At the Miette Hot Springs, a new pool, long contemplated was begun. The Federal government set aside $65,000 for the construction of a stone and cement pool. Last dips were taken in the historic old log pool.[19]

[19] I was six years old and spent several weeks of this summer camping at Miette with my mother. I had cut my foot on a broken beer bottle in the log pool. The road and construction crews were dressed down thoroughly by the foreman in charge. As a conciliatory gesture I was allowed to choose the dessert and as I was a Jello lover, for two weeks men coming to the huge mess tent joined me in every conceivable variety of a Jello dessert. They were probably happy to see our tent come down so they could again have apple pie. — Toni Ross

At Cadomin F. W. Faulkner sold his interest in the theatre to R. B. Fairclough, manager of the Cadomin Mercantile Store.

Messrs. R. Lovett and A. Morrison, president and secretary of District 18, UMWA were business visitors to Mercoal November 1st, negotiating a new wage scale agreement which resulted in a 5% increase on all union rates.

At Edson construction began on the $50,000 water tank in the CNR yards. When completed only one stop between Edmonton and Jasper would be required by trains.

Police court was held at Coalspur in December presided over by Magistrate Thurber of Edson. The sawmill just west of Robb, formerly owned by P. A. 'Baldy' Robb was the direct cause of all charges heard.

The Mountain Park Co-operative Society which had catered to the people of Mountain Park for 16 years in general merchandising turned their business over to W. S. Knight of the Luscar Mercantile. Art Leonard, recently of Safeway Stores, arrived to take charge of Mr. Knights new store.[20]

1936 - Luscar Wins Provincial Senior Amateur Championship

The Coal Branch was elated when for the second time in three years the Luscar Indians brought home the Provincial Senior Amateur Championship.

Bill Lewis writing in the Edmonton Bulletin Sports Pages March 11 stated:

Hockey followers throughout Northern Alberta will be highly pleased with Luscar Indians winning the Provincial Senior Amateur Championship ... Here is one who is willing to stand up and lead the cheering for the fighting band of pucksters A. N. Scott gathered together to represent the mountain mining town.

In Calgary they showed their fighting spirit by winning their second consecutive victory over Coleman Canadians after dropping the opening game to them here last week.

Copping two in a row in the south after losing what was supposed to have been their 'home' game takes plenty of what the writing boys refer to as intestinal fortitude and the Indians proved they have plenty of that.

So once again it is not out of place for all hockey fans in this part of the province to give them all of the congratulations that are their due, and to wish them the very best in the approaching interprovincial playdowns.

[20] See Leonard story.

Luscar Indians 1941–42 Alberta Champs, Western Canada Finalists. Back Row L. to R. Hamilton, Art Jerwa, Mike Onychuk, Walter Holden, Jim McVey. Front Row L. to R. Bandy Ross, ??, Sandy Domenichelli, Claude Bartoff (Goalie), Curly Kulyk, George Bonner, J. A. Protti.

Edmontonians take a particularly keen interest in the Luscar team, and are all the more pleased with their triumph because of the fact there are a number of former local players on the Indians Lineup . . . Lindsay Carver, Dee-Ay Gillies, Eddie Shamlock, Leo Lemieux, all were practically raised on the ice of Edmonton rinks, while Bob Kennedy and Rollie Hills played their hockey here for quite a few years with various local aggregations. So it requires no persuasion at all for fans here to join with those of Luscar, and the entire Coal Branch for that matter in wishing the team continued success in their drive for titular honors.

From the southern city the story read: Calgary, March 11 — With a great display of courage team play and determination, Luscar Indians won the Alberta senior hockey championship and the right to meet Prince Albert Mintos in the Allan Cup playdowns, defeating Coleman Canadians 4–3 in the third and deciding game of the provincial final in the Arena last night. Coleman had taken the first game 2–1, and Luscar the second 3–2 before the rubber match.

Indians rose to great heights in turning in a spectacular victory before a capacity crowd of more than 4,000 and it was really a brilliant win for the Northern Coal Branch Team. They earned it by cool and deliberate play under heavy fire, and are worthy champions of the province for the second time in three years.

Michael Onychuk, in a way was the hero of the contest for he laid down the pass from Kennedy to secure the tying goal six minutes from the end, and with two and a half minutes left to play ran in the winning tally on a solo effort that brought down the house.

Luscar had a good margin of the play in a scoreless first period before Jimmy McVey opened the count for Luscar with an end to end rush. Kennedy picked out the narrow side on Stewart's pass to make it 2-0 but Jimmy Joyce got one of those goals back for Coleman.

It was a thrilling close. Duke Kwasnie, burly Coleman defenceman, getting away on a centre ice pass from Brown to beat Goalie Davie Pow with a close-in shot. Coleman continued the pressure and Joe Fisher, former Edmonton junior, belted in Billy Fraser's rebound to send the Crow's Nest champions ahead.

It was then that Luscar came through with a closing charge that just couldn't be denied. Their plays clicked with smooth regularity as McVey, Kennedy and Onychuk backed by the spirited play of Lindsay Carver and Rollie Hills, clamored for goals. They came. Kennedy and Onychuk doing the scoring with another scoring effort by Kennedy being disallowed through a Luscar player being in the goal crease.

Canadians put up a game fight, though a losing one, and the Indians made a host of friends with a grand display of hockey. They were a credit to Coach Frank Coulsen and their former mentor Duke Keats. Lineups:

Luscar — Pow, Carver, Hills, Onychuk, Shamlock, McVey.
    Subs: Sanders, Kennedy, Jerwa, Stewart.
Coleman — Scocarello, R. Kwasnie, J. Kwasnie, W. Fraser, J. Fraser, Fuher. Subs: Joyce, Lopichuk, Brown, Johnson.
Referees: C. S. Campbell, Edmonton; Earl Overand, Okotoks.

* * *

However the Luscar Indians lost their chance to enter the Allan Cup finals when Prince Albert tied the score at Calgary the next weekend. The Luscar team weakened through the absence of Onychuk who was in the hospital at Prince Albert suffering from a severe attack of influenza, saw Robbie Hill benched through an injury in the second period. However there would be another year.

* * *

Unemployment was still rampant and at Jasper 40 married men, all residents of Jasper started on relief work widening roads. No provision had been made as yet for the single jobless. On the Coal Branch too, the widening of the 'trails' continued.

J. H. Unwin took up the cudgel of the road situation in the legislature. On March 20, 1936 the Edmonton Bulletin carried the following story:

Effective immediately the 500 single homeless unemployed men in the nine provincial work camps will be paid 50¢ per day for every day worked, instead of 20¢ a day as in the past, according to Hon. Dr. W. W. Cross, Minister of Health and in charge of relief.

Under this plan a maximum of $15 a month will be available to any man in addition to his food, clothing and shelter.

This new provision is also to prevail in Dominion works camps in the province.

It is provided that the men will be paid the 50 cents for five days a week if they work. If they do not work, there will be no pay. Under the former scheme they were paid 20 cents a day whether they worked or not.

* * *

In early May 1936 the Mountain View Hotel at Cadomin burned to the ground. The building was owned by the Cadomin Coal Co. and the business managed by Peter McKenna. A number of men who resided at the hotel lost all their personal effects. Excellent work on the part of Fire Chief W. Muldowan and his men kept the flames from spreading to adjoining buildings. One man attempted to enter the burning building heedless of the flames. Chief Muldowan turned the hose on him to deter this plan. Loss was estimated at $10,000 partly covered by insurance.

Plans were drawn up almost immediately by Architect William G. Blakey, an architect from Edmonton for a new Cadomin Hotel.

It was in June that the town of Cadomin became aware of a multiple shooting through the night. The files of the RCMP read:

GEORGE PANEK—Cadomin, Alta. — Attempted Murder

On the early morning of 12-6-36 our Constable at Cadomin received a telephone message from Coalspur that the above named had shot and wounded Mrs. John Jess, John Harco and Andy Istevan of Cadomin. Immediate investigation was made by our constable and it was ascertained that Panek on the night of the 11th, after drinking freely in the beer parlour with John Jess, had accompanied the latter to his home, taking six bottles of beer along with him. Mrs. Jess expressed her displeasure and told him that she did not like to see him come to her place, to which Panek replied "All right, I fix you." Later, however she was induced to drink a bottle of beer and prepare a little supper for them. When the beer was all consumed Panek left after announcing his intention to return later with some whiskey. Mr. and Mrs. Jess retired, and about 2:30 a.m. Panek came into the bedroom occupied by Mrs. Jess, and after a slight altercation announced that he was going to kill her, her brother Andy Istevan, John Harco, Mike Klapkan and Mrs. Irastinsky, and then himself. Carrying the gun in his right hand Panek took a loaf of bread out of the breadbox, returned to the bedroom and after saying good-buy fired two shots at Mrs. Jess the second of which struck her in the right breast. After going again to the bread box, he went back into the bedroom and, remarking to Mrs. Jess, "You are still alive yet," fired another shot at her which missed. He then said, "Goody-buy, you have got enough." John Jess, the husband, who was occupying another bed, told Panek that he was going to get the police. Ordering him to stay on the bed as he intended to shoot the police too, Panek left the house.

Panek next went to the house of Bill Lobos and on Andy Istevan going to the door he fired several shots at him, also at John Harco, wounding both men. Just before leaving the house, he fired a shot at John Lobos who was lying in bed, but missed him.

113

Panek returned to his home for a club bag and left Cadomin about 3:20 a.m., and in spite of well-organized search parties and the use of dog 'Dale' he has not been seen or heard of since. As the country around Cadomin is a wild, wooded, hilly country and Panek is known to have no knowledge of the woods, there is strong reason to believe that he has committed suicide as he threatened to do.

The only motive that can be assigned for this man's actions is that at different times he had quarrelled with the various parties concerned. All the victims have made a good recovery.

Inspector Tucker, RCMP Edmonton was in charge of the operations and Cadominites continued to speculate on Panek's whereabouts for many years.

* * *

The fight for the Coal Branch Road continued. At a meeting of the Edson Board of Trade, Mr. M. Burleigh of Mountain Park stated there were over 100 cars in Mountain Park, Cadomin and Luscar and only 17 miles of road. Mayor W. B. Low referred to the revenue the government received from the district, and the Board's president R. E. Thurber introduced the guest speaker, J. H. Unwin, M.L.A. who talked of Alberta Prosperity Certificates or 'script'.

Mr. Unwin declared he was astounded to learn that the council of the Town of Edson had passed a resolution declaring that the town was only prepared to accept "cheques or legal tender" for any accounts payable to the town. "You are asking the Provincial government for a lot of things," said Mr. Unwin. "You want the Coal Branch road and you want other roads. Are you prepared to co-operate with the government in getting these things?"

"There were only two ways of providing these things, one was by the use of our own credit and the other was by borrowing the money. We can use the credit of the province to build these roads, using script to pay for the work, or we can build the road and then owe some guy in New York two million dollars."

"The government was willing to build the Coal Branch road and other roads, but they were not willing to go into debt," said Mr. Unwin. "The amount of script to be issued will depend on the amount of co-operation the government receives," continued Mr. Unwin. "At the present time it is proposed to issue $5,000.00 worth of certificates to each constituency. If it is found that this is doing the work, more will be issued, the government at all times standing ready to redeem it."

At the same time retailers were notified that certain wholesales and manufacturers connected with a specified list of Boards of Trade and Chambers of Commerce would not accept Provincial script in payment of accounts.

The notice read as follows:

To all Retail Merchants:

"In fairness to the retail trade, and for its protection the wholesalers and manufacturers of the undersigned trade organizations are anxious that you should understand their position with respect to the proposed

114

Alberta Prosperity Certificates to which they have given serious con-
sideration.

"They have therefore requested us to advise that they will be unable to accept the Prosperity Certificates if issued."

The notice was signed by the Edmonton Chamber of Commerce, Calgary Board of Trade, Lethbridge Board of Trade, Red Deer Board of Trade, Medicine Hat Chamber of Commerce and the Canadian Manufacturers' Association.

Confusion reigned throughout the province.

A story from Drumheller read:

"Work and wages programme with script as payment got underway in the Drumheller industrial area this week. 15 men out of a total of more then 700 recipients turned out on the Midland Vale highway project.

According to some members of the unemployed, Works Official John Gray discouraged men who had large families from accepting the script proposals stating that they would be better off on the existing relief scale.

The majority of grocerymen were at a loss to know what action to take if script were presented at the month-end. "It can be confidently stated that no grocer will accept the script in Drumheller unless wholesalers have a change of heart before the month-end."

By the middle of July the staunch Social Credit group at Cadomin passed the following resolution:

As the Government of the Province is issuing Prosperity Certificates for the purpose of building roads, and as the merchants in some parts are refusing to accept said Certificates, and, as the merchants of Cadomin, Alta. have signified their willingness to accept said Certificates and co-operate with the Government to the fullest extent:

Therefore be it resolved: That we urge the government to commence work on the Alberta Coal Branch road at this point, to give the Certificates a start;

That as this road is surveyed and partly graded and stumped between Coalspur and Cadomin;

That at the present time work is slack and road work commencing immediately would be of great assistance to us all;

That our winters start early in this high altitude and summer is really the best time for road work;

That this group is convinced that we have suffered enough from our past mis-government and look hopefully to our Social Credit government to do something for us in the way of road work and employment by the use of our credit.

The Social Credit group at Marlboro also agitated for the road. The resolution was signed by Hugh Munroe, president, D. M. Miller, vice-president and J. Ledray as sec-treas. and declared to be the view of '150 members'.

At Edson 150 males from Edson and the Coal Branch gathered in farewell to Corp. "Bob" Matheson, RCMP who left to take up duties in Red Deer.

"Corp. Matheson has been on police duty in Edson and district for the past fifteen years, first with the RNWMP, then with the Alberta

Provincial Police and later with the RCMP. Previous to this he was engaged in farming east of Edson."

* * *

In baseball circles the Cadomin Maroons finished their Northern Alberta Title Series. The Bulletin describes the lineup as follows:
Frank Lewis: Manager and shortstop, a real veteran, played with Calgary Bronks and is still going strong.
Ken Stewart: Catcher, age 24, Played senior ball with the South Side Athletics, three years with Cadomin.

W. Stene: Second baseman, lead off man, has played all his baseball with Cadomin, a good hitter.
N. Melnyk: First base. The team veteran, played with Chev Cubs in '29 and with Cadomin ever since. One of the finest first basemen in Alberta ball.

Dave Pow:'Age 24, third base, a good hitter and worthy manager of the hot corner.
Alex Matheson: Age 21, utility man and a real comer.
L. Dietz: Centre field, only 21 and a veteran for his age. Played with
Spokane in Timber League, a fine ball player.
F. Braben: Age 28, utility fielder. Steady fielder and fence buster, having played a lot of ball in central Alberta.
W. Zazulak: Right fielder, age 26, a ball hawk and dangerous at plate. Played on Pacific Coast.

John Gerlitz: Another veteran. Home run king of the circuit, formerly with Calgary White Sox and Army & Navy Club, Edmonton.
Dick Benott: Pitcher, age 29. A steady moundman and also dangerous at plate.
Harold Croft: Pitcher, age 19. Southpaw ace of the squad and a good prospect for fast company.
Guy Simpson: Age 27, played ball all over the province, a fast ball pitcher. Worked with Webb King's Bulls.
Henry Graham: Local bat boy par excellence.
Peter McKenna: President of the team, and well known sportsman.
W. J. Dick: President and General Manager of Cadomin Coal Co.
J. A. McLeod: Supt. of Cadomin Mines.
Colin Campbell: Manager of Cadomin Mercantile Ltd. Eric Collins, Sec.-Treas. of the club.

But in a six game series Cadomin lost out to the Lethbridge Galt Miners for the Alberta Senior Baseball Championship, a first for Lethbridge.

Back on the Coal Branch, tennis, soccer and football enthusiasts continued to play as if they too were headed for provincial championships.

Miners throughout Alberta prepared to vote on the proposed amalgamation of independent and Canadian mine workers unions with the United Mine Workers of America.

Confusion continued to rein over the script plan, both at the street level and contradictory statements issued at a higher level.

At Cadomin construction began on a new $50,000 hoist, one of the largest hoists of its kind in Western Canada. It would be capable of lifting 1,000 tons each 8-hour shift. Building began on the brick hoist room measuring 38 × 61 feet which would be covered with a metal roof. Steel headframe for the shaft made by John Woods and Son, of London, England would be 56 feet high with two 14 foot sheaves.

And in Washington, W. A. Selvig, U.S. Bureau of Mines geologist predicted the nation's known oil reserves would be exhausted by 1951.

Early in 1937 the Edson Girls Monarch Team captured the Northern Alberta Intermediate Ladies Hockey and the Alberta Provincial Championship in Intermediate Ladies Hockey. They brought home with them the Twin City Trophy and the Coffe Memorial Trophy and to the best of all information this title is still retained by Edson. No intermediate ladies hockey team ever challenged the group for the title, after the Varsity Co-Ed game was played in Edmonton. Billy Macdonald was manager of this team and coach, G. G. Farewell.

Lines-ups were:

Co-Eds: Rose, Hazlet, MacDonald, Hewett, Dean, Stevenson, Laidlaw, Chesney and Stone.

Edson: Willis, Armstrong, Blasius, Zelinski, Dutka, Hardacre, McCuish, McKeever, Switzer, D. Hardacre and Morris.

Referee, Pat Costigan.

* * *

May 1st, Workers' day was celebrated at Cadomin. Proceedings opened with a Workers' parade headed by the Cadomin band, followed by organized workers carrying the International Red Flag of Labor. After an afternoon meeting addressed by James MacPherson of Edmonton, the meeting closed with the workers' salute, the half-raised arm with closed fist.

The evening's attraction was the Boxing Card with promotor Jimmy Maddams drawing from the Cadomin Gymnasium Club. In the 1st event Donny Mclaren won from Stan Morgan Jr.: 2nd event Jim Logan and Bob Chapman fought to a draw; 3rd event, Kid Dombrowski and Battling Willis were a draw; 4th event Louis Joy and Martin Sinal were a draw; 5th event Sid McLeod knocked out Spud Dombrowski in the third round, 6th event Henry Kwasney and Flying Shearer were a draw.

Mr. S. Travers, Fisheries Inspector, supervised the distribution of 30,000 Loch Leven trout fry in four locations in the Mountain Park area in June of 1937. They were placed as follows: 4,000 in Ruby Lake; 4,000 in Cardinal River; 4,000 in Grave Creek and 18,000 in Medicine Lick Lake, all these tributaries of the Saskatchewan River. Pack horses were used to get them to the locations.

Disappointment was felt by many when work at the Miette Hot Springs pool closed down through lack of funds. More than $65,000 had already been spent on the project. The road was open to the public as a scenic drive, but no camping privileges were allowed the summer of '37.

The Cadomin Maroons retained their title as Northern Alberta Champs by defeating Cadogan in a two game series.

In September Robert Stone 69-year-old postmaster at Pocohontas closed out what was believed to be the smallest area sized post-office in Canada.

In December, J. Simon of Cadomin interviewed the Minister of Public Works and presented a petition of 2,000 signatures from Coal Branch residents asking that winter work be undertaken on the Coal Branch Road.

1938

Late in 1937 a local branch of the International Woodworkers of America was formed in the Edson area district, and early in 1938 three camps, Sibbald, Menarie and the Frank Corser camp workers went on strike.

One of the main arguments was over the cost of camp board, which government regulations set at 75¢ per day and for which some camps were charging $1.00 per day. Wage cuts under the union were also a bone of contention. J. H. Unwin, M.L.A. met with workers, and the strike was concluded but feelings were still bitter over the new Order-in-Council, Order No. 5.

The miners met too at a two-day conference in Mountain Park. They hoped that with a united front prevailing many of the adverse conditions of the depression years would be rectified and an appreciable increase in wage be effected when contracts expired April 1st.

Board member C. E. Payne presided and M. P. Susnar acted as secretary. Delegates present were A. Susnar, Kaydee; Thos. David, T. Gates, Mountian Park; M. O. Susnar, J. McKay, J. H. Ferguson, Cadomin; Ted Cowling, Luscar; Frank Knesovich, Mercoal; Art Stevenson, Foothills and A. J. Henderson, Robb.

Accidents once again made the headlines. Overcome by coal gas about 650 feet below surface in No. 2 slope at Luscar Collieries, Eldred Ambury, 42, and Harry Buttermur, 36, died of asphyxiation. The next day was to have been Ambury's last day as he had given notice that after ten years of mining he was quitting to enter a trucking business in Edmonton.

At Hinton an underground explosion took the lives of five miners and five others were seriously injured. Killed in the explosion were Tony Pastushak, Martin Sprela, George Bilcha, William Ileck and Peter Phillipino. Injured were William Aitken, Sr., Tony Baumgartner, Gus Kubek, J. Pallo and Reg Williams.

The multiple funeral took place in Edson with over 60 cars following the remains to Glenwood cemetery. Stores in Edson were closed for a short period of time in respect.

No mine rescue equipment was at Hinton at the time of the accident and the only mine rescue car in the district was at Cadomin, where because the car had been condemned it remained, because the railway would not move it.

The Hinton U.M.W. of A. asked that the provincial government as well as the CNR establish telephone and telegraphic communication at Hinton.

At Cadomin May Day was again observed. It was pointed out that the first May Day celebration was held in Chicago in 1886 and on that occasion was used to draw attention to the workers' desires, the eight hour day. This time the six hour day, five day week and 20 per cent increase was discussed.

At Mountain Park, the collieries announced intention of installing a 350,000 ton capacity wet washing and drying plant. M. M. Mauovic, Jugoslav Consul in Canada, paid a visit to Cadomin and Mountain Park where many of his countrymen were employed.

On June 15 the Miette Hot Springs officially opened to the public after two years under construction. Jasper, Edson and Coal Branch residents took advantage of the mineral springs.

By August the Attorney General's department had laid fines against officials and miners of the Hinton Collieries in connection with the March accident. The miners were fined $10 each and the overman fined on two charges, $30 and $25 respectively. The mine manager was fined on four counts in a separate trial.

In August, Tommy Waddell of Cadomin, wire rope splicer died in the Miette Hot Springs pool.

On September 17, 1938 the Edmonton Journal carried the following story:

> Scots Mine Owners Visit in Edmonton.
> Harold Mitchell, wealthy young Scotsman who represents the London constituency of Brentford in the British House of Commons and his brother, A. M. Mitchell, both directors of Mountain Park and Luscar Collieries, Ltd. arrived here Saturday.
> During the day they discussed mine conditions with officials at the company offices here. They are sons of the late Alexander Mitchell who founded the two Alberta mines.

In October R. G. Drinnan, managing director of Luscar and Mountain Park coal mining companies for almost twenty years announced his retirement as Managing director of Luscar and Mountain Park Collieries. He would continue as vice-president. A. N. Scott, superintendent would take over as successor.

District No. 18 voted to accept the majority report of the Drumheller Conciliation Board which recommended a general increase of 5% and in the lower paid workers, 10% besides adjustment in contract irregularities.

119

1945 — Luscar townsite — razed and levelled in 1963.

Photo courtesy Provincial Museum and Archives of Alberta

Renewed agitation for a definite road building program began on the Coal Branch. Three bridges were in the process of construction but residents felt that money was being expended and the work was still far from completion.

That fall the Mercoal school was closed for two weeks because the teacher, Mrs. L. V. Kirkwood was sick.

* * *

The spring of 1939, fund raising events throughout the district were geared to the purchase and freight charges of the 'Iron Lung' ordered from England for installation in St. John's Hospital. Leading contributions came from the C.G.I.T., A.Y.P.A., Dr. Macdonald, Sterco; Coal Valley Mining Co. Ltd., C. E. Payne, Mountain Park; Dr. H. C. Begg, Cadomin; Dr. P. Melling, Mountain Park; Mr. F. Seabolt, Hinton; Mr. J. Neff, McLeod Valley; Rev. Father Landrigan, Edson, who all headed fund-raising committees.

On the night of May 27, 1939, seven optimistic men ventured forth in a 1928 Pontiac sports roadster headed for Coalspur. Armed with everything from haywire to planks for portaging rivers and muskegs, they arrived in Coalspur in something like three hours. Distance 24 miles.

They reported the highway from Mercoal to Coalspur in A-1 condition, but a stretch of seven miles between Mercoal and Leyland taxed the ingenuity of the driver, Elmer Tronsgard, However with stumps to the right of them, stumps to the left of them, they got through. The adventurers included passenger John Braben, Cadomin, Williard Matheson, Cadomin, Carl Wagner, Luscar, Allan McLeod, Happy Pyne and Jimmy McVey all of Luscar.

* * *

A 1,200 foot eight inch diameter high pressure steam line, one of the longest, if not the longest in Canada was put in operation at Cadomin. The welded pipe would be used to convey steam from the mine shaft for operation of the large hoist installed two years ago. Installation costs ran about $25,000.

The biggest event of the year was the Royal Visit, June 2, 1939 when King George and Queen Elizabeth stopped in Edson, a scheduled three minute stop that turned into twelve minutes.

Special trains from the Lovett and Mountain Park Branches brought over 1,100 people early in the day to Edson. Youngsters joined the Edson children and 2,000 strong began a march-past waving flags and led by the Edson Town Band. Thirty scarlet coated RCMP were on hand to assist with the arrangements. The Queen accepted a bouquet of roses presented by Sheila MacLean and chatted for several minutes with Edson Mayor W. and Mrs. Wilson.

A sports day, free show, and the distribution of 1,700 lunches for visitors followed the events before the Coal Branch train departed. Many stayed on for the Royal Visit dance, the biggest of the season.

The management of the various coal companies paid the railroad fare of Coal Branchers who made the trip. While the adults of Coal Valley were in Edson, members of the 1st Brazeau Troop of Scouts were in Edmonton for the Royal Visit. The troop was picked out as one of the smartest and best dressed in spite of the fact they had just recently been organized. Const. Foster, RCMP, Mr. Findley, scout master and a group committee from Sterco, Coal Valley and Foothills were responsible for the organization.

Cadomin residents were saddened to hear of the death of J. H. McMillan, who had died in Nanaimo, B.C. in May. The former general superintendent who had resigned in 1935 because of poor health had had a profound influence on the mode of life of Cadomin citizens.

The resignation of W. J. Dick as president and general manager of the Cadomin Coal Co. prompted new appointments in August. J. A. McLeod and W. H. Parmell became manager and sales manager respectively. Directors at the meeting which made the appointments included F. L. Hammond, chairman and president; A. C. Emery, vice-president; and S. W. Field, K.C.

Weekly, men from the coal mining towns began to offer their services to the Canadian army. A number of Poles left to join the Polish Division financed by a fund provided by people of Polish extraction.

In Cadomin the first contingent from town consisting of 17 men were given a royal send-off with flags flying and the Cadomin Band playing military music. David Stene acted as chairman at a complimentary smoker given the evening before their departure.

121

In the group leaving Cadomin were William Ince, Imperial veteran of the Gallipoli landing, James Varley, Neil Gilchrist, Robert Davidson, William French; Robert Roberts, Roy Rice, James Waddell; James Paterson, Harry Croft, Albert Sutria, David Jenkins, Jack Riddel, Ronald Hall, Henry Graham, Albert McLeod and John Shellack.

Branches of the Canadian Red Cross Society were formed on almost every camp of the Coal Branch, and the women brought out their knitting needles.

Motivated by a pioneer spirit and a desire to get to their home in Marlboro, G. C. Lovell and R. Kent, who had been trucking at Foothills drove into Edson one day in August and delivered a lump of coal from P. A. Robb, at the Bryan Mine, lack of a Coal Branch Highway notwithstanding.

From Mile 32 they drove to Embarras, to Weald, across the McLeod River and followed the old tote road most of the way. They had to cross the Embarras River several times and had to roll boulders out of the way to get through in many spots.

They made the trip in four days driving time. The two said the most difficult part was crossing Schwartz Creek where the banks are very steep.

* * *

Tragedy stalked through the Cadomin mine Saturday night during the last shift of the last working day of 1939 when deadly methane gas trapped a group of miners about 6:15 p.m. and took a toll of three dead while six others barely escaped with their lives.[21]

Dead were James Maddams, Jr. age 29, John Burnside age 41 and Dan Spinazzi, 48. Maddams lost his life in an heroic attempt to save

Jimmy Maddams, who at age 29 died a hero's death in a valiant attempt to save his fellow workers . . the last shift of 1939 — Cadomin.

his comrades. He was out of the danger area and went back to face the blast of deadly methane.

Fireboss Peter Nicholson suffered painful face and body bruises and injuries to his back in a fall down an almost vertical 150 foot coal chute dragging miner Hugh Docherty who had been overcome by the gas, with him.

Nicholson and Docherty had just dragged miner Charles Lockhart to a safety zone with successful resuscitation efforts. They had returned to attempt the rescue of more of their comrades when they were caught by the gas and just managed to reach the head of the chute when they collapsed.

Docherty went down first and Nicholson dragged him the remaining few feet. Nicholson lost consciousness just as he reached the chute opening and down he went pulling Docherty along with him.

Joseph Nickjoy was pulled out by the gallant efforts of miner Alex Woods and was revived in a safety zone. Heroic efforts were made by Cadomin's crack mine rescue squad under Peter Shearer, superintendent of mine rescue, before the bodies of Dan Spinazzi and John Burnside were recovered by Steve Trstensky. The body of James Maddams was recovered by Pit Boss Robert Muir.

Three and a half hours of steady artificial respiration by Peter Shearer and his men were futile. The three men had received a full charge of the deadly gas, one full inhalation of which is sufficient to bring about death.

The fatality took place in No. five panel, a panel in which the 'pillars' were being drawn. Normally a warning sound indicates the presence of gas when it frees itself. But there was no warning. Fireboss Nicholson had made his rounds of inspection only a few minutes before and almost within seconds of his return, the tasteless, odorless terror crept down, leaving in its wake the stricken men caught in a merciless gas trap.

There was frantic anxiety on the part of wives, children and those 'on top' until the message was brought to the surface revealing the dead, injured and rescued. The scene at the shaft mouth where hundreds were gathered was poignant. Common to mining towns when word that tragedy has struck below is received, feelings of joy and prayerful thankfulness at the sight of those close to them safely returned, were sobered by the utter despair on the faces of the members of the families and friends of those who had put in their 'last shift'.

Whistles did not blow at midnight signalling the New Year, and all social, public and private gatherings were cancelled as Cadomin paid tribute to its dead.

Funeral services took place, January 2nd, 1940. Rev. Father McGowan officiated at the services for James Maddams who was popular in athletic and hunting circles, and for Dan Spinazzi a bachelor, in the Roman Catholic Chapel; Rev. S. Reikie conducted services for John Burnside in the United Church.

After the church service Mike Susnar, secretary, Cadomin Local U.M.W.A. read the miner's service in the Community Hall.

A procession was then formed for the march to Leyland, where the bodies were put on the train to be taken to Edmonton for interment. The Cadomin band, aided by Luscar and Edmonton bandsmen, hundreds of people from all points on the Coal Branch marched six abreast behind the three trucks bearing the caskets.

Members of the Cadomin branch of the Canadian Legion: Robert Steel, Bert Ward, S. Davis, James Chapman, William Laing and Roy Simmonds were the pallbearers for Mr. Burnside.

J. L. Nickjoy, H. Docherty, H. McKenna, W. Jaschke, Eugene Sadoway and Sam Hudyma were pallbearers for Mr. Maddams.

Louis Raffin, John Luccini, John Vadrasco, John Passamero, Max Ongaro and Attili Esquenni, who came from Mr. Spinazzi's home town in northern Italy accompanied his casket.

A little more than a month later Paul Ciputa, 50, and Anthony Resek, 44 were killed in a cave-in February 7th in the Mountain Park Collieries. Fellow miners recovered their bodies soon afterward 1,800 feet underground, in the area where the men had been working.

* * *

Death in the mine was always a possibility and as Vic Riendeau stated, "At Mountain Park you could count on at least one a year."

Miners went to work and didn't dwell on the possibility. It was part of the job. Miners went to the washhouse which was always kept at a very warm temperature in order to dry the work clothes, changed from street clothes to work clothes, went to the lamphouse, then to the toolhouse then down to where they were assigned in the mine that day. Jack B. Roome says that overhead props in the mine were not only for support, they would give warning and crack under pressure. At the end of the shift you would turn your tools in to be sharpened and turn in your check number. "You would sweat so much during the day you'd have to put some salt back in," so it was a 'stop at the bar' after a wash and a return to street clothes.

Mrs. Greta Jeffers of Mountain Park recalls, "I used to see the men coming from the mine going to the washhouse. You couldn't tell one from the other, they were so black."

Working so far underground miners were totally unaware of the elements. Jack Roome said, "I went to work one day and it was 60 degrees below. When I came off shift it was 45 degrees above." The top of Mt. Cheviot would often serve as a weather vane. "When the snow would start blowing at the top of Mt. Cheviot you'd know a chinook was coming. Within an hour it would warm right up."

* * *

Luscar again captured the Provincial Intermediate Hockey Championship in the total point series winning over the Canmore team at

Camrose. The victory advanced the Coal Branch team into the western Canada semi-finals against the Vernon, B.C. Blue and Whites. Lineup for the Luscar Indians was: Bartoff, Holden, Art Jerwa, Onychuck, Bonner, McVey, Kulyk, Newsome, Dominchelli, Protti, Ross, Stene, and Bello.

* * *

At Mountain Park a statement was issued in March.

The members of the Mountain Park Local No. 2655, U.M.W. of A. are idle in protest against the employment as a mine official of L. G. Chavignaud, who was mine manager at Hinton Collieries at the time of the explosion in that mine in March, 1938, when five miners were killed and a number injured.

The workmen offered to continue work providing that the Mountain Park Coals would lay off Chavignaud pending negotiations for settlement of the dispute. This proposal was rejected by the management.

"The men, orderly and cheerful are determined to stay with the stand they have taken and ask all unemployed men to stay away from Mountain Park while the dispute is unsettled."

Single men who are unable to pay cash for their own meals as required, are building their own cookhouse and call their tent restaurant, "Mount Harris Hotel".

The strike continued for three weeks affecting 340 men. After this time an agreement was reached where the men would go back to work providing Mr. Chavignaud could not be employed in any position over that of fireboss until after July. The men would express their grievances further by taking them to the provincial government.

* * *

At Sterco a public library was built by voluntary labor under the direction of Percy Mellet. Mr. Mellet aimed to collect 1,000 books to start the library on its way. Residents pitched in to help.

* * *

At Coal Valley that March the community mourned the death of Charles E. Barry, president and managing director.

The eulogy read, "The passing of Mr. Barry will be felt very keenly by the whole personnel of the Coal Valley Mining Co. for he was more than a managing director. He took more than a passing interest in the comfort and welfare of his employees, and was continually striving to better the living conditions that are usually met with in a small mining camp.

The whole camp was well constructed and kept freshly painted. Running water has been installed in every house in the townsite, several of the houses have complete bathrooms and septic tanks installed.

Mr. Barry was also very keenly interested in the social and sporting activities of the camp, and it was only on account of his generosity and co-operation that Coal Valley has a community hall, picture show, skating rink, tennis court, school and church.

CHAPTER NINE

An Ugly Side Effect of the War

A meeting of residents in this district met at Sterco on Sunday afternoon, June 2nd, 1940 when 55 British subjects were in attendance to discuss the employment of enemy aliens to fill the positions left open by men joining the C.A.S.F., and it was moved that a petition be sent to the management as follows:

1. No enemy aliens or any naturalized since 1939 be employed for the duration of the war;
2. Preference be given to British subjects as foremen;
3. Positions vacated by men enlisting in the C.A.S.F. be filled by British subjects.

The motion was carried unanimously.

Methods of combatting fifth column activities were discussed and it was decided to report all anti-allied activities.[22]

A clipping from an Edmonton paper was read with regard to the employment of enemy aliens by the Edmonton city authorities, and a report of activities of a fifth column on the Coal Branch. A circular was also read with regard to the danger of careless talk on information which might be of assistance to the enemy. This was put in the form of a motion and drafted on the original petition.

22 Edson-Jasper Signal

In a discussion regarding seniority of enemy aliens on the waiting list, Mr. A. A. Deacon, local union representative stated, "Loyalty to the British Empire stands before seniority."

A committee of T. Rankine, M. Lanquett and W. Wilson were elected to present the petition to the company in the proper manner.

The knitting needles of women of all nationalities clicked merrily as they sent endless socks, sweaters, scarves, wristlets and mitts to the Red Cross depot in Edmonton from the groups on the Coal Branch.

* * *

Coal Valley[23] — On Thursday, June 27, 1940, a very enthusiastic meeting was held by loyal British subjects in the Community Hall at Coal Valley. The following motions were put to the meeting and passed unanimously:

1. That the Coal Valley Mining Co. Ltd., be requested not to hire any enemy aliens or sympathizers during the war.

2. That only loyal British subjects hold positions as foremen, or any other position of responsibility.

3. That any enemy sympathizers in the employ of the Coal Valley Mining Co. Ltd., at the present time, be discharged.

4. That any man leaving the employ of the Coal Valley Mining Co. Ltd., for service with His Majesties Forces be granted leave of absence until his services for the country expire.

5. That this meeting expresses itself as being against immigration of nationals of any country with which we are at war during the present conflict, for a period of 25 years after the cessation of hostilities, and a copy of this resolution be forwarded to the member of Parliament for this constituency for action in the House.

6. That the Coal Valley Mining Co. Ltd., be requested to have their employees refrain from speaking anything but English or French.

7. That a committee of four be appointed to submit the minutes of this meeting to the Coal Valley Mining Co. Ltd. and to the unions representing the employees.

* * *

Charles Jacoby, an old-time miner of the Coal Branch and a resident of Cadomin for sixteen years received patent rights for a new safety catch device for shaft cages and elevators.

The catch worked on the wedge system and its simplicity of construction made it comparatively inexpensive. Mr. Jacoby had worked on his invention for two years, after the death of a brother in a Nova Scotia mine disaster. The brother died when the rope on a 'trip' broke and plunged a group of miners to their deaths at the end of an incline.

* * *

Another 45,000 rainbow trout fingerlings were released on the Coal Branch this summer. W. C. Hales, district fish and game warden

[23] Edson-Jasper Signal

128

said the fingerlings would be evenly distributed between Cadomin, Mountain Park and Luscar. Fish and Game Associations at each of the camps met the train and assisted in the speedy releasing.

* * *

In September of 1940, A. Corsor, a lumber camp operator stated he intended to construct a logging road from Erith towards Coalspur sufficient for his own needs that winter. He felt that if the businessmen of Edson felt they could assist with either men or money it would enable him to do a greater amount of road work than would be possible with his own resources.

It was pointed out to the Edson Board of Trade that this route was the one favored by the Government surveyors who have looked into the situation, and it was further revealed that Mr. Corsor said he could build a passable winter road for around $4,000.

A committee was formed to raise as much money as possible from Edson and towns on the Coal Branch. Committee members included A. S. Maxwell, T. Fowler, W. B. Low, Wm. Wilson, Dr. R. E. Johnston and H. C. MacDonald.

On October 25th a large crowd from the area met Angus J. Morrison, M.L.A. to discuss the Coal Branch Road.

Mr. Morrison said, "It is a fact that the people of the Coal Branch are virtually prisoners and that this situation has no parallel in any other part of Alberta. My first consideration was to secure an outlet for the people concerned and I asked Mr. Fallow (Hon. W. A. Fallow, Minister of Public Works) to appoint engineers to survey the possibilities of both routes." (One route was a road from Leyland to Hinton along an old trail route using Craig's lumber road part of the way. The other was from Coalspur to the Big Eddy, and to Highway 16, out of Edson.)

"In ordinary times it is the duty of the government to provide money out of taxes for the building of roads. However in these abnormal times there wouldn't seem to be any law against people helping themselves."

Mr. A. E. Deacon of Sterco said the outstanding thing about life on the Coal Branch was the isolation, and that whatever was decided he would assist in every way he could.

Mr. Morrison said that "When the time comes when I am in possession of all the facts I will then, and then only, declare my stand on whichever route will do the greatest good to the greatest number."

Mr. A. S. Maxwell informed the meeting that the gang working out from Bickerdike was as far as Weald and that a winter trail would be put through to Coalspur by fall.

In the meantime the camps on the Lovett Branch had taken up a collection for work on a road between camps to Coalspur. The mines supplied the cat and fuel, while the collection paid the operators wages. A trail was cut through to Coalspur and this became known to residents as the 'Burma Road'.

A new wage order affected wages in October. The order came from the Board of Industrial relations headed by Clayton Adams. Basic wage for miners was set at 50 cents an hour. Certain underground helpers got 45¢ and surface workers 40¢. Machine workers on the long face wall got 65¢ and boys from 16 to 19 were to get 35¢. Under previous Minimum Wages orders adult minimum must be paid at age 19. The new rates compared with the old minimum of 33 and one-third cents. Hours of work regulations stipulated an eight hour day with time and a half for overtime.

* * *

Youth training classes were proving popular with the younger set this fall with Miss M. V. Stene in charge of the Cadomin classes and Miss Vivian McLeod supervising the classes at Luscar.

In November Fireboss Peter Nicholson and Miner Alex Wood went to Vancouver where they were presented with medals by the Canadian Institute of Mining and Metallurgy.

The awards were made in recognition of the rescue work they had undertaken at Cadomin December 20, 1939. The two men had been responsible for bringing out three men.

* * *

In December 1940 the Coal Valley correspondent writes:
At last — after many years and many promises the people on the Lovett Branch have a road through to Coalspur. Not by any means a No. 1 highway, but a road cars can travel on. The people grew sick and tired of waiting for the Government to build this road so they raised enough money among themselves to build it. Already cars from Luscar and Cadomin have been seen in Coal Valley and Foothills.

The tipple at Coal Valley which was totally destroyed by fire October 29, 1944. The newer more modern tipple was built after this. Mrs. Marie Barry of Edmonton who sent the picture says, "My father Napolean Allard was stationary engineer at the plant. Our family lived in Coal Valley from the 30's till the early 50's."

130

If weather conditions do not become too unfavorable the road will be used extensively this winter. People who have only been a few miles from each other and total strangers will now have an opportunity of getting to know each other.

After making this effort on their own initiative the people on the Lovett Branch are entertaining hopes that the Government will make such necessary improvements as that will make this an all-weather road.

* * *

During the war years and the post war years the Coal Branch area began the 'swinging years'. Miners made top money on a contractual basis and good money on any job connected with the mines. Miss Rose Antoniuk, now Mrs. E. A. Q. Bown, was a desk clerk at the Imperial Hotel in Edson through the early forties. She says,

"I can remember the miners coming in from the Coal Branch to register at the hotel. Many of them had diamond stick pins, diamond and gold cuff links, and I was really impressed. They had money to burn and spent freely. Many of them couldn't speak English very well. They'd dress up and walk up and down Main Street, then come back to the hotel. Louis Stupar, the owner knew them all and they'd talk by the hour. (Louis Stupar had an ownership in a mine on the branch but sold out, not having the necessary capital to expand. Louis and Alex Susnar were credited with the discovery of the seam at Gregg River.)

"Frank Willis was the manager at the time. Once in a while Mr. Stupar, a tall imposing Serbian with a bristling moustache would ask me up to their room for a drink. They drank one of two things. Either very good Scotch or Jack the Frog's moonshine. The moonshine was supposed to be such pure alcohol the miners said it was used at the University of Alberta. When they drank the moonshine it would be poured into tumblers, then filled with very hot water and set on the windowsill to cool. I used to think this was so some of the alcohol would evaporate. They would talk of events of the early days on the Branch. Many of them had gold teeth and I can still see them laughing and the gold teeth glinting. They talked of a visit to the hotel in the early thirties when several men had boasted of being APP special police and bullying picketing miners. That night the loud-mouthed men had been beaten in the alley behind the hotel. The drinkers roared appreciatively when Louis Stupar said he hadn't heard a thing that night."

* * *

1941

In February James Saltz, 48, was trapped in a Mountain Park mine cave-in. His working partner, Steve Zuk scrambled to safety as the rock and coal began to fall, but Saltz was caught by the rubble.

Fireboss James Burton was in charge of crews that worked three shifts daily for five days to reach the miner. The body of Mr. Saltz was found at the 90 foot level of the mine, about one-half mile back in the shaft. The cave-in was over 900 feet deep in the mine.

* * *

A Journal reporter who toured the processing plant at Mountain Park in January was astounded at the maze of equipment required to separate and clean coal sold by the plant. He wrote:

> 'The coal is glamorized like a chorus girl before making her first public appearance. Machines and hand-pickers eliminate unworthy chunks. Hot water baths, coupled with gravity, eliminate dross. Coal floats. The dross sinks. Hot air driers like those used in beauty parlors evaporate moisture, after the baths. The noise of automatic shakers that separate the coal lumps by size resemble an artillery barrage. Modern coal mining, like modern warfare, is mechanized. Electric locomotives pull coal cars through miles of tunnels that burrow into the mountains that overlook Mountain Park, Luscar and Cadomin. Where locomotives can't penetrate, cables haul the cars. Only where locomotives and cables can't be used in twisty tunnels are horses used. Picks and shovels used to be the standard equipment of miners. Now, in the 'big three' they're secondary to electric drills and chutes that use gravity to load the cars.'

* * *

All was not rosy in the mining industry. A further report reads:

> 'Contributing to the problems which mines face today, were the minimum orders given out from week to week and the minimum prices paid for the coal by the CNR during the years preceding the outbreak of war. This practice starved mining operations to a point which did not permit the companies to maintain the necessary mine development work that would enable the mines to cope with a national emergency such as has arisen. Production, due to lack of development work, is far below that of several years ago.'

The operators stated with regret that the average price received for coal was below $3.00 a ton.

In June, after nearly doubling their Victory loan quota with a total subscription of $31,500 the citizens of Mountain Park sought a way to mark the event. Boy Scouts and Cubs caught the ebullient spirit and paraded, carrying an effigy of the 'Führer' through the town to the tune of bugle and drum music. Makings of a bonfire had been placed previously around a stake on a nearby hillside and there they took their prisoner of war, tied him to the stake, and lighted the fire. Fresh mountain breezes soon fanned them into a vigorous conflagration, and that was the end of Herr Hitler at Mountain Park.

* * *

In 1941 Mountain Park had a population of 1,000 citizens. Average daily production in the mine was 1,400 tons per day. Miners and mine workers numbered 407, of whom 306 worked underground. The payroll averaged $60,000 per month.

Citizens enjoyed visiting the Cheviot Hotel and chatting with D. J. Macdonald who had by this time been identified with Mountain Park for 25 years. The hotel and its annex provided rooms for 110 miners, while eight rooms were kept for visiting salesmen, visitors etc. Mrs. John Lotnick (Nellie) worked there as second cook after coming to visit her aunt Julia Monroe, who was also one of the 14 employees at the hotel. Mr. Macdonald backed Mr. and Mrs. Lund who purchased the Mountain View Farm at Bickerdike. His idea was an assured source of cream, beef and chickens for the hotel. After a few months Nellie Marion moved down to help take care of the chickens at the farm, met and married John Lotnick and remains to this day on the next piece of property at Bickerdike.

Residents could now take a bus on intercamp roads. Soren Madsen who had spent 19 years in the employ of the two mines at Mountain Park and Luscar had started Branch Lines Ltd. with a partner E. Holmes of Edmonton. One 17-passenger bus and one seven-passenger bus offered daily service to Coalspur and points between. G. Philbrick and Ralph Wright were drivers and competent mechanics.

Soren Madsen contributed much to the business centres of the town. His theatre offered two changes of pictures a week. The theatre with moveable cushion sheets also doubled as an entertainment centre with an excellent stage and hardwood floors. Scenic paintings on the walls and velvet hangings made it a favorite choice for gatherings.

Soren Madsen was also the owner of the Summit Confectionery which became a social hub for the younger set as well as adults. The basement boasted a barber shop and billard room, while the ground floor provided a tea room, confectionery, ice cream parlor, light lunch and fountain counter, newstand and office space for the Branch Bus.

Ralph Gould offered excellent tailoring as well as dry cleaning, pressing and repair work.

Mountain Park residents in this year did their banking at the more industrialized camp of Cadomin. Cadomin Coal company had 4,300 acres under lease, extending seven miles in length, a mile wide and running with the coal seam. Of the several workable seams, only one, 25 to 30 feet thick was mined. The yearly output approximated 350,000 tons and a yearly payroll of $500,000 was distributed among some 350 employees.

At least 50% of the miners owned their own homes, and unlike other camps who employed a large number of single men, a good percentage of miners at Cadomin were married, resulting in a stable population. Though the company owned the townsite, various buildings such as the school, community hall, hospital and commercial property, they did not operate the stores, hotel or other business places.

In 1941 some of the business places were the Cadomin Cafe owned and operated by George Mow; the Cadomin Dairy owned and operated by Talgo and Moxness; the Gillespie Meat market managed by

George Petrie; the Matheson Bros., Chris and Willard who had the Studebaker line while Cadomin Motors with S. A. McIntosh local dealer for Ford and Mercury and Peter McKenna, the General Motors dealer; the Cadomin Bakery operated by W. Osada, Riverside Grocery operated by Charles Jacoby and J. A. Wrigley.

This business was purchased by Mr. Wrigley in the spring of 1933 and in December of 1935 Mr. Jacoby became his partner. The store, located at Leyland station was a short distance from the Cadomin townsite.

The Cadomin Barber Shop and Beauty Parlor was owned by Mrs. M. Beach with Jack Kansky barber and Miss Florence Bard, beauty operator.

The Cadomin Recreation Hall was operated by the Cadomin Miner's Association for its members with Wm. Muldowan as manager. Bowling, billiards, snooker were enjoyed, and cigars, soft drinks and confectionery sold.

Two shows were put on each week at the Cadomin Theatre by R. B. Fairclough, proprietor.

The Cadomin Hardware was owned by R. A. Craig and managed by E. S. Reid. R. A. Craig had been in the district since 1926 carrying on his lumber activities. His present camp lay 11 miles northwest of Cadomin and his planing mill and lumberyard were north of the highway. "The road serving his timber limit goes within 26 miles of Hinton, built necessarily to serve his timbering operations." Craig's road was highly advocated for the highway route, but many supporters including Edson's Mayor William Wilson plugged for the present Highway 47 route.

In 1941 Luscar Collieries found that 250 miners had produced 250,000 tons of coal the preceding year with a total payroll in excess of $500,000.

Luscar had pioneered the first plant embodying 'the static process' of pneumatic dry cleaning almost seven years before. Though the process was developed in England, its introduction at Luscar was a radical departure in Canadian coal mining. Total cost of this coal dry-cleaning plant was $175,000 and it would be capable of treating 880 tons of coal in eight hours.

Luscar, through their War Service committee raised more than $10,000 for the dominion government's war fund, this being accomplished by way of an accepted three per cent wage deduction. This was raised the following year to five percent through the employer-employee payroll plan.

Population of the vigorous residents at Luscar numbered around 650 in 1941.

The Luscar Hotel provided excellent accommodation for the travelling public as well as the local steadies. Owned by Archie Mitchell, the beverage room in the annex was in the charge of C. Bartoff with Mrs. J. Lee supervising the housekeeping. Mr. Mitchell operated the Miner's Dining Room which provided meals for some 90 miners as well as visitors.

The Palm Cafe and Confectionery was owned and operated by D. Giovinazzo and Mrs. Y. McVey. The beauty parlour upstairs was in the charge of Rose Onychuk, and in the basement there was a billiard hall and barber shop managed by Fred O'Reilley. The Palm was situated close to the Luscar Hotel and was 'the' gathering place for locals. D. Giovinazzo was also the proprietor of the Luscar Meat Market while George Beaton owned and operated the Luscar theatre with two changes of program each week.

* * *

By 1942 Red Cross organizations were knitting furiously for the 93 Coal Branch men who had joined the services.[24] Early in 1942 AB Louis Joy was home in Cadomin on leave. Louis, one of the former members of the Cadomin Junior hockey team that had met the E.A.C.'s at Edmonton for the junior crown in the 1939 season was taking it easy. He had served with the Restigouche overseas for several months and was one of the 44 survivors of a Canadian corvette which had sunk with a loss of 22 lives. At that time he was in the icy waters of the Atlantic for more than two hours, thus the extended leave.

The Cadomin School Cadets First Aid team received the Strathcona First Aid cup awarded by the Department of National Defence to the Cadet Team placing highest in First Aid work.

Captained by Danny Shearer members of the team were Peter Shearer, Jr. George Sival, Ted Hird, Reg Hird, Tino Dotto and Bill Stene.

Peter Borken died Valentines Day from injuries received while employed at the Luscar Collieries prospect mine.

In Jasper the spring of 1942, the Government of Canada brought 'alien residents', the Japanese, to work on the opening of the road west of Jasper to the Pacific Coast.

"At the present time there are fifty of these gentry at Geikie; fifty at Lucerne, fifty at Red Pass and fifty at Rainbow. It is expected that more will arrive shortly."

Many residents of the area will remember the remnants of these camps in evidence years later; arched bridges that were woven of willow on lodgepole over tinkling mountain streams; interwoven pagoda-like huts, wild flowers, rock and sand arranged in startlingly beautiful formations. All were evidence of the leisure activities of the Japanese during the war years.

* * *

In March of 1942, S. H. Cliffe writes caustically:
"According to reports there will be considerable activity on the Coal Branch road this season. As soon as conditions permit the Department

[24] Edson-Jasper Signal.

*of Public Works intends to send out crews to commence construction
from the Jasper Highway towards Coalspur.*

*Included in this will be a sounding crew to find the best spot for cross-
ing the McLeod river.*

*Presuming the government intends to carry on this work to com-
pletion, it will have to be taken into consideration that a great deal of
work needs to be done on the Foothills section as well as the Mountain
Park section, from Coalspur in both cases. It is true that a bus arrives in
Coalspur from Mountain Park each day, but from the point of view of
the average motorist the journey is still something of an adventure.*

*It is fourteen years since an organization was formed to get this job
done. Since then there has been plenty of promising, jockeying, starting and finishing. During this period we had a major depression with
unemployed men and machinery, but nothing was done apart from a
relief project which got us nowhere."*

* * *

At Craig's Mill, 12 miles north of Cadomin co-workers gathered to
honor Cory 'Grizzly' Simmonds on his 70th birthday. Jimmie Poy,
camp cook baked a cake on which there were 70 candles. Mr. Simmonds had worked on the G.T.P. Coal Branch line from its inception
and was in charge of the famous Robb tunnel. In 1912 he worked on
construction of the line from Coalspur to Mountain Park and in 1914–
17 operated the store and post-office at Coalspur.

In March too, Luscar was awarded the Alberta Intermediate Hockey Title. The Medicine Hat intermediate team received a telegram
from C. V. W. Stanley, vice-president of the Alberta Amateur Hockey
Association in charge of intermediate playoffs which read: "Impossible to get ice. Do hereby declare Luscar winners on their one game
victory."

The Luscar Indians prepared to meet the Nanaimo Clippers in the
Alberta-British Columbia playdowns.

* * *

In Jasper, vigorous protest about Japanese roadworkers in the
area being permitted to wander at large about Jasper without guards
was sent to Ottawa by residents of the town.

Townspeople complained that Japanese without guards were permitted to come into Jasper, shop at local stores and visit public places
such as motion picture shows.

"If there happen to be any among them who are able to contact
enemy agents they are certainly getting a fine opportunity to gather
any information they might need," a citizen stated in the columns of
the Bulletin.

Mountain Park people found themselves in the position of having
to drive to Cadomin for gas this spring. Residents offered to improve
the saddle trail from Mountain Park to Miette Hot Springs so the
thirty odd miles could be travelled by motor cycle but were forbidden
to do so by National Parks officials.

At Mountain Park the local union of the U.M.W.A. elected new officers headed by president William Micyk; vice-president Fred Kipiak and Sec. Treas. Chas. Payne.

In June the Hon. W. A. Fallow announced a road-building project to link up Coalspur with the Jasper Highway at Bickerdike. "Gravelling would also take place the 18 miles between Coalspur and Leyland and if feasible this year to Mountain Park."

Residents along the entire Branch breathed a collective sigh.

At long last.

The first wire-wound wood pipe in an Alberta mine began use in Foothills, in July. When installation of a compressor and cutting machine in the mine were completed, hand-mining "will be done away with."

The capricious McLeod River (1942) caused the death of two Cadomin men.

Farewell parties were given for a teacher, Miss Eckenfelder who left for Edmonton, for the principal of the Foothills school, Miss J. Filipkowski and Mrs. T. Jackson. Mrs. W. L. Hammett and daughters moved to Edmonton, and Mr. Hammett conducted church services at Foothills during the Rev. Brylant's absence.

At Cadomin Danny Doherty, 22, and John Sromek both met death by drowning in the McLeod river. Following exceedingly heavy precipitation the McLeod was a raging torrent and it was presumed both men fell from a bridge near town which had almost been washed out. It was presumed they were watching the heavy rush of water. Danny's drowning occured Friday night, and a constant search was set up for the recovery of the body which was found Sunday by George Nikiforuk one of the searchers, on a sand bank three miles below Cadomin.

It was not known at the time that John Sromek had also been drowned until his body was discovered a mile from Danny's. The body of Sromek was first seen by A. J. McEvoy, trainman working out of Edson who reported to the RCMP.

* * *

Introduction of Japanese into the area west of Jasper for road work proved to be a very unsatisfactory arrangement. Protests were kept up by the Jasper Park Chamber of Commerce. The Signal reported in July: "Now the Japs themselves have settled the question. By slowdowns and strikes on one pretext or another the project has been so unsatisfactory that the Dominion Government decided to close the camps, leaving only a few key men there, and move the Japanese to British Columbia, such points as Slocan being mentioned."

Immediately it became known that this work was to be stopped protests were lodged by the Alberta Motor Association and the National Parks Highway Association.

* * *

CHAPTER TEN

Five Die in Cadomin Mine Flood

For the second time in three years Cadomin mine faced a multiple tragedy. The mine whistle blasted its eery message of disaster on Wednesday, August 5th 1942 at 7:30 p.m.

Grief stricken relatives and miners gathered at the minehead hoping against hope they would see their men alive as each trip of the hoist reached the surface bearing miners who had escaped. Women sobbed. Men suppressed lumps in their throats. Wild cries of elation escaped when a husband or father was recognized.

A torrent of water had broken through panel pillars from old mine workings into the No. 9 panel below. A double shift of men began toiling, shovelling debris from the main and back angles to clear the way. With tons of the mixture hanging blocked by pieces of timber careful proceedings were highly necessary. Several times tons of the muck broke loose endangering the lives of the rescuers.

The body of John Vallance, age 52, was brought to the surface Wednesday night. Weary rescuers replaced others through the long night's siege. Early Thursday morning the group, some who had waited all night watched as a rescue party approached the head of the mine shaft. The party halted and lay down its stretcher. On the stretcher was the body of Victor Alleggretto, aged 41.

All day Thursday, rescue parties spelled each other off. Mine officials off duty came and took part in the rescue work. Weary miners snatched a few hours sleep and came back.

139

During the early hours of August 7th, the badly mangled bodies of Joseph Dombrowski, age 55, Carl Stocks, 52, and the pitboss, John Logan, age 63, were brought to the surface.

Three of the miners who escaped death from No. 9 panel where the five met their deaths were Peter Laghi, Michael Kapusinski and Harry Tyson. At the inquest held a week later fifteen witnesses testified to a jury composed of P. McKenna, J. Bochenko, Neil MacKinnon, A. Bennedetti, E. Hagglund and Frank Fallis.

Miner Peter Laghi, an escapee, in a faltering voice told of having changed places with his partner Joe Dombrowski, while eating his lunch at number seven crosscut. He stated he heard a loud noise but at first could see nothing. He jumped into the coal chute, seeing a light, presumably Dombrowski's. He called to him but got no answer. He then jumped from the chute, caught his hand in some planks of timber and lost his light. He then went down to the counter through the mixture that was coming down, but could not find anyone. He was down the raise to the entry before he saw lights. He endeavoured to tell the men what little he knew but was very excited. He was sent to the surface soon after.

Thomas Mason was working with his partner Harry Tyson at No. 6 battery, above the scene of the accident, a fact which saved their lives. Hearing an unusual noise, something different to anything he had ever heard underground he and Tyson stopped work and began to look around. They sensed that their air had been cut off, presumably by blocked airways and remembering what Fire Boss John Logan had always cautioned them to do, they dropped down number 4 main angle and kept on going till they hit the counter where some of the haulage men were.

Mike Kapuscinski stated that after finishing his lunch, he emptied the coal chute and waited some time for more coal. Allegretto had gone up to see what was holding the coal up. Immediately after he left Kapuscinski heard a loud unusual noise and in the next moment was thrown against the hanging wall by a rush of water and coal. He swung himself up onto the pipes running along the roof and let himself down into the chute. From the chute he went to the man-way and then down to the bottom of the entry. Finding this blocked he came to the doors and after pushing his way through the first and second doors without seeing anyone he went through the third door and saw some lights. He stated the only warning was a rush of air seconds before it hit his location and that he never saw Allegretto alive again.

Tony Kwasney, partner of Mike Kapuscinski said that a tremendous roar came through to them and before he knew what it was, he was covered to the hips with a mixture of fluid coal. He too jumped for the pipes and made his way out.

Driver Boss William Shearer said that Allegretto had been sent up to see what was holding up the coal. He also stated there had been no change in the moisture conditions prior to the accident. Jack Chesney and Ignace Banar, miners and partners of the shift previous to the accident both stated that apart from damp coal there was no sign of free water.

Pumpman George Deans gave evidence stating he had worked the previous shift and had been called out again when the accident was first reported. He stated there had been no increase of water from number 9 panel before the accident; that no water had gained on the pump and further there had been no appreciable increase since the accident.

The fault had not been man's. The Town mourned.

* * *

In the summer of 1942 military exemption was advocated for Alberta coal miners. The industry was imperilled by an estimated shortage of 1,500 mine workers.

* * *

Mercoal was booming. Living accommodation for the increasing number of employees was badly needed and building could barely keep up with the need. Canadian Collieries (Dunsmuir) Ltd. who had taken over from McLeod River Hard Coal Co. made plans to increase production from 500 tons per day to 1200. It was expected that the 150 employee payroll would climb to 250 in short order. President of the firm was J. A. Boyd, general manager H. R. Plummer and H. Wilton Clark, superintendent.

* * *

At Foothills Alex Marconi died when pinned under a fall of coal. He was 41 and a bachelor.

At Cadomin Robert Muir, 57, fireboss and Charles Swanson, 64, timberman died when overcome by gas. Two other men, Conrad Doherty, Sr. and Fred Gosney were pulled to safety by their fellow workers. Just why the two deceased did not get out on time is not definitely known, but it was suggested that Swanson was slow in getting out of the mine and Muir went back to assist him.

* * *

By November extra ration coupon sheets for tea and coffee were issued to miners in Alberta.

Mountain Park residents bid farewell to Charles Payne, secretary of Local 2665, who had been appointed to the Emergency Coal Production Board by Finance Minister Isley.

Empire Day, 1944 brought scattered showers throughout most of the province. Residents of the Alberta Coal Branch spent the holiday digging themselves out from under 55 inches of snow.

The mountain valley snowstorm which swept from Mountain Park to Robb blanketed the whole area in the most concentrated snowfall since the memorable July 1st storm of 1917. The snowstorm isolated the branch for four days, and then was followed by floods.

The soggy snow at Mountain Park burdened the big ice skating rink building to the breaking point and the roof collapsed under an estimated 250 tons.

* * *

Empire Day, 1944 brought 55″ of soggy snow.

Collapsed roof on skating rink at Mountain Park.

1946

By the end of July, in 1946, the basement for the projected new hall for the Mercoal Branch of the Canadian Legion was bulldozed. Volunteer members set to work with zeal.

142

In August Peter Wetyk, a miner employed by the Foothills Collieries for only five days was discovered dead of a broken neck.

A. Davidge and sons began work on the New Mercoal Mercantile.

Cadomin had one of the most severe electrical storms they had ever experienced on August 13th. Transformers were severely damaged. The prompt action of an attendant at the local garage averted what could have been a serious fire when lightning struck the base of a gas tank.

The Luscar correspondent writes:

> 'It was an unusual sight to see Billy Kulyk, clad in a fur collared jacket and cap pulled over his ears, bringing snow laden boxcars down to the loader. What is unusual about that: The Date — August 16th.'

The Croatian Society held a successful picnic on August 25th with a charter bus bringing guests from Mountain Park and Cadomin. Everyone enjoyed the lamb barbecue. Proceeds of the event would go towards building an orphan's home in Yugoslavia.

Josephine Ferguson of Cadomin was awarded a University of Alberta matriculation scholarship, and the Cadomin Juniors were nosed out of the Northern Alberta Junior championship by the Edmonton Canadians.

The homes of Mr. and Mrs. P. Pavich and Mrs. Oslund were destroyed by fire at Mountain Park.

Berry pickers found the raspberries a bumper crop this year and were grateful to lumberman R. A. Craig who kept his eye peeled for the best patches and provided transportation to the hard-to-find sites.

* * *

A radio message was received at Brule on Saturday August 31, 1946 for Mr. Don Buck, forest superintendent at Edson, stating that Ben Knutson, a lookout man for the Grave Flats area, that district between Brule and Mountain Park, was missing.

Mr. Buck immediately radioed a message to Mr. H. Parnall at Leyland, notifying him of the occurrence and requesting that he organize a search party.

On Sunday morning, September 1, Mr. Buck left for the branch by car and contacted Const. Clarke, RCMP who left Sterco on Monday morning travelling the Grave Flats Trail.

Ranger Dino had already left on the High Divide Trail, and Ranger Crawford by the Big Horn trail, so this meant that when all had arrived at Grave Flats the usual travelled territory had been covered. Thirty volunteers from Mountain Park took part in a Labour Day search but it was unsuccessful.

The fall term of Sterco school found pupils ready but no teacher. Five high school boys left for the Evansburg dormitory for the ensuing term.

Young Tommy Seaton and Merril Pyne of Luscar had the thrill of their lives when in October they encountered three grizzly bears.

143

They had gone to Grizzly Flats between Luscar and Miette to make some repairs and close the 'summer place' for the winter. The two boys had taken their rifles along as a matter of course.

Suddenly three bears loomed before them. Tommy took a bead on the first bear, shooting it through the head with his first shot. Both boys fired five or six shots at the others, one escaping, the other hide spoiled. They then spent four hours skinning their trophy. The skin weighed over 100 pounds and had to be brought out by packhorse. The Seatons would have a fine rug measuring eight feet one inch.

At Cadomin Eddy Maddams took out a party of American hunters who had chartered a seaplane in Edmonton and landed at Brazeau Lake. All four hunters were successful in obtaining their quota of sheep, goat and elk.

In October too, some excitement was created at Coal Valley when a ukelid operated by the Mannix Company went over the bank and into the Coal Valley pit, the driver just managing to jump clear as the machine hit the water.

The new modern dance hall at Coalspur held its official opening on November 1st.

At Sterco the correspondent writes:

"One can stand in camp and listen to one shot being fired after another this hunting season. Sometimes one would think it wasn't safe to venture outside the camp limits. But don't think the game doesn't know it is open season! Two moose have ventured right through camp, and at noon hour at that. Deer tracks have been seen on the paths inside camp in the morning the animals having eaten off hay piles during the night."

The new hall at Mercoal was opened on November 9 with a dance sponsored by Mr. B. Spanach, owner, as a treat for the public.

William Chadwick who had been Cadomin's station agent for 27 years, having arrived in 1919, was honored at a farewell party.

Mountain Park started a new stripping venture with M. A. Voire as contractor. A new road was built to accommodate the tracks.

CHAPTER ELEVEN

Explosion at Luscar Mine

On May 12th, 1945 an explosion occurred at Luscar Collieries. The bodies of two men were recovered almost immediately, these being D. Davies and M. Hlushka.

Three days later the mine was flooded to prevent further explosions and fire.

Searching operations continued, continued and continued. On December 7th 1945, the bodies of W. Belik and M. Zozuk were found. The search went on. On May 3, 1946, the bodies of D. Astley and P. Zozuk were discovered and finally on May 5, 1946, the body of the last missing man, Steve Zayezierski was found.

The enquiry into the deaths of these men opened at Luscar in June 1946. Court proceedings instituted by the Attorney-General's department opened in Edson January, 1947. Charges were laid against Mr. A. Hnatyshyn mine manager at Luscar at the time of the accident.

The following witnesses were called, then the case was adjourned to Luscar to March 1, 1947: Mr. A. Hnatyshyn; Mr. A. N. Scott Sr.; Mr. Andrew Scott Jr.; Mine surveyor H. Evans, at the time, mine manager; J. Jones, fire boss; R. Evans, driver boss; J. Domnichelli, pipe fitter at the time of the explosion; Mr. W. Healy who was the chief investigator for the Mines Branch when rescue operations were in progress; and Mr. A. Muir District Mines Inspector.

* * *

Hockey is hockey, and a game scheduled must be played. The Edson Seniors left early Sunday morning in January, 1947 for a game at Sterco. The van left at 9:00 a.m., and had difficulty making several of the hills on the Coal Branch Road. The real trouble began when the van left Coalspur and turned up the Burma Road on the Lovett Branch. After baling snow up and down a dozen hills, the boys called it quits, loaded their gear on their backs and proceeded to hoof it the rest of the way. After a good hot meal at the Sterco cookhouse, the boys were ready to play. The time 7:00 p.m.

Their victory left the boys in good spirits but this was dampened by the three mile walk to the van, then a rough ride to Coalspur. They arrived back in Edson at 3:30 a.m. Monday.

The Sterco team returned the visit the following weekend and returned 'on the drag' from Coalspur Monday morning. All, of course, were late for work.

Arrangements were completed early in 1947 for the formation of an enlarged school division on the Coal Branch to be known as Coal Branch School Division No. 58.[25]

The schools included in this arrangement were Foothills, Coal Valley, Sterco, Robb, Coalspur, Mercoal, Cadomin, Luscar, Mountain Park and Gregg River.

Miss M. Fulmer, of Edson was appointed temporary secretary and C. R. Ford, Inspector of the Edson School Division official trustee.

* * *

In Mercoal a most successful dance was sponsored by the Canadian League of Croatians and the Association of United Ukrainians. Later in the spring ninety-one meritous citizens were initiated into the Mercoal Lodge of the B.P.O.E.

* * *

The Postmaster at Luscar, Jack Richmond found his premises entered overnight by a pseudo Jack-the-Ripper. Eight mail bags had been slit.

* * *

"Due to extremely bad weather conditions which made the road from the Gregg River Mine to the Cadomin mine a sea of mud, the Cadomin Coal Company were forced to close the Gregg Mine. A large number of truck drivers and other employees entered an enforced holiday period."

* * *

Luscar's Eddy Thomas, who, with his brother had been playing for the Edmonton Canadian Hockey Club left for Victoria. Paul Thompson of the Chicago Black Hawks was operating a hockey club in that coastal city and Eddy had hopes of being one of the forwards.

At Mountain Park, the 'Tipple Cleaners' tangled with the 'Outside Essentials' in the first inter-town ball game of the season.

[25] Read John Finlay's story.

At Foothills residents checked their meat sheds each morning to see if a hungry bruin had paid a visit during the night.

On May 27, 1947, Sydney Lain, the 21 year-old son of the master mechanic of the Foothills Coal Company met his death in a mine accident. A union service was held at Foothills and the body shipped to Edson for burial.

Foothills residents were on the alert for a cougar reported seen in the area.

Ambitious gardeners who had their gardens planted early lost them when a severe frost hit the area June 5th.

A crowd gathered this day, too, and watched with interest the efforts of the Edson Wrecking Crew. A CNR 'extra' had tangled with a number of cows in the Robb tunnel causing much excitement, blood, and the derailment of one car.

* * *

At noon, Saturday, July 19th a sudden storm that lasted one half hour caused an unbelievable mess. The storm hit with a sudden fury preceded by a five minute darkening of sunny skies. Six dogs, terrified by the furious clap of thunder raced madly through the open doors of 'The Summit' and took refuge under the seats of the booths. Nothing the management attempted could persuade the frightened creatures to make their exit. In the torrent of rain that followed, mud and ashes were swept down onto the railway tracks to a depth of two feet in places. Sections of hard-packed roads were completely washed out, other roads were strewn with boulders. Low buildings were flooded with two to four inches of water. Just over a half hour later residents emerged to skies that had once again turned sunny and looked with dismay at the mess.

* * *

July 21st, George Lorne Paul, a drag-line operator employed by the Mannix company at Cadomin, was crushed to death in a coal slide.

The next day a hailstorm hit the area playing havoc with buildings and gardens. Hailstones picked up in the McLeod River crossing were brought into the Signal office by Joe Fronchuk and measured as much as one and a half inches in diameter.

An unusually heavy rain on Monday, July 28th was a factor in the death of a young Sterco man.

Ray Walker found water overflowing into the pit at Sterling Collieries and asked a group of men, A. McMaster, James 'Bud' Irving, J. McRae, A. Holmes, William Nichols and Ray Walker to help stem the flood. Mr. Walker found the ditch full of water and called the men to put sandbags in front of the break in the bank. While four men returned for more bags, Mr. Walker and Irving stood on the bank, about eight feet apart, talking.

Mr. Walker found the bank breaking and was hurled over the edge of the pit. The men were away for possibly twenty-five minutes and when they returned there was no sign of the two left behind. Mr. Nichols heard a cry for help and succeeded in locating and pulling out Mr. Walker who was covered with silt. The men searched for Bud Irving without success. Pumps were put to work and water and silt removed but it was not until August 17th, that the body of Bud Irving was recovered.

Bud was the son of the former CNR agent at Sterco Mr. and Mrs. A. Irving.

* * *

Organizational work for the proposed hospital building for the Mercoal Municipal Hospital District progressed favourably that August, with Peter Berkosha as chairman and organizer.

At Cadomin Peter McKenna, proprietor of the Cadomin Hotel for some twenty years sold his interests to A. B. Westworth of Coleman.

In September James O'Rourke was killed at Mountain Park when buried in a strip mine cave-in. Jim was standing between a truck and a power shovel when the bank of coal crumpled and buried him.

The train caused some excitement when it hit a section speeder at Mile 5. The men on the speeder jumped clear, but the speeder kept on down the track all on its own finally stopping at Coalspur when it bumped into a track-car.

Five polling stations were set up, one each at Mercoal, Foothills, Coalspur, Coal Valley, Sterco and Robb for one of the first municipal district plebiscites ever held. A disappointingly small vote saw 345 for and 24 against the building of a new hospital at Mercoal.

Hunters at Mountain Park were out in force the first week of October with the following residents bagging a silver tip grizzly each: Archie Embleau, Nick Antonenko, W. Sampson, Les Marshall and F. Parker. Mr. Parker bagged his silver tip a mile and a half from the townsite.

* * *

The Mountain Park correspondent wrote: Sunday, October 12th, the wind was in a playful mood and blew around corners and finding everything as usual decided to have some fun, so in the most playful pre-Hallowe'en mood blew little shacks and buildings over. Then remembering it was Thanksgiving on Monday decided to blow some chimneys over and spoil dinners. This was not enough so it puffed its cheeks and blew in windows . . . not to be caught at this joke it whistled away, rolling trees and taking all loose papers and cans in its stride.

Deciding this was not enough, it whistled away out of town to wreck the new bunkhouses and injure one of the carpenters rather badly.

Realizing wrong was done, the wind circled around and went away leaving people to sweep dust from their homes and survey the wrecks.

* * *

The annual convention of the Edson Constituency Social Credit Association was held in Edson October 22nd. The Hon. Norman Willmore pointed out that gravelling had been completed as far as Coalspur and would be continued to Mountain Park. Work on the Foothills section of the road was progressing as possible and would be continued, until it had been completed, including gravelling.

One proud owner of a car claimed to have made the trip to Coalspur and back in one day with little trouble. The Foothills correspondent asks, "How come? Is the 'Burma' passable?"

* * *

At Mercoal the Mercoal Garage, renamed by its owner Bob Spanach, was gutted by fire. Under construction at the time, much new equipment, some not even unpacked, two trucks, tools owned by the plumbing firm working there, were destroyed. One of the mechanics who was sleeping in the office of the old garage only became aware of the fire when he was awakened by citizens who had seen the blaze. Loss was estimated at $30,000 partially covered by insurance.

One Sunday morning in October private truckers and trucks of the Luscar Coal Company gathered en masse for 'Operation Sawdust'. The contingent worked all day to load trucks from a large sawdust pile out of town and transport it to cover the bottoms of the Luscar skating and curling rinks. The day would have passed without incident except that Louis Guent's truck suffered a broken axle when fording the McLeod River. Carl Wagner hooked a chain on to the truck but it wouldn't move until the combined power of three trucks took up the strain and pulled him from the water.

* * *

A shooting accident occurred in mid-November concerning visiting hunters. A 30-30 rifle in the hand of Robert Shaffer of Dapp, accidentally discharged while he was removing it from the front seat of a truck. The bullet struck Jack Seatter of Jarvie, Alberta. Other members of the hunting party were William and Henry Seatter and Fred Mitten, all of Jarvie, Alta. Bleeding profusely from the bullet wound Seatter was taken to Cadomin, 20 miles away. Dr. P. Melling discovered that due to the heavy loss of blood his veins had collapsed and blood plasma supplied to the victim was transfused as the accident victim lay on sleeping bags in the truck. Travelling to Edson, Seatter was given two more transfusions while still remaining in the vehicle. A mattress was purchased for the injured man to lie on and he was then taken to Edmonton. The entire trip to the city took twelve hours.

* * *

In mid-November too the pioneers mourned the death of Cory Wellington Simmonds. His friend Charlie Payne talked of the summer in '29 when the two had gone by boat from Lovett down the Brazeau and Saskatchewan to Edmonton.

Deep snow had by now fallen on Mountain Park. Men questioned each other at the washhouse. "Have the horses from the West come in?

149

Have the horses from McKenzie come in? Cheviot? Blue Berry Ridge? Sulphur Springs?" Each man worried about his own. They looked forward to their next day off so they could look for the animals and herd them into the corrals. The next concern would be Tommy Chapman's car of hay, which he doled out carefully so that all would have some and no horses suffer; as carefully as a physician prescribed medicine ... and all the horsemen were grateful.

* * *

Visiting hunters Leon Huoto and Norman Guoin of Vimy, Alberta got a thrill of a lifetime when guided by Paul Huoto the trio sighted a herd of forty elk. The visitors were equally proud to bag one grizzly bear, two moose and one elk.

* * *

Early in 1948 Alberta and British Columbia miners went on strike. Chris Pattinson left for Calgary as a U.M.W. of A. representative on the three man arbitration board endeavouring to find a satisfactory settlement to the strike.

* * *

At Mountain Park Mrs. Steve Baluch was happy to be home again after the war interfered with her holidays, which extended them to eight and a half years in Bavaria, Germany.

In February the Lovett Branch of the Canadian Legion, B.E.S.L. was formed.

Assisting in the organization were Zone Commander Jack Pattinson, Edson; Mr. R. A. Ansell, president of the Edson branch of the Canadian Legion, and Mr. George Graff of Edson.

Officers elected were: president, T. Ferris, Coal Valley; 1st vice-president W. Buedett, Coal Valley; 2nd vice-president P. C. Smith, Foothills; sec.-treas. J. Wyllie, Coal Valley. Executive: R. Adamson, Sterco; E. G. Miller, Coal Valley; C. Roscovich, Foothills.

* * *

Early in April 400 pupils of the Coal Branch School Division participated in a drama and musical festival. Nine one-act plays were presented.

In April, too, the coveted John Ryan Trophy was presented to J. A. McLeod, general manager of Cadomin Coals Ltd., who accepted it for the company and men, at the Canadian Mining Institute meeting in Vancouver.

In the year 1947 the Cadomin Coal Company had the lowest accident frequency and received the regional award for the Prairie Provinces. As this was the lowest accident count for the three districts, it also received the Dominion award. In the seven years of competition this was the first time the Dominion award had come to Alberta.

N. Melnyk, mine manager, S. Douglas, Jr. and R. Carr, pit bosses, District Inspector of Mines, Alex Muir and all the employees felt a deep glow of satisfaction.

In June of 1948 harbingers of spring, the mountain flowers, excelled themselves with a glorious burst that seemed to spring forth overnight. Carpets of richly hued flowers that extended up crannies, down gullies, across valleys for as far as the eye could see.

That spring, Assembly No. 49, Canadian Daughters League, Cadomin celebrated their 16th birthday party.

Throughout the summer teams practiced for the Mine Rescue and First Aid Contest, competing for the Coal Branch Championship.

Out of a possible 750 points Mercoal scored 732, Luscar 724 and Cadomin 721.

Judges for the events were: First Aid: Dr. W. A. Wilson, Dr. H. D. Hebb, Mr. James Young, Workmen's Compensation Board; Commissioner H. Darling RCMP and provincial president of St. John's Ambulance Association, and Mr. E. C. Emmott, St. John's Ambulance Association, Edmonton.

Mine Rescue: Mr. J. Thomson, District Mine Inspector, Edmonton; Mr. James Thomson, Superintendent Mine Rescue Station, Edmonton; Mr. J. McAndrew, General Superintendent for Alberta, Calgary and Mr. Alex Muir, Mine Inspector, Edson.

Teams competing were: Cadomin: J. Herman (captain), S. Hudzma, (deputy captain), L. Engley, G. Dotto, E. Sadoway, J. Gosney (patient).
Mercoal: W. James (captain), W. Mazur (deputy captain), R. McIntyre, T. Miserva, A. McQueen (patient).
Luscar: W. Thomas (captain), R. Davis (deputy captain), T. Mitchell, E. Gitzel, M. Kapach (patient).

* * *

In the fall local guides prepared for the season. Andrew (Lolly) Bello headed for Brazeau Lake where a hunting party arrived from the United States by plane.

Included in Mr. Bello's outfit were locals Alex Stene; Eddie Maddams, Eddie Kwasney, guides, Wrangler Billy Robertson and Fred Jones who would cook for the group.

At Weald Forest Ranger Gordon Ramstead, accompanied by 12-year-old Joe Gilbertson attributed their escape from an enraged bull moose to a sudden coyote-like agility on their part and to heavy underbrush. The moose charged from a distance of 75 feet, and the huge hornspread slowed him up in thick growth. A full half hour of pursuit and repeated charges ensued before he gave up the chase.

In October at Foothills James Pascoe lost his life in a mine accident while Edward Belrose and M. Dziwenko were injured.

At Mountain Park in November Ranger Angus Crawford was thrown from a horse while preparing to leave Grave Flats with Assistant Ranger Bradshaw. The two managed to make their way back to the Grave Flats cabin and telephoned for help.

Kenneth and Donald Crawford, sons of the injured man, left Mountain Park with a dog team for the 21 mile hike. With very little snow the two did not reach the cabin till midnight. Leaving at 9:00 a.m. the morning of the 19th, with a rest at Mile 10 on the Big Horn Trail the party arrived in Mountain Park at 8:00 that evening. In many places the dogs had to pull the sleigh over bare ground which slowed the pace.

* * *

Residents of Cadomin packed the Community Hall December 18th to honor Mr. and Mrs. M. P. Susnar. The Susnar's were leaving for Calgary as Mr. Susnar had been appointed organizer for District 18, U.M.W.A.

Mr. Susnar had been secretary-treasurer of the Cadomin Miner's Union for fourteen years, U.M.W.A. and during the war was a member of the Regional War Labor Board. Active in all phases of community affairs, the affair was sponsored by Cadomin Local No. 7296 and supported by all local organizations.

* * *

Wind Tears Roof off Houses

Winds of unbelievable velocity and 14 inches of snow in January of 1949 left the people of Cadomin, Mountain Park, Luscar and Leyland staggering under the impact.

At Cadomin the roof and two walls of a three room house occupied by Mr. and Mrs. W. Coupland and baby were torn away while they were in bed. The entire roof of the house occupied by Mr. and Mrs. D. Rocchio and family was lifted off and carried 100 feet.[26]

Old-timers recall it as the worst storm in the history of the Coal Branch.

The wind started on Wednesday, January 5th at Mountain Park in the afternoon and by evening had reached an estimated force of 90 miles per hour. Not a building in the village was left without a mark of the storm. Miners in each town were let off shift and went home to

Building moved out onto road after a windstorm at Cadomin.   Photo — V. Melnyk

Aftermath of a windstorm.

Windstorm — Cadomin, 1950.   V. Melynk — Photo

try and protect their property. Heavy planks were boarded across
each window.

People living on the hill suffered most as windows were blown in,
not only the glass but frames as well; rocks were picked up by the
wind and hurled through the air like baseballs; doors not hinged
from the inside were torn away; roofs were blown from garages and

barns, shingles ripped from roofs, chimneys blown down and houses shaken so badly the plaster fell from walls.

The full fury of the storm reached Cadomin and Leyland about 2:00 a.m. Thursday with a steady wind velocity of 50 mph with occasional bursts to 90 mph and left behind the same story of broken windows, damaged roofs, power and telephone line damage. At Luscar it was the same story with afternoon shifts disrupted. Damage to the water power deprived the people of their special water delivery until Sunday. The wind abated Thursday but with the 14 inches of snow, and temperatures ranging around 35 to 40 below zero, it was a dismal picture.

* * *

At Coalspur the roundhouse had burned down. A stationary boiler was set up and a building gang erected a house over it.

At Luscar, company employees and local citizens fought a fire which broke out in the coal bin. The bin had a capacity of seven hundred tons and was nearly full when in March a fire of unknown origin broke out. Live steam was applied to the building which smothered the first flames, but concentrated heat from the coal blew out sections of the walls, and it was only a matter of minutes until the large structure was a flaming inferno. Bulldozers demolished the building finally.

Flames had leaped hundreds of feet from the ground and would suddenly swing out at ground level driving workmen and spectators to take cover.

The fire which had broken out on a Sunday did not stop work Monday morning. Coal was dumped straight from the trucks onto the tipple.

* * *

Wolves were prevalent in the area, and lumber operator Aron Berglund found a partially eaten moose on the road south of Erith, with wolf tracks in abundance. Bounty on wolves was $12.00.

* * *

In 1933 the CNR superintendent's office had been moved to Edmonton in an economy move. In the spring of 1949 this was moved back to Edson with W. Frame the new superintendent.

* * *

The first week of April at Mountain Park a few rumors circulated about the underground. Rumours, rumours. There was always some rumour or other circulating.

Saturday, April 9, 1949. Pay day! A day that was always a jocular event, with much kidding and cat-calling. Men opened their pay envelopes. A little slip of paper advised them that their services were no longer required.[27] Stunned, they turned to each other. What did it

[27] Read Tom Gates.

154

mean? This couldn't be. Why some of them had been in Mountain Park for twenty years. The men were also advised to come back Monday the 11th to get their tools. One hundred men out of work. Just like that.

Many headed for the bar, a regular habit at any rate, but this time the atmosphere was a different one entirely. What would they do? While some union employees made immediate transfer to the sister company Luscar Coals, Ltd., others remained in a state of seemingly suspended animation. They made no move whatever, unable to comprehend the enormity of the situation.

Gradually as weeks went by the men found work at other points on the Coal Branch returning to be with their family on weekends. A few families moved to Edson, with the man of the house continuing to work on the Coal Branch.

* * *

Coal Valley residents complained as there was no doctor in the village. While the Medical Committee advertised in hope of luring a doctor to the camp, two nurses coped with the bulk of the problems.

Mrs. C. W. Smith of Robb suffered multiple bruises of the body and leg lacerations when struck by a freight train while crossing the track and was taken to St. John's Hospital in Edson.

At Cadomin guests turned out ninety strong at a shower for bride-elect Alice Cebuiliak, held in the Community Hall.

On August 26, 1949, Luscar Collieries Ltd. was presented the Ryan Trophy for having the lowest accident rate in three prairie provinces the preceding year. The presentation was made in the Mercoal Theatre with a free show given to the community by Luscar Coals Ltd.

At Cadomin the community presented newly wed Mrs. L. Johnstone (nee Miss A. Lucchini) with one of the magnificent showers the towns on the Coal Branch were noted for, with 121 guests present.

At Mountain Park school had opened with the following staff: Mr. J. Mclnychuk as principal, Mrs F. H. Parker as grade 5 and 6 teacher, Mrs. Bothwell, grades 3 and 4, and Mrs. Melnychuk, grades 1 and 2. Grades 10, 11 and 12 would be bussed daily to the new high school in Cadomin.

September 10 a heavy fall of snow was reported with a temperature of 17 above.

* * *

September 12 was an unfortunate day for Luscar. Young George Shipka sustained a serious arm injury when caught in a gear in the local briquette plant shortly after the day's shift started. He was taken to the local hospital and then by ambulance to the city. A few hours later Walter Lewicki capsized his bulldozer over the hill in the townsite, then George Slynski, blinded by the sun, missed a curve on the road and turned his car over.

Hunters complained this year about the scarcity of game in the area. Melio Bello, assistant ranger at Mountain Park, coming in from

Mile 10 one day in September saw a cow moose charging towards him followed by a pack of nine timber wolves. The moose rushed right by him, brushing against the pack boxes.

Clem Curtin, 34, was killed in a car accident between Cadomin and Mercoal. Missing since Wednesday of the previous week, the wreck was found at the foot of a steep hill on Sunday. Such is the terrain of the country that hundreds had driven by without seeing the car.

* * *

Residents of Mercoal and district were shocked to hear of the accident and death of Mr. Robert (Bob) Spanach, age 39, on Tuesday, October 25th.

The accident occurred at his planing mill at Steeper about 8:00 a.m. Tuesday morning. Mr. Spanach started the machinery and was putting belt dressing on the belt when his clothing caught and he was flipped against the end wall. He was survived by his wife, Amelia, two children, George 5, and Diana 4, a sister, Mrs. Berkovich of Kamloops, B.C., his mother and three sisters in Yugoslavia.[28]

Teachers at Cadomin this season were: Mr. H. O. Harper, principal, Mr. W. Johnston, math and science, Mr. L. Way, commercial and social studies; Mr. G. Fancier, industrial art and physical education, Miss M. Kochalyk, home economics.

Junior high school teachers included Mrs. G. Harper and Mr. V. Sharman.

Elementary school teachers were: Mrs. W. Thirlwell, grades 1 and 2, Mrs. Cantrell, grades 3 and 4, Miss E. Stevens, grades 4 and 5, Miss L. Gordey, grades 6 and 7. Mrs. S. Yelland was caretaker.

* * *

In November the Robb correspondent wrote:

"Our boys here were let down when it came to getting their wages. First it was Mile 32 mine, then Mile 33. Thought these companies had to have a bond to cover wages or don't they? Makes it a pretty slim Christmas for more than one."

30,000 tons of coal were mined in November, 1949 in Mercoal. To celebrate this record breaking month the McLeod River Hard Coal Co. sponsored a free dance in the theatre on the first Friday in December and refreshments to all on Saturday at the hotel and the Legion Hall.

Sunday fire broke out twice in the boiler room but was quickly checked by employees.

In December a human skull was discovered by T. Davis of Edmonton on the Embarras river. Residents speculated on the identity. It could have been one of a half dozen missing persons.

---

[28] Read Amelia Spanach story.

CHAPTER TWELVE

1950

January and one snowfall followed another. Coupled with temperatures that hovered between 20 and 45 below zero, residents of the Coal Branch battled the winter.

At Sterco Mr. and Mrs. Fraser made an attempt to get to Cadomin but turned back after making it as far as Mercoal. The Robb correspondent writes, "We are really in a bad way here, no phone, no road and not even the horses show up."

Sterco residents cancelled plans to watch Cadomin and Wetaskiwin play hockey and the Sterco correspondent writes, "Our local train, due in here Saturday night arrived Sunday about twenty hours late."

In early February W. H. Kankewitt and Don Riggan on their way to the Luscar carnival with carloads of Edson skaters stopped near the Wadley farm on the Coal Branch Road. Sid McLeod and Danny Shearer of Cadomin dazedly watched as five hundred gallons of gasoline poured from an Imperial Oil truck which they had just overturned. The skaters doubled up while Mr. Kankewitt drove the two young men, suffering from shock, into Edson.

At Mercoal the new $4,000 curling rink was opened up. Volunteer labor and volunteer contributions had kept the costs down.

At Coalspur residents watched as a small band of Indians from the Saddle Lake reserve loaded six head of game; moose, elk and deer, for transport to the St. Paul area.

Fifty mine officials gathered at the Cadomin Community Hall to pay homage to Mr. Alex Muir, District Mine Inspector who was to leave for Calgary to take up his new position as Mines Inspector. Simultaneously Mrs. Muir was honored at the home of Mrs. D. R. Young by fellow sisters of the Eastern Star.

At Sterco thirty-five cars were counted among the forty-eight families. The correspondent asks, "Do we get gravel and just how soon?"

Frank Knezevic, a well-known trapper in the Lovett area, warned Branch residents of the prevalence of wolves. Black Frank, as he was better known, reported running into a pack of 15 wolves, shooting one he estimated at 200 pounds. Black Frank recommended carrying a rifle for protection. Bounty on wolves to March 21, 1950 was $12.00 and $15.00 on cougars.

Two deer in a quest for food entered the E. Anthony logging camp on the Coal Branch. Timber wolves attacked and killed the deer right in the camp.

The Lovett Fish and Game Association was formed the spring of 1950 with an enrolment of 120 expected from the combined camps. Elected were: President, A. A. Fraser, Coal Valley; Vice-President, W. Wilson, Sterco; Secretary-Treasurer, R. Muir, Sterco; E. Stollings, Lovett, was in charge of game animals; R. Butts, game fish; and C. Roscovich, game birds and song birds.

At Cadomin Eddie Kapuscinski said good-bye to his parents for the season, which he would spend pitching for Cal's Dodgers in Edmonton.

April 22nd, fire broke out in the bunkhouse at Mercoal, which accommodated forty employees. Men moved over to the old bunkhouse with residents providing blankets. Others were invited into private homes.

At Luscar, the Palm Confectionery burned early one morning. Frank Knapp, owner, was asleep on the second storey and escaped by dropping from the window onto the poolroom annex.

In early May residents at Mountain Park watched as 'The Summit', the gathering place of the younger generation burned to the ground. Young Bobby Fleck morosely kicking at the ruins later that day, kicked a can which exploded, burning his eyelashes and eyebrows off. The lad spent the rest of the day in hospital.

Another 14 inches of snow fell on the Coal Branch area in May.

At Wagoner's Camp, a bear, lunching off the carcass of a dead horse, was shot by a Robb resident, the bear weighing 600 pounds.

At Mercoal the Bank of Nova Scotia opened a new branch.

Yet another fire, this time the three storey Home Cafe at Mercoal burned to the ground May 21. Roomers upstairs were warned in time to escape with some of their belongings. Hoses were turned on the Legion Hall and favorable winds kept this too from burning.

A group of men at Robb, backed by that community, decided to gravel a hill near that settlement when a '35 Ford truck went out of control on the loose gravel and turned over. Lucien Lavoie, 41, sitting on the flat rack with three other men was thrown out. Rushed to Edson by car he was pronounced dead on arrival.

Then Came June

Yet another snowfall, the first part of the month, added to the still heavy cover. The weather suddenly turned gloriously warm, melting the foot deep snow. The tenth of June the weather turned to a steady drizzle, the rain depressingly dismal and wet, adding to streams and rivers already swollen with the spring run-off.

Then almost without warning, the full fury of the McLeod River rushed down upon Cadomin, sweeping mud and water over the town with what eye-witnesses called 'a terrific impact'.

The flood crest rushed through the town, completely isolating the Cadomin mine and the Cadomin hotel.

The entire south section of the town was cut off by the swirling McLeod, risen four feet above the normal level in three hours time. The wild river struck three privately owned houses in the low-lying area of South Cadomin, wrenching them from the ground and floating them away.

A mile from Cadomin, at Leyland, the flood washed out two bridges and completely inundated the Riverside grocery store.

Meanwhile swollen mountainside tributaries of the river hurled two mud and rock slides of three feet depth across the CNR track at Leyland, halting all railway traffic.

Highway traffic was also halted as the surging waters washed over the Coal Branch road for 12 miles south of Coalspur. All bridges between Mercoal and Cadomin were washed away. Only one bridge, between Mountain and Cadomin withstood battering by the wild river.

And Five Men were Trapped in the Cadomin Mine

Fireboss Roy Carr, 38, Mike Kapuscinski, 58, Pete Morris, 66, Rade Kasonovich 62, and Steve Tomlenovich, 53, were high up in the east workings.

Two hundred and seventy feet above them was the surface — and a cave-in. A hole, large enough to hold about 6,000 tons of coal had formed as a result of the cave-in of what had once been a surface working or a section of strip mining.

Heavy rain overflowed a ditch along the top of the high hill and went into the cave-in. The water roared through to the miners working up from below.

Four men 100 feet below made what pit boss Joe Henderson called a 'miraculous escape'. Twenty-three others also were in the mine but 'felt the air reverse and their fire boss got them out'.

Wives, families and friends waited. A friend keeping vigil at the Carr home watched as Mrs. Carr ironed a yellow shirt, a favorite of Roy's. She remembers thinking that Roy Carr almost had not gone to work that day. He had given his resignation earlier that month and planned on selling for Investors Syndicate. He'd mentioned to his wife that 'I'd better work out my time because I might not make a go of it as a salesman', so thought it best to leave with a clean slate.

Rescuers toiled and the town waited.

June 16th and hope rose when a five man party turned in a broken miner's lamp 36 hours after the entombment. Hopes fell when Joe Fedynak disclosed that a man's leg wearing a heavy shoe and dismembered below the knee had been found by a rescue party earlier.

By this time thirty-eight truckloads of muck had been taken from the mine as parties worked clock-round, in six hour shifts to clear the mud-clogged passageways.

It was to be a long, long search.

The bodies of Red Kasenovich and Pete Morris were found.

Sixty miners continued round-the-clock rescue operations.

Funeral services were held for Michael Kapuscinsky on July 17th.

By July 27th, 4,000 tons of debris had been removed from the mine since the search started.

John Crawford, Department of Mines stated: "Progress has been slow, owing to the fact every foot cleared has to be blocked and timbered to prevent further cave-ins. We have to establish ventilation for the workers. There is no use of opening up just one end of a pipe."

In August, funeral services were held for the last two victims, Red Kasonevich and Roy Carr.

* * *

Disaster of Another Sort

On June 20th the last working whistle at Mountain Park sounded signalling the death knell of mining operations. Miners were stunned; their jobs gone. "On June 30th mine company officials gave 30 days notice to miners and their families living in company houses to vacate". Home owners have been given 30 days to remove their dwellings off company property."

Light and water service would be discontinued at the same time.

In an article headed 'Miners at Mountain Park Mourn Over Town's Death' Marjorie Jones wrote: MOUNTAIN PARK, July 24 — In a few more days Pete Cheisa will no longer be able to look up at ever-changing Mt. Cheviot and feel at home.

Mountain Park's oldest miner is making his last rounds at his last job as watchman in this dying town.

At the end of July his work will be finished. So will the town.

The Mountain Park Coal Mine whistle which first blew 39 years ago, blasted its last on June 20, when the mine was shut because of lack of orders, but its echoes still ring in the mountains.

Reluctant ears of 110 miners whom it threw out of work, and their worried wives, hear it yet.

As they pack to leave they hear it. As they say quick goodbyes to neighbours who in 30 years are more like family than friends they hear it.

They hear other unnerving unfamiliar sounds now. The squeal of nails being pulled, the thud of boards falling, sounds of their homes disintegrating . . . their small spic and span green and white houses a mere pile of old lumber.

Mr. Chiesa watched those houses going up and lived in one of them. Seeing most of them torn down one by one makes even his leathery old face a bit wistful.

"These are sad days for me," he says.

But he's better off than many men. He'll have his mine pension to fall back on. It's men between 50 and 60 who are hardest hit and those with large families. Younger men can adapt themselves to new jobs and surroundings but everyone is in the same predicament for housing. They must find a place to live.

The company has sent eviction notices to everyone. Those in company houses have been asked to get out by July 21 and those owning their own little homes on company property must also move. They must sell or tear them down.

Either way they stand to lose. They can't move them over narrow mountain roads. If they sell, they may get $140 for them, some are going for less. If they dismantle them they must rebuild someplace else.

The Company-owned hotel, its annex, the store and other public buildings are being torn down. The United Church has been given to the neighboring Mercoal congregation.

The half million dollar tipple is idle, much of the mine machinery has gone, the underground mine has been flooded and entrances blasted for safety. Strip operations are fenced.

"Perhaps a war will reopen it," station agent R. L. Jones said. But he's planning to leave in three months. The leased railroad will be operated by the CNR for at least a year, he believed.

Hardworking Tom Stevenson, a jolly Scot, now concerned about his future thinks the mine is done for. "I'm not sure I'm not either," he says.

161

The question on every lip is where to go and more tragic than the question is the answer, "We don't know."

Young Nino Chiesa who with Jack Roome took over the store only a year ago on borrowed money, plans on peddling goods he can't sell by July 31st.

Luckier than most, in that her husband has a job and a place to go but admittedly 'broken hearted' about leaving, Mrs. Vic Riendeau says she 'can't believe it has really happened.'

She came as a bride from Montreal 29 years ago. Before she left for Luscar this week the still vigorous woman climbed the slopes back of the tipple to pick forget-me-nots and mourn it would be her last climb.

One of the trucks which have been loading all week pulled up to her door and took her household goods and she, as other women and children, followed her husband to a new life.

Some without much money, feel they must stay and live a lonely hard life with the deserted dogs and cats and the mine horses that gallop through the streets among empty buildings. How they'll manage without lights and water which will be cut off July 31st, possible curtailed railroad service, poor roads, no telephone, doctor or hospital, they don't know.

The Archie Emblau family of 13 have no place to go. Here they lived cheaply, paid low rent and could hunt and fish to help out.

Telephone operator Mrs. Covey Fleck, her jobless husband and eight children will stay until the office closes, then what, they don't know.

Even ranger Angus Crawford can't stay without conveniences for his family.

Mrs. John Baruzzini has known no other home since she left Italy. Here her husband lost his sight five years ago and with three of eight children still at home this courageous little woman must try to make ends meet.

It hasn't been too hard owning her own house, but when she leaves she must find another house and pay rent. If she stays her children will be without a school and she will have no way of getting her groceries.

Mine Manager D. F. MacKinnon himself is a bit uncertain about his future. But without coal orders the mine can't continue and without the mine, the town, once 900 people, can't continue.

And Pete Chiesa, the watchman, who will soon have nothing more to watch, says text books will have to change because Mountain Park will no longer be the highest (6,200 feet) inhabited town in Canada.

* * *

In July, Luscar Coals announced a quarter of a million dollar expansion program. The company proposed to install a new briquetting plant to double its output of briquettes. The plant would be in operation to meet the winter demand. Luscar Coals Ltd. would then have a capacity of 1200 tons of briquettes daily, coupled with 1200 tons capacity of screen coal.

162

The announcement was received on the Coal Branch with relief, and many of the 100 odd men of Mountain Park found work on this payroll. Many others moved to Mercoal, but here there was already a real housing shortage. With the cafe rooming house, and the bunkhouse recently destroyed by fire, the camp was hard pressed for living space.

By August Mountain Park residents had to go to Cadomin for their mail, and residents tried to remember where each family had moved. The mass exodus was hard to keep up with, and former families were delighted to meet each other again in a new location. Neighbors, once more! Others had to contend with a railroad strike. By the end of August eighteen families still remained, some waiting for homes to go to, others waiting for transportation for their furniture.

Bryan Mine Goes Into Production

So while one mine died, that fall another opened, or rather re-opened. The first loading of coal from the newly re-opened property of Bryan Mine began October 31, 1950. The strip-mining project was a new operation carried out by North Western Coal and Oil Limited with Frank E. Ruben as president. The company was a wholly owned subsidiary of the New Pacific Coal and Oils.

Bryan was first opened in 1923 as an underground project by James Bryan, well known northern fur trader. When the local market declined in the mid 30's operations gradually ceased. In 1939 the mine was re-opened and operated intermittently on a small tonnage basis until 1948 when it was taken over by Mr. Ruben.

The seam from which this coal is being taken is known throughout Western Alberta as the Val D'Or Seam.

* * *

And as if fires, mine closures and deaths were not enough, an epidemic of scarlet fever broke out on the Coal Branch this fall of 1950. Hardest hit was the camp of Mercoal when 15 cases were reported. Schools operated only intermittently and a mass innoculation of 400 children was carried out. Dr. K. Trentin of Coal Valley and Dr. Thomas Moore were in charge.

The year wound up on a happier note when Alberta Coal Miners voted to accept an 80-cent a day wage increase.

The Fifties

Shifts in residence were very much in evidence when line-ups were posted in one of the numerous inter-town hockey games played. Old Coal Branch names were prominent in the Edson line-up: Hendricks, Kowalchuk, Cebuliak, Ramstead, Bochek, Lovsin, Chiesa, Dunphy, Pavich, Congrave.

163

Familiar Mountain Park names cropped up in the Luscar Tigers lineup: Bartoff, Mahoney, O. Hicks, Baruzzini, Harrison, Tomich, Bracko, Kulyk, Carriere, D. Hicks, Mitchell and Chalus.

At Luscar the Third Annual Ice Carnival was produced with 'Cinderella' as the theme. Twelve hundred spectators viewed the two highly successful performances. The event chaired by Phil Morris saw everyone in the mining village involved in some degree.

Cadomin won the District High School Hockey Tournament which included participants from Evansburg to Jasper, and Cadomin lady curlers walked off with the Grand Challenge at Edson. Not to be outdone the Cadomin men took the same honors at the Men's Bonspiel at Edson.

Russell J. Butts, 43, was killed early in March by a fall of coal at the Foothills Colliery, with Dr. P. J. Kimmitt, coroner, presiding at the inquest held in Edson.

At Coalspur the King Coal Mines began to close for intermittent periods . . .

At Luscar W. Zazluk took over management of the store which would be renamed The Luscar Mercantile Co.

And at Sterco three well known families, E. Finnen's, R. Haigh's and J. Stanock's were honored at a joint farewell party in the local community hall. Residents on this branch still complained of the conditions on the 'Burma' road.

Wm. A. Hughes by using a chemical method instead of soil in his greenhouse at Luscar managed to grow onions nine inches high in a period of thirteen days. Cinders in combination with chemicals were used as a base.

The Coalspur correspondent writes in May, "Our little village is very quiet since the mine closed down, but we hear rumors it will open up again shortly."

Cy Thomas, one of Luscar's hockey personalities arrived home for the summer after studying medicine at Halifax and playing for the top team there. Brother Ed had spent the season playing for Vernon.

A derailed car on the CN Tracks at Luscar contributed to the accidental death of two Edson men working on the wrecking crew there. George Congrave, assistant car foreman was killed instantly, Arthur Leach died in Luscar hospital and Ted Madge lost an arm, and was treated in Luscar hospital.

A general shifting of the population of the Coal Branch was much in evidence this summer, with many families leaving to make their homes elsewhere. Families who had lived on the Branch for decades decided it was time to pull up stakes. Generally declining coal markets precipitated a good many of the moves. At Mercoal as many families moved in as moved out and the overcrowding at the school necessitated a class of grade three pupils being moved to the community hall basement. The housing and boarding situation was so acute

LUSCAR CARNIVAL COMMITTEE

Presents

Their Fourth Annual

ICE CARNIVAL

"The Wedding of the Painted Doll"

SATURDAY and SUNDAY

February 23rd and 24th

that a single teacher Miss Beale exchanged teaching positions with a Mrs. Parker at Cadomin.

Coal Branch residents once again left for Edson for another Royal Visit, this time Princess Elizabeth and Prince Phillip. Paul Marshall of Mercoal, Captain of the Coal Branch Cadets and his corps were delighted when the Royal Couple stopped to chat for a few minutes. Because of the 14 inch fall of snow and resultant icy and drifted roads, many could not get through to Edson.

At Cadomin Marilyn Basso won the Governor General's Medal in Grade 9, no mean feat as this was the second largest division for these awards in the Province.

Early in January, 1952, Walter Kaasa arrived to do the choreography for routines for the up-coming ice carnival this time centred about the theme, 'The Wedding of the Painted Doll.' One of Luscar's top figure skaters, Noelle McVey scored second, 85.5 in the Western Canada Figure Skating competitions held in Vancouver. The entire cast presented this show twice in Luscar and then cast, scenery and props moved to Cadomin for a third showing.

The Foothills Community Hall which doubled for church services went up in flames on a chilly Wednesday night in January.

Luscar's Noelle McVey, Janet Bartoff, and the fifty piece Edmonton Schoolboys Band contributed to Edson's 1952 annual ice carnival, called Circus Capers.

Robb formed a Home and School Association with Wm. Curtin, president, Mr. Bennette, vice-president and Mrs. W. O'Boylce, secretary. Their first objective was the installation of electricity and water suppy for the school.

The Wrigley rink from Cadomin entered the Luscar 'spiel with J. A. Wrigley, age 39 as skip, Mrs. A. Wrigley 36, third, Bonita Wrigley, 16, second and Walter Wrigley, 16, as lead.

The Foothills mine closed for one day in March, a first for the year 1952. Soon many Sterco men switched to working the Coal Valley Mine during succeeding lay-offs.

T. Kurp, 46, of Coalspur found himself an uncle for the 29th time.

Lovett Branch residents were shocked to hear of the death of Mrs. Carol Muir and her daughter Sharon in Vancouver. Roy and Carol (nee McAloney) had moved to the coastal city from the Lovett Branch. Roy had gone off to a store to buy ice-cream in celebration of a family birthday party and Carol and Sharon were burned in an apartment fire.

At Coalspur the tipple of the mine burned.

At Mercoal fire broke out in the mine in September of 1951. Failure of dry ice to combat the mine fire forced officials to attempt to block off the flames and allow men to return to other workings in the mine.

First blocks constructed soon after the fire broke out proved ineffective and new blocks nearer the entrance were built, bringing the fire under control.

Hon. Gordon C. Taylor, Minister of Highways, A. Frame, Deputy Minister, A. M. Reid, district engineer and Norman Willmore, M.L.A. toured the Coal Branch highways. As a result improvements were scheduled on the road between Sterco and Foothills and the road gravelled between Coalspur and Sterco.

Residents of Sterco were downcast when the post office was closed out and the sub moved to Foothills.

At Luscar the collieries continued to work steadily with two shifts a day.

Post offices switched again, and now Mercoal served the camps of Foothills, Coal Valley and Sterco. This necessitated a trip of up to 21 miles for some residents to collect their mail. After much complaining a sub reopened at Coal Valley with Mrs. V. Fraser as post-mistress.

Lovett Branch residents gathered at the Coal Valley Community Hall to pay homage to Mr. Sam Sutherland, retiring CNR conductor. The name 'Sam's Train' was to linger.

In June 1952 another flood hit the Cadomin area and the McLeod River flooded a section of the 4,800 foot level of the mine, the richest coal seam being worked. The railway line, roads, bridges and sidings also were washed out adding to the mine's problems.

Without much ado the Cadomin mine closed down in July, 1952. Just under a hundred men were given final notification.

Cadomin, the biggest of all the camps on the Coal Branch with a population that had reached 2,500. Cadomin the commercial core. It had been inevitable. Coal contracts had dwindled and the writing had been on the wall signaled by periodic shutdowns. However, unlike Mountain Park there had been a feeling of preparedness for this eventuality. The population had already thinned in the last few years, and others carried out plans already half formulated. A few of the old time diehards shrugged and prepared to retire. Where? Right in Cadomin of course. Where else could you live as cheaply. Fuel there for the taking. They weren't forced to move. Perhaps they could pick up some work in the limestone operation that seemed to be plugging steadily along. Others found work in Luscar. While some sold their homes or prepared to move them, others decided to leave them as they were and use them as summer homes. They would be back and back often to visit 'home'.

Even before the flooding the coal marketing conditions in Western Canada, said Colin Campbell, executive vice-president, had been working a hardship on the company, as they had been on most Alberta underground mines. One main factor was the decision to dieselize Canada's two railways. Another main factor was the collapse of the Japanese market for export coal from Canada at the year end.

Rails, pipes and other equipment would be left in the mine, so that the mine could be pumped out and work resumed if it was decided that conditions warranted revival of the operation.

In August of 1952 Richfield. Oil Corporation of California announced location of its first Canadian drilling venture, located on farmout lands from Hudson's Bay Oil and Gas Company. The site was 20 miles up the Coal Branch with Drident Drilling of Calgary in charge of operations.

This was to be the beginning of many such ventures and the Coal Branch area would become crisscrossed with the marks of oil and seismic exploration. While some hailed the exploration, trappers and hunters watched with trepidation, and made dire predictions.

In September the population of Cadomin had dwindled to less than a hundred families, but a well attended meeting of the Cadomin Sports and Amusement Association discussed plans for the purchase of the Community Hall so that shows and winter sports could be continued. Heads of many of the families there, now worked at Luscar, a bus service transporting them to and from work. By October the Cadomin Coal Co. had agreed to turn over the Community Hall to the United Church and Catholic Church committees until April 1, 1953.

On the Lovett Branch remaining residents of the three camps attended the opening dance of the new Quanset Hall in Foothills.

At Mercoal the new $50,000 hospital was opened to the public November 22nd, 1952 at a formal Visitor's Day. The hospital containing eight beds would have a staff of two nurses, a housekeeper with Dr. P. Melling as attending physician and surgeon. It was open to non-residents as well as Mercoal people.

In December an area of forest west of Cadomin and southeast of Luscar was destroyed by fire. Believed started by the sparks carried by the wind from a burning abandoned mine the fire lasted for two days with forestry officials and employees of the Luscar Coal Co. bringing it under control. Little snow had fallen this fall of 1952, so the fire managed to cover a considerable area.

Cadomin proceeded along and optimistically elected a new slate of officers for the Cadomin Legion. J. H. McKenna was president, with Joe Moar and N. Kulyk, first and second vice-presidents; N. K. Matheson, secretary-treasurer; W. Docherty, recording secretary. Executive included B. Roberts, J. Palwoda, R. C. Haigh, B. Bodenchuck; Sgt.at-Arms, H. Docherty and auditors J. L. Nicholson and J. C. McLeod.

Early in 1953 Mah Chow, after spending 30 years in Coalspur decided to return to his wife and family in China.

At Sterco the store closed completely and the remainder of stock moved to Coal Valley.

Jack Lee in a letter to the Signal writes in May of 1953: A trip over the Coal Branch these days brings into sharp focus the sad plight of the coal mining industry of Western Canada. One feels the sense of insecurity in towns where miners work short time and lay-offs threaten. There is the town of Cadomin now, so forlorn, with the mines closed down, business places boarded up and miners trying to sell their homes at give-away prices before leaving in search of work

Despite boarded business places the Cadomin High School bustled with life during the graduation exercises for the 1952-3 term. Graduands included: Lillian Supsak, Luscar; Rose Pilichowski, Luscar; Beate Bernedt, Luscar; Shirley Downie, Luscar; Lydia Huyma, Cadomin, Estelle Philbrick, Coalspur; Arnold Flohr, Mercoal; Peter Marcetta, Cadomin and Edward Bealle, Cadomin. These were to be the final graduates. The school was advertised for demolition the following year.

"Soren Madsen was the successful bidder for the recently built high school and the public school buildings at Cadomin."

By the summer of 1953 the Sterco correspondent writes: Sterco is beginning to look like a village on stilts with so many buildings jacked up ready to move. It is a sad state of affairs when a man doesn't know where to go 'home'.

* * *

Black Frank

In October of 1953 Frank Knezevic, better known as 'Black Frank' was declared missing.

'Black Frank' was a tall fiercely independent individual of Czechoslovakian descent. He had worked the mines for a number of years and then moved to full time trapping.

He was seen periodically in Edson, a colorful figure in fringed buckskin, clothes he had made himself. He was a master blacksmith, tanned his own leather, made his own saddles.

Held in much esteem by Coal Branch residents he had prior to his disappearance promised to bring Mr. Romeo Brassard and his staff

Frank Knezevich better known as Black Frank.

169

at the Coal Valley Hotel some elk steaks on the occasion of his next visit.

On October 26th a ranger took his mail down, saw no one around, but as the dog was tied in the kitchen and three horses penned nearby assumed the trapper was near or checking on his trapline. A week or more later, an Indian friend went down to the cabin situated on the Pembina about ten miles below Lovett. The mail was untouched and he notified forestry officials, RCMP, forestry and residents immediately launched an all out search.

On November 10th examination of the cabin revealed the end link of the chain which had secured the dog was straightened out and the snap was missing as well as the dog. Black Frank was an exceedingly neat man and nothing was disturbed.

Residents informed police that Black Frank had suffered a heart attack earlier that spring. The Constable in charge was N. H. Greenwood-Madsen, while Chief Ranger Don Buck and Ranger C. Chapman of the Forestry Service assisted.

On the morning of the 15th of November, 1953, the bones of a bull elk which appeared to have been recently killed were found about three miles downstream from Black Frank's cabin. The animal had been completely devoured by wolves. The remains of this animal were closely examined but none of the remaining bones showed any signs of a bullet hole.

After many fruitless forays, the search was given up. In 1962 Mr. Justice Primrose of Edmonton pronounced Frank Knezevic officially dead. The estate was looked after by a god-child and it was necessary to obtain affidavits from the then Corporal Greenwood-Madsen who was serving at Lamont, and Cst. C. J. Barry serving at Andrew, Alta.

Almost twenty years later, on October 4th, 1972 a hunter in the Pembina River district southwest of Robb came across the skeletal remains of a human body. The hunter recovered a rusted rifle which he found lying a few feet from the skeleton and took it to Edmonton where he notified the RCMP. The hunter, RCMP search party and Forest Ranger Ken Wheat arrived by Air Detachment and then on foot and on October 5th, 1972 located the skeleton. Among other items a cigarette lighter with the initial 'K' was found. The skeletal remains were turned over to Dr. R. J. Swallow at the University of Alberta. The pathologist considered the condition of the bones to be compatible with exposure to the elements for 15 to 20 years. The Crime Detection Laboratory of the RCMP in Edmonton minutely examined the rifle. The chamber of the rifle contained a live round of 6.5 mm ammunition. Staff Sgt. Major Greenwood-Madsen, Chief C.I.B. Clerk with the Edmonton RCMP took a keen interest in the procedures.

The rifle was in a cocked position ready for firing.

* * *

In November, 1953 two bunkhouses and the 'innards' of the tipple at Sterco were moved to Coal Valley. Early in January Coal Valley mine was idle for four days of one week, and residents grew restless with uncertainty. By March the Coal Valley correspondent wrote: 'The mine is still going three to four days a week. Men are drifting away slowly for other jobs, yet we all hope it isn't the end.'

The Western Signal ran a red headline for the first time in years with the banner line reading: PULP MILL AT YATES IS DEFINITE. The story following stated that North Canadian Oils, who acquired the interest of North Western Pulp and Power Limited and Bryan Mountain Coal Company Limited would become associated with a large American paper company interested in sharing the development. 'Operations at the mill will be done with coal from Bryan Mountain, there being ample supplies at the mine to meet all the power requirements of the mill.'

Cadomin   couresty — Alberta Government Photo Service

In April the Robb mine closed.

'The announcement of the closing of the mine at Robb has brought serious repercussions to the railway industry in Edson. Railway officials from Winnipeg are in the district this week and it is expected that the terminal facilities at Coalspur will also be closed down.'

The banner headline was wasted. The pulp mill was to become an actuality but not at Yates.

Meanwhile retired miners at Cadomin extolled the virtue of living in a home purchased for as low as $50 with luxury types selling for up to $200. Annual $5 rental fee for the lot was payable to the Alberta Department of Lands and Forests. You could dig for fuel in the abandoned mine; ample water was available from the McLeod and fishing was good. Life could be worse.

Residents there nodded with pride when a former Cadomin girl, Helen Margaret Smyth became a double-award winner, receiving the President's Gold Medal in Nursing and the William Fulton Gillespie Memorial Prize at the University of Alberta School of Nursing, in 1954. She was, after all, a Coal Brancher.

In July of 1954 the Signal again ran a headline, this time in conservative black type — Pulp Mill Site To Be At Tollerton. Area residents by this time had become inured to rumours concerning the site of this much talked about pulp mill, and read the story with a jaundiced eye.

Tex Byers died in Mercoal Hospital, September 23, 1954, and many a story was recalled centred about this well liked, intrepid pioneer of the Alberta Coal Branch.

By October, 1954 a headline read Immediate Start on Spur Line to Pulp Mill Site: The first important step towards construction of the pulp mill since land purchases were made a few weeks ago is the letting of the contract for the building of the spur line to the mill site.

The contract has been let to The New West Construction Ltd. of Edmonton. The spur will start out just west of the SNA Lumber Co. spur line and will turn south parallel to the Glenwood Cemetery road, then west on the old Tollerton grade to the site.

Edson Town Council met frequently to discuss the building of pulp mill workers houses in the town; the Council through the Department of Municipal Affairs secured building jurisdiction over the type of buildings, business places or residences within a five mile area of the town.

January 1, 1955, mail to and from the Coal Branch was carried by motor vehicles. The switch from rail to highway allowed the postal service to maintain better control over times of delivery and pick-up, it was stated.

Rail service too, was cut on the Coal Branch. Service on the Edson-Foothills line was cut from three days to one day a week effective January 31st. Edson-Luscar service also dwindled from the three day schedule to one day leaving Edson on Wednesday and returning Thursdays, weekly.

January, 1955 and officials of the St. Regis Pulp and Power Commission were in Edson inspecting the clearing and progress of the mill site.

H. Anker Construction who had the contract for the clearing of the site reported that to date he had approximately 70 of the 300 acres cleared. The contract stated clearing must be finished by April 1st, and Mr. Anker felt there would be no problem meeting that date.

In the inspection party were Mr. McArthur, Chief engineer of the St. Regis Pulp and Power, New York; Mr. P. V. Hart, General Northlands Forestry Manager of the St. Regis Pulp and Power; Mr. F. Ruben, Chairman of the Board of North West Pulp and Power and Mr. R. Ruben, district representative.

The Edson Town Council discussed a housing development of 500 houses.

The end of February citizens were perplexed with the announcement that the pulp mill would not be at Tollerton.

The Signal reads: 'Hon. Norman Willmore, M.L.A. for Edson constituency, made a special visit to Edson in order to meet with representative citizens and inform them that the officials of the pulp mill project would be moved from Tollerton to a site near Hinton. The reason for going west, according to the company was the more favorable water situation in the Athabasca River and the soil conditions in the proposed new location to carry the type of building the mill would require.

The company asked for, and tentatively received timber reserves north of the Athabasca in the Little Burland area. This area was not included in the original agreement, and "whether the timber in that area was any reason for the change in plans is a moot question."

This bombshell was not very well received by those who attended the meeting.

"It still remains something of a mystery why, after the McLeod River water supply had been fully investigated; an engineer had surveyed the river for a dam site; land had been purchased and partly cleared; a superintendent of construction whose business it was to supervise the construction of such projects as pulp mills had arrived in Edson for a two-year stay; the grade for the spur line had been built; the provincial government had built a road later in the season than is usual for road work, it should be discovered that the site and water supply were not suitable."

The Edson Board of Trade immediately directed a telegram of inquiry. A long involved reply was received from Mr. Willmore, and after the technical question of the issue was explained he added:

'I feel it may be proper for me at this time to point out that with the exception of three or four major lumber companies and a handful of smaller independent operators the history of lumber operations in the Edson area in the last 25 years, of which I have some knowledge, has not been a happy one. It has been too often a history of failures and bankruptcies resulting in unpaid accounts at stores and garages and other business places and in some cases the loss of wages to the lumber worker. At best many small operators and sub-contractors were operating on

short seasonal basis with too little security or stability in their operations.'
Edson. Foiled again!

* * *

The bustling camp of Mercoal lost three buildings in one night when the Mercoal Hotel, a private residence and the pool room went up in smoke in early April, 1955. The hotel was owned by J. Askew and A. Lyseck, Mr. John Van Least owned the pool room and the residence owned by the mine company had been occupied by William Kolbe and family.

* * *

In October of 1955 work started on the pulp mill townsite at Bliss, cheek by jowl with Hinton. Anker Construction was making satisfactory progress on the 41 mile road from Hinton to Mercoal. This road would be used for hauling wood from the Coal Branch area.

By the end of October 600 persons were employed in the construction of the new mill.

"Operational cruising in preparation for next year's timber cutting is now under way on the 3,000 square miles of timberland on which the company has a long-term timber grant from Alberta. In addition, 3,000 square miles of timberland have been granted to the company as a reserve. These 6,000 square miles of timberland are sufficient to support a pulp mill with an ultimate capacity of 350,000 tons annually."

Mercoal now called itself the Capital of the Coal Branch, a claim that was not disputed. Townfolk gathered at the Forester's Hall to help Mr. and Mrs. Walter Mazur celebrate their 25th wedding anniversary. Dr. I. G. Waugh proposed the toast to the couple.

Over 40 youngsters at Mercoal took part in a boxing event November 11th with Neil Madsen, RCMP and Jack Hogg judging while Malcolm McGregor was timekeeper. Sponsored by Walter Austin and Robert Todd the card featured such personalities as Fly Wheat; Baby Face Jarvie, Pee Wee Relling, Bull Dog Waugh, Flash Teasdale, Bruiser Timchak. Combined weight of the named sluggers was 332 pounds.

Chopper Spanach, Slasher Kapalka, Mauler Liske and Gentleman Boles were of a much heavier weight, each well over the 100 lb. mark.

* * *

In November too, Jasper Elks Lodge travelled by charter bus to Mercoal to deliver the travelling gavel. Enroute Brothers watched the presentation of a Past Exalted Ruler's Jewel.

The presentation made to Past Exalted Ruler Bro. Ingle was unique in that it was presented on the travelling bus. The presentation was made by D. D. G. E. R. Bro. Wachter.

* * *

1956

In January a fire which started in the presses of the briquetting plant owned by Luscar Coals Ltd. caused $250,000 damage and closed down the plant.

The briquetting plant run in conjunction with the stripping operations was two miles from the town site. All available manpower was called out in an effort to extinguish the blaze with sub-zero temperatures hampering the efforts. Six men employed at the plant became temporarily unemployed while the loss of the plant slowed down operations of the stripping site.

Residents speculated while officials did not state whether the plant would be rebuilt.

In March the Hin-Del Corporation was incorporated with a capitalization of 500,000 shares without par value issued at a maximum price of $500,000. This company following an agreement with the Alberta Provincial Government would develop the new town-site of Hinton. Business and residential sites were offered to the public.

In July, Mr. and Mrs. Mike Romaniuk of Foothills were the lucky ticket holders of a beautiful summer cottage raffled by the Edson Kinsmen club. The cottage would be taken to a site on Lake Wabamun.

Oil Discoveries north of Edson this summer would become an important factor to the economy of the town. This would offset the dwindling railway revenues.

The summer of 1956 was hot and dry with severe electrical storms rippling over the Coal Branch area. Lightning strikes started a raging forest fire. The fire increased in intensity until it became a very real threat to the town of Mercoal.

Provincial Civil Defence authorities, and Commissioner Pringle, RCMP advised the CNR of the necessity of having a relief train at Mercoal. This train consisting of two engines, a coach, three cabooses and twenty freight cars left Edson at 2:00 a.m. July 22nd.

Mayor W. H. Kankewitt called an emergent meeting of the Edson Town Council and in conjunction with the Civil Defense laid plans in case it became necessary to evacuate the people of Mercoal, with a population of over one thousand. The town was canvassed by eighteen Edson girls and by 11:00 p.m. the town was ready to accommodate the evacuees.

All available manpower in Mercoal, men from the North West Pulp and Power Co. of Hinton, men from Luscar, a special detachment of RCMP from Edmonton and forestry men from throughout a large area fought the fire. A group of men eighteen miles from Mercoal had been cut off at four different intervals by the roaring blaze. Another group of men told of having to wade across the McLeod River to escape the flames. The lookout at Luscar Tower reported 14

Luscar Lookout Tower just after the road was bull-dozed up to the Tower. Previously it was only accessible by a foot path. — Shipka

new fires breaking out in new locations of the Yellowhead Trail, Mercoal Creek and McLeod River.

Late Sunday night with the fire creeping to within three miles of the Mercoal townsite, the wind changed. Monday, residents of Mercoal, although still keeping a wary eye at the black smoking clouds, began to feel a tentative relaxation. By Tuesday tension eased as the fire, forced back by the use of five tank cars and bulldozers was gradually brought under control. Tuesday night, the standby relief train was ordered back to Edson, and Wednesday it began to rain. A good soaking rain continued through Thursday and the emergency was over. Thousands of acres had burned.

Letters of thanks arrived from various Mercoal organizations. Another arrived from Canadian Collieries (Dunsmuir) Ltd.

General Manager's Department, Cumberland, B.C.

Dear Mr. Mayor:

I visited Mercoal last week and reviewed with Bob Erikson, the mine manager, the dangerous situation which arose there resulting from the recent forest fire. I also have Mr. Beland's, the fire Commissioner's, report and details of his protection plan for the Mercoal townsite and our mine plant.

Both Bob Erikson, in his remarks to me and Mr. Beland, in his report, emphasize the feeling of confidence and reassurance which replaced the atmosphere of uncertainty as soon as they knew that your town had accepted the responsibility of becoming a reception area for evacuees from Mercoal.

I am therefore writing to express my own personal thanks, the thanks of my Company, and the gratitude which the people of Mercoal feel towards yourself, the Town Council and the citizens of Edson for so readily preparing themselves to receive evacuees from Mercoal, should the necessity have arisen. I feel quite confident too that had evacuation from Mercoal become necessary your citizens would have received the unfortunate victims of the forest fire with unbounded hospitality and kindness. I would be very grateful if you could somehow convey to all those who worked during the crisis and who expressed willingness to give accommodation, should it have become necessary, our grateful thanks and appreciation.

> Yours very truly
> E.O.T. Simpson,
> Vice-President, Mining.

At Hinton, school attendance had jumped from 235 to 750 in one year. School construction lagged behind and pulp mill officials offered to divide a portion of a new warehouse into classrooms until construction was completed.

The Hon. Gordon Taylor and Hon. Norman Willmore attended the official opening ceremony of the completion of hard surfacing of Highway 16 to Jasper Park on Friday, October 19th, at Jasper.

* * *

Luscar Closes

In October, 1956, officials of Luscar Coals Ltd. announced that disappearing markets had forced them to order the strip mines closed. Notices were posted and the three hundred odd remaining townspeople prepared to leave the settlement by November 30th. About 75 employees remained on the payroll.

Officials of Luscar Coals said they must shut down the mine because they had lost the contract to supply slack coal to the British Columbia Electric Co. for processing into manufactured domestic gas at Vancouver. Vancouver would be getting natural gas and wouldn't need the artificial variety any more – another chapter in the same story of coal losing out to other fuels.

The B.C. Electric contract called for 70,000 tons of coal per year, and without that market there was no reason to keep the mine open.

John Ferguson, employment liaison officer for the province headed a special committee appointed to rehabilitate miners thrown out of work by the closing of coal mines. Mr. Ferguson visited Luscar October 30 to interview miners and determine whether all had made arrangements for other employment. In extreme cases, the committee would provide the money to move families and effects.

The closing of the Luscar mine left only two mines operating on the Branch – Foothills and Mercoal. Vic Riendeau in a taped interview said "In 1944 there were 14 different mines operating on the Coal Branch."

Luscar became another 'ghost town' following the fate of Mountain Park in 1950, Cadomin in 1952, Coal Valley, Sterco and Robb in 1954 and 1955.

Foothills closed in February 1958 and then finally Mercoal in 1959.

* * *

For almost a decade it was a common sight to see houses and parts of houses coming down to Edson from the Coal Branch Road. Some had been dismantled twice, as in the case of Charlie Lee's home. When Mountain Park closed in 1950, Charlie left to work in Mercoal. His wife, Jane, daughters Mary and Sandy spent the summer tearing their home apart, board by board, piece by piece. This was rebuilt at Mercoal. When the mine closed at Mercoal, the house was split in two and brought down to Edson by truck. Too wide for the bridge, the McLeod River in the fall of 1959 was at an accommodating low level, perhaps in expiation for ravages wrought in the past. Truck and house forded the river. To-day the house now proudly stuccoed, is occupied by Sandy Lee Senyk, her husband and two children, in Glenwood, a suburb of Edson. Other houses are scattered throughout Alberta, newer owners not even aware of their past.

Mountain Park a decade after the mine closed.

Mountain Park during the winter. Mrs. Jane Lee, 10304-115 St. Edmonton says of her late husband, "Charlie wasn't too much for hunting with a gun. He always preferred to go hunting with his camera."   — Charlie Lee photo

Mountain Park — Charlie Lee photo

Sandy Senyk of Edson says, "Dad (Charlie Lee), Allan Godby and a lot of others climbed Mt. Cheviot in the twenties. They put their names in a tin can, and then built a cairn around it. Whether the cairn is still there or has since fallen apart, I don't know."

181 — Charlie Lee photo

Ruby Lake — near Mountain Park. For many years the whereabouts of this lake was a jealously guarded secret by the ardent fishermen who knew its location.

— Charlie Lee photo

PART II

Allan E. Godby

ALLEN E. GODBY - by himself. Born April 2nd, 1889, Frogmore, Ontario, Township of Houghton, County of Norfolk, near shores of Lake Erie.

I don't know know why I was born in Ontario - but I think it was so I could be with my mother. I do know I was born very young, unemployed at the time, lived on nothing but milk for weeks and it took a little pull to get even that.

I had very few playmates, especially of the opposite sex. In fact my mother never told me which was the opposite sex. I was about eight years old when I first went to school. It was there I got acquainted with girls, and darned if I didn't kind of like them when I found out they weren't boys.

When I grew up and might have cared for a girl, you had no idea what you were caressing. All wore those long dresses down to their instep. (It's different today, they wear them up to their step-ins). Then, it was real naughty for a woman to show her ankle.

I just never could get excited over a female in those days. How could you. They wore those corsets - what a contraption they were; steel stays about a half inch wide and six or eight inches long. Why putting your arms around a female's waist was just like loving up a roll of baling wire. We used to take the steel stays out of old ones - corsets that is, take them to school; chew up wads of paper, bend them

183

back with wad on the end and let them go shooting across the school room.

Looking back, some of those old timers were very clever in many ways. Many had a large pile of wood cut up ready for the cook stove right next to the outside plumbing which were mostly quite a distance from the house. Women were very modest in those days. They would not let strangers see them go in one of these outhouses, so if someone came in sight while they were going out to one they'd just pick up an armful of wood and come back. Just a few interruptions and the woodbox was full of wood.

Allan Godby plays while his dog howls on porch at Mountain Park.
— Mrs. Charlie Lee

I can still see those old outhouses plain as ever. Most were one holers, a fair sized hole. Small people had to use a little judgement backing in, or you'd end up with your shins in front of your face hanging on by your elbows. Some of the better off people had fancy affairs known as the old 'eight family three holer'. Much safer as the three holes were of different sizes, you could pick one to fit you.

But yet what stands out in my mind most of all is good old Timothy Eaton's catalogue hanging up on a nail inside. I must say they served their purpose very well indeed because with the average family you'd be just about into the harness section by the time the new issue came out. But do you know, I've never quite forgiven Eatons for putting the harness section on glossy paper.

I came to Edmonton in September, 1912, and stayed at the old Edmonton Hotel in the flats by the Low Level Bridge. The High Level Bridge was half way across. It was very cold, 50 below sometimes.

I wasn't off the train one hour in Edmonton when a fellow wanted to sell me lots in Moose Jaw. When I was leaving Moose Jaw a fellow wanted to sell me lots in Edmonton. In Edmonton they were selling lots in Edson and according to them it was going to be a real city in time. One fellow had bought some lots in Edson, got off the train when I did, looked up his lots and they were covered by a fair sized pond. It is part of the town today, so he may have done alright at that.

A friend of mine from Ontario whom I had known was in the fire department and got me the job at Lovett on the Coal Branch. My pay started the day I got on the train and my fare was paid. If I remember rightly the mine was called Pacific Pass Collieries, but changed to Fergie, and finally ended up called Lovett. There was a mine at Coalspur called the Yellowhead, but no Foothills, Sterco, Coal Valley then.

I remember when a miner from Lovett went to what is now Cadomin and started prospecting there for coal right along the track. I remember John Gregg camped in Cadomin Flats when he prospected for Luscar (but that was later when I was in Mountain Park).

When I went to Lovett in February, 1913, Peter Christensen was the manager and met me at the train. I had sat for Alberta papers for Steam Engineer, so he said, "Are you the steam engineer?"

I said I was, so he took me up to a large log building with bunks made out of poles and said, "You sleep here. Go to the store and order any bedding you want." I did, had supper and went over to the pool hall and sat down not saying a word to anyone.

A fellow staggered up to me and said, "I'm Mickey Joyce; I'm the fire boss here."

I had never been in a mine before, I thought that a Fire Boss was someone who fired you or laid you off. He said "I know your kind, you are just one of those smart provincial engineers and you do think you are smart don't you."

"I just got here tonight on the train. I haven't even worked yet. I'm not bothering you at all so leave me alone." I got up, walked away

A washout at Sterco. The road to the dump.

185

from him and sat down again. He followed me and said the same thing.

"Look mister, I'm moving once more and don't you bother me again."

A fellow tried to talk to him but he wouldn't listen. He came to me, stepped on my feet and started all over again – so I hit him.

He fell against the pool table, his peanuts fell on the floor. He picked them up and walked out. 'Dutchy' who ran the pool hall came over and said, "He's a very nice fellow when he is sober. I don't know what he has against you."

"Neither do I, I just came in on the train tonight. What is a fire boss? Can he fire me?"

He laughed and said "They work in the mine and fire the powder that blasts the coal loose. He has nothing to do with you. Your boss is the master mechanic, Harry Pallet."

Next day I went to work hoisting coal in the little hoist room and got along fine. That night when I was going home, Mickey Joyce came up to me, apologized and said I should have hit him harder.

The mine worked only a day or two a week in summer. The railroad said the coal made too many sparks and set the forest on fire. Anyway they didn't take coal in summer. But nobody, or I should say very few would leave the place. They would fish, shoot a little game and seemed to get along fine. The stream now known as Lovett Creek we called the 'Little Pembina' as it ran into the Pembina about five miles down the trail. Fairflax Lake we called 'La Hore Lake' as Jimmy LaHore drowned there.

Peter Christiansen the Mine Manager thought so much of his men that when the company wanted to cut wages Peter wouldn't have it.

"No I won't cut my men's wages." he said. "A man worth $4.00 a day in Edmonton is worth $5.00 up here."

So he quit and Andrew Miller became manager. Andrew was a good Manager and a fine person.

In 1913 going up to Lovett on the train the rabbits were running ahead of the train, beside it and everywhere. I never saw so many rabbits in my life. I think it was 1915 they died off. In the spring there was dead rabbits everywhere, and they never became so thick or numerous again.

The fishing was good, catch a feed of fish anytime but so many fishing they kept getting harder to get as the years went by.

Before Peter left I worked in the power house near the track. It was my job to blow the whistle. I asked one of the railroad engineers for the correct time, and then blew the whistle. Peter came and said "What did you blow the whistle two minutes fast?" I told him I had got the correct time from the railroad engineer. Peter said "Never mind about railroad time. I got a $100. watch and I'll keep the time here."

186

Mountain Park's new power house built in 1930.

Sometimes he'd come around, stick his head in the power house and say, "I guess this is about the best place you ever worked eh?" As it was, I said "It sure is Mr. Christiansen." He'd say, "I tought so, I tought so." Never say thought.

He had a daughter Phebee so he named one little creek after her and other one Peter Creek. He'd say, "Dat's Phebee Creek, my daughter, and Peter Creek, dat's me." He was one of the finest men I ever worked for.

A Romanian woman had a child and he delivered it and left her in bed. The next morning he came to see how she was feeling and she was up working as hard as ever. Peter couldn't talk her into going back to bed.

During the First World War in 1914, all who had guns had to have them registered. Two of the fellows went hunting, and while walking in single file, the unregistered gun went off just missing the leg of the fellow ahead. He jumped and said "You almost shot me." The other replied, "Well that wouldn't be right would it? I have no license you know." And they walked on the same as ever.

The coldest weather I experienced was in Lovett. Just one day. It went down to 70 degrees or nearly so. Our thermometer went to 68 degrees below and it was down below that a little. I had to walk to work about 200 yards and I froze my nose. I felt it tingle a little but had no idea it would freeze that fast. When I got in the Hoist House I soon found out as it pained me a lot, and freezes easily to this day. It was calm out and I could hear people talk a quarter mile away quite easily.

As they couldn't move the empty box cars under the tipple to load the coal, they called it off and we all went home. We had coal heaters

187

and coal cook stoves. The houses were built fairly warm, we'd had no trouble keeping warm before, but this one day we sat very close to the heaters.

In 1916 I remember hearing about the railroad being washed out as it rained steadily for six weeks. They drove cattle up the track to Mountain Park for food.

I was hoisting coal. The rope from the hoist went up through the top of the hoist house to the tipple, so when pulling a load of coal it had a tendancy to want to lift the hoist. Even though there were tons of gravel and bags of cement they put this hoist on timbers. All the time the hoist was pulling up the loads of coal the building shivered and shook up and down a little. After a few months of that it affected my legs and they ached sometimes until I couldn't sleep. The doctor said I'd have to give it up. I told the boss and he gave me a job in the Power House which was fine. All I had to do is sit around as long as everything was going okay. It wasn't long until the hoist went out of kilter and they couldn't get the coal out. They asked me to go back, fix up the hoist and just stay there until they could get someone to run it. This happened so many times that I knew I'd have to leave the place to get off that hoist. So on a Sunday in February, 1917 I took the train to Mountain Park and got a job in the Power House there at more money.

When I saw the mountains in Mountain Park I felt it was the grandest place I'd ever been in. For years there was no road between Cadomin and Mountain Park. Seems to me it was the hungry thirties that they had men working for board and a few cents extra building a road. They used shovels and wheelbarrows, and had a camp just past the Whitehorse Canyon about a mile.

Water wagon at Mountain Park.

188

Pack train ready for a few days ride in the mountains.

(Godby)

The power house, Mountain Park, A. Godby at table.

Many had horses in those days; I did myself and spent many a day out in the mountains. You'd wake up in the a.m. and moose, elk and deer would be mingling with your horses. I loved every minute of it.

One time coming from Edmonton in 1922 we would get as far as Cadomin on a passenger train from Edson then take the coal train up to Mountain Park. We rode in the caboose. We got as far as the Whitehorse Canyon and got stuck in the snow. An engine came up from Cadomin to help out and it got off the track. We were there nearly two days and eating with the crew. We got down to pancakes and were nearly out of them. The grade was fairly steep. The engine would bring up only about ten empty box cars. Frank Liverio ran the engine in Mountain Park which the company rented from the railroad, to move the boxcars in the yard after they were loaded, but the

Mountain Park school in the twenties.

engine was not allowed out of the Mountain Park yard. One night he stole the engine, took a box car and a crowd of men, women and girls to Cadomin to a dance. I'm sure Ray Jones the station agent knew about it as he was conveniently away from the station at the time. Years later Frank Liverio told me, "You know Godby, I sweat now when I think about it. I could have got ten years in prison for stealing a railroad engine and taking it on their line." I rode down on that engine that time. I sat up on the running board in front of the cab just ahead of Frank. The car full of people went off the track but they had devices that you put on the rail. The wheel will run up on it and onto the track.

Frank Liverio was Italian and what a guy he was. He had large black eyes and could look real mean. He'd go in the store and start bawling out one of the girl clerks, or maybe a waitress in the restaurant – pound the table with his fist. The look on strangers faces was something to see. The girls would just smile and pay no attention. The fun was watching the faces of the strangers.

When the trainmen were bringing the cars in the yard, there was always a trainman on top. Frank's job was to let the cars down to the tipple to be filled with coal. When they were shoving the cars up in the yard, Frank would be on the ground walking beside the cars, and Frank would be shouting abuse and bawling the trainman out. The trainman on top would be waving his brake stick at Frank down below telling him what he'd do to him, calling Frank a damned Dago, etc. It was a real show and worth seeing. Once or twice the trainman

190

did it out of place and got told off by an official. Frank just smiled and said it was all in fun.

I cannot recall the name of the fellow who got thinking too much of this married woman. She treated him like anyone else and kept him in his place. He broke into the railroad station and stole a rifle. While trying it out it went off and put a hole in the floor. He walked down the railroad track a ways and came up the creek to this woman's house. She was in the kitchen. He shot her, she got to the bed and died. He walked out, went up on the hill, sat on stump, put the barrel of the rifle in his mouth and pulled the trigger and blew the top of his head off. A couple of people walking by saw his cap go off his head and up in the air.

We used to use wood alcohol in the airlines to keep them from freezing. Three boys batching together, thought by boiling this wood alcohol it would take the poison out of it. So when they were not at work one morning someone went up to see why, and here were two of them dead, the other nearly so. He managed to pull through with the doctor's care.

I played guitar, banjo, ukelele; Tommy Robertson played a accordian, Fred Steffie played piano and mandolin.

Hundreds of times we would be asked to play at parties. At that time they would have a keg of beer up on a chair and many times I've had glasses lined up at my feet on the floor. It was for me to drink, I never did drink much of anything but the beer was put there just the same. People would be dancing and kick them over and the floor covered with beer. It was quite a time. I never liked people bending over me and trying to give me a drink while playing. They would spill it on my clothes and instruments. Many times I'd have to go to work at midnight and I went. In the years from 1917 to 1950 I never went to work drunk or ever missed a days work.

Sometimes when they would bother me too much to drink, I'd just start for home. They would call me back and leave me alone after that. On a paynight nearly every other house in town would have a keg of beer. Little Tommy Robertson the accordian player, liked his giggle juice and many times he could hardly stand up but it never seemed to effect his playing, and could that little fellow play.

I got tired of being called out to play every Saturday night and many times two or three times a week. I got married in April 1924 and played in the dance orchestra on holidays and Saturday night. We had a good orchestra and I lived a more normal life after that.

Water was delivered to the houses by a large tank drawn by horses. We sat on that tank played a tune at every house where the driver filled the barrels with pails of water. The women would laugh, clap their hands and being around breakfast time would want to give us a sandwich, pie etc. Oh, not all, some of the old sassor bills would give us a real talking to, but very few.

191

A Welshman, Tommy Griffiths would drink ten glasses of beer as fast as the bartender could set them on the table. He would just open his mouth and pour it in, didn't seem to have to swallow.

Yet I'll never forget the joy there was when the road was finished to Cadomin and we got cars. Oh, we'd get stuck in the spring or in real wet weather, but there were lots of rocks and gravel everywhere and with a shovel and jack to raise the car, fill the hole with rock or gravel, and perhaps with the help of others we'd get out okay. Then when we could drive as far as Coalspur or even Mercoal that was really something. Some spent every minute they could out in their cars.

During the war all we had was one permit a month for $5.00 worth of booze. Hundreds of women who never had a permit or ever bought booze had one. I can remember when Dyllis worked in the store, I've seen miners offer to take her down to the vendors in Cadomin, pay her days wages and give her extra money if she'd use her permit and get liquor for them. She'd just smile and say 'I never got a permit. I didn't want one.'

One fellow had an old model Ford with those large wheels. He must have had six children. The glass was broken in the windows and they'd all pile in with kids and a dog with their heads out the window. He had so many flat tires that if it wasn't too far, he'd come home on the rim. If he had only one flat in a trip, he had a good day.

The electrician had an Essex. One day he took me for a ride and we got about a mile from home and the car stopped. He said, "We're out of gas." I'll go get some I offered. He said, "Oh, that won't be necessary. I'll just get a pail of water and put it in the gas tank."

"What?"

He said "It's okay." He did just that and away we went.

"Well that has me beat."

He just smiled and said, "I'll tell you. The intake pipe is broken off and only reaches about halfway to the bottom of the tank, so when I put water in, gas stays on top of water and raises it up to the gas pipe. I've intended to repair it but so far haven't."

We used coal in our stoves and of course had coal to bring in and ashes to take out. It was impossible to wear a white shirt a day without the neckline being dirty. Coal dust was in the air. Even with storm windows on, and storm doors all closed you'd go away for a couple of weeks and when you came back it was all dusty inside. Yet no one seemed to mind it too much.

Being over a mile above sea level water boiled at about 199°, instead of 212° as at sea level. So it took eggs at least five minutes for soft boiled . . . would have to cook beans many hours longer. Women had to learn all over again. Also you had to have plenty of wood for the cookstove as they just could not get the coal burning. It was coking coal and would just sort of melt and cover the fire all over like tar. It had to be poked and broken up. Lignite coal like at Mercoal, Coal Valley and those places was no trouble at all, as it burned like wood. I could be mistaken in some details but don't think I'm too far off.

Coal was very cheap, but even so many bought electric stoves as the charge for electricity was very cheap. So many bought electric stoves and heaters the load on the engine at night was too much. So then the company put in meters. However it got so bad that the women at the far end of town couldn't use their washing machines. The electrician went out looking for the trouble and found it. One of the officials had eight electric heaters in his henhouse keeping his chickens warm.

Soren Madsen ran the picture show in the hall and there were always raffles and the draw was made at the picture show.

The strike came off on April 1, 1922. We were off work for six months. My pay cut was from $7.40 to $6.10. In 1924, the second strike came lasting nine months. My pay was cut from $6.10 to $4.90. In the first strike we got food sent up by our Union U.M.W.A. In 1924 we got money every week. I cannot recall how much it was now. I was doing okay, I guess because I got married and we spent our honeymoon on horses out in the mountains, camping, hiking etc. We always had plenty of food. It was all a new experience for the wife and she made the best of it. I'll always remember Tex Byers. When the women would start cooking a meal, he'd start picking up bits of food and eating, and so help me when the meal was ready, he'd had plenty and would sit down and drink a cup of tea but seldom eat. I've seen this happen many times.

No one was more of a green horn than I was when I came to Mountain Park. But I had the best folding Kodak I could buy. It was folding postcard size #122 film and cost me $105. in 1922. So as it was my

Left to Right: Mary Voytecheck, Marjorie Jones, Elsie Godby, Mrs. Fay Falkener.

A. Godby, Ray Jones with goatskins — 1926.

L. to R.: Mrs. Horace Haddock, Mrs. Wagner, Miss Foster, Mrs. Pascoe, Mrs. Jones, Thelma Berry, Mrs. Martin.
2nd Row: Mrs. Osland, Mrs. Ben Haddock, Mrs. Melling, Mable Hobbins, Barns, Jean McLeod, Miss Farley.

hobby and I was fairly good at it I was asked out on hunting trips to take pictures.

Can remember one trip. Dr. Hill's wife and daughter Ethel and friends were camped nearby. I was out with Cam Matthews. We were

194

out on the Ruby. Cam shot at the sheep, missed it, but hit a large rock ahead of the sheep. It turned and came back running right towards Ethel. Cam shot it and it dropped not two feet from Ethel. I can still see Ethel with her hands in her pockets taking it all on so unconcerned like. It was the first Big Horn I'd ever seen and it looked to me as if it had a rocking chair on its head.

Trappers used to set snares by bending a tree over so when the animal took the bait it would snare them and lift them off the ground. One time we were out hunting and Billy Scott, an Englishman got in one of these snares. It had him hanging by the leg upside down. All the yelling just like he was being murdered. It never hurt him but did we ever laugh. I still laugh when I think of it. His head and shoulders were on the ground. He could have reached up and taken it off himself. He was really frightened.

Albert Wright was from Lancashire, England, and came to the mines in Mountain Park. He soon adapted to the way of life over here and liked it. His father owned a store over there, and when his father died they asked him to go back as it was left to him. Oh he said over there the store is their pantry. They just buy what they need for each meal. So when he got back his friends asked him if living was as good in Canada as in England. He said, "Look, when we buy tea we buy at least half a pound, a pound of butter, five pounds of jam, 50 or 100 pounds of flour, 5 to 100 pounds of sugar and other things accordingly." Well he said, the way they looked at one another and winked, and said he was as bad as the Yankees. They just would not believe him. Nellie, 8, and Charles, 7, had been free to run in Mountain Park for miles. Over in England they were miserable. "I couldn't see them so miserable so we came back." Nellie and her husband Eddie Harrison now live in Cadomin. It is worth while listening to Nellie when she tells how she hated it over there, and she says, "never, never, will there ever be a happier moment in my life than when Father said he was coming back to Canada."

Then I went to Coal Valley to work. Coal Valley had the best board for the least money of any place I boarded. The company ran the boarding house and I'm certain they lost money as we paid very little for such grand meals. Many times I saw one fellow 'Carl' take large T-bone steaks to feed his dog. On a Sunday many would come from Foothills for dinner and pay 75¢. There was no underground mining, it was done with steam shovels. Men were busy and did a fair amount of work but never did I see men eat as little as they did there. Cook would come in and say, "Somebody eat this steak. Finish this pie, I don't want to have to put it in the fridge again." Many of the older men who had been there for years had jobs with not too much labor would eat only a bowl of soup for dinner, but a bowl of that cook's soup was a meal in itself.

There were many French Canadians there and I liked them very much, and enjoyed their hospitality many times.

195

Everyone at the Coal Valley mine could have up to $16.00 a month taken off his pay and the company would put in the same amount. I had $4.00 a month off and in nearly five years I was there had close to $800.00. Many had $2,000. or more. What a difference between Coal Valley, Mountain Park, Luscar and the other places. In Mountain Park it was pitiful to see women there while their husbands looked for work elsewhere when the mine closed. They just couldn't seem to believe it — were sort of dumbfounded. At Coal Valley of course many hated to leave, but there was such a different atmosphere as the majority had money.

When Coal Valley closed down I went to Luscar. It was known that Luscar would close down in the near future so engineers wouldn't come up. Louis Voytechek and I worked 12 hours a day, seven days a week for months. It was time and a half for overtime. All I did was work, sleep and eat. I got up to 200 pounds but never again. I could hardly tie my shoes. How so many can stand it, I'll never know as it was the most miserable time of my life. For over one month I took nothing but orange, grapefruit or vegetable juices and in six weeks got back down to 145 pounds.

The underground was closed at Luscar and it was strip-mining with steam shovels. Many of the older single miners just stayed in the hotel and spent most of their time in beer parlors as long as their pension money lasted. A few were very thirsty before the end of the month and borrowed money till their next pension cheque.

After working hard in the mines most of their lives, then suddenly doing nothing but sitting around and drinking, many died within a few years.

Now I belong to the Senior Citizens Orchestra of the Lion's Club, 111th Ave. 113 St. in Edmonton. We have to be 60 and over to join it. And somewhat like the days I just mentioned, we are asked out to play at nursing homes, hospitals, clubs etc. In Klondike Days we play in the streets at the Town Hall on the steps, Macdonald Hotel etc. We make no charge and are kept quite busy. At places in which we play we are treated much like the old days in Mountain Park.

Allan E. Godby, 12028–95 Street, Edmonton

. . . The Whole Camp Shared in the Booty

PETER ROMANIUK remembers the steep hill at Foothills very well. Not only because he plodded up and down it for many years to go to work, but because he still carries part of the hill wherever he goes. Literally. The cinders of the hill still embedded in his face and left hand came about through an accident. He smiled wryly, "Not a mine accident."

196

One afternoon in Foothills one of his granddaughters came to visit. She left soon after with friends, leaving her English style bicycle. Pete decided to return the bike. After all, what was there to riding a bike even at the age of 57. So he clambered on and took off down the hill. Swiftly gaining momentum he tried to brake with his feet. No brakes! Faster and faster he careened down the hill, frantically trying to footbrake, when the bike threw him. He slid, face, hands, throat, knees scraping through cinders, and landed semiconscious in the ditch.

Foothills mining crew.   (P. Romaniuk)

Walter Hammet found Pete lying in the ditch and notifying the doctor, Pete was rushed to hospital in Mercoal. An awful looking face, shuddered the hospital staff. They cleaned him up and sent him to hospital in Edmonton where the doctor did his best. Mr. Romaniuk was told to return for more surgery but somehow didn't get around to going back. He still retains dark marks on his little finger and a dark area on his face.

Mr. Romaniuk was born in Bergthat, Manitoba, July 17, 1896. He met and married Magdalena Wisniewicz in 1916 and the couple worked at farming in the Chipman area. Tom Parfeniuk, a brother-in-law was employed at Foothills so Peter decided to join him. He started with Foothills Collieries as a timber packer, got a miner's certificate in 1927 and started digging coal.

Two months later his wife and children Annie, John, Mike and Mary joined him.

The family lived in a two bedroom company house and paid $4. a month rent. They obtained water from a nearby spring in the summer, and in winter periodically put dynamite in a well to blow the ice and start the water running again. After a few years the company built a water reservoir and water ceased to be a problem.

Soon after moving to Foothills four-year-old Mary became ill. Dr. Macdonald, the regular company doctor was away on holidays and an older substitute doctor gave the child castor oil. A fire-boss, Jack Mitchell, saw the worried parents and advised brusquely "Take your daughter to Edson. That's the way I lost my son."

The train was due to leave so the Romaniuks bundled the child warmly and hours later came to Edson. "It would take a whole day to get from Foothills to Edson because they loaded freight all down the line; at Foothills Mile 50; Coal Valley, Mile 48; Sterco, Mile 47."

The child was operated on by Dr. Tiffin who removed a ruptured appendix and Mary was hospitalized for six weeks.

Elsie was born in 1927 at Reco with Dr. Macdonald in attendance. Then the family moved into a larger four bedroom log home and paid $12. a month rent. Eddie was born in 1930, then Peter was born; a premature daughter who died; then Rosie attended by Mrs. Walter Hammett and finally Deanna.

During the early thirties work was slack. Peter supplemented his salary by hunting and fishing. He along with many other miners were laid off. Many families were put on relief and allowed $17.50 a month credit at the store for groceries. Pete went to work on the relief camps set up to build the road to Mountain Park.

"I think it was 1932. We lived in tents and I'd hop the freight weekends to see my family. The men on the road camps didn't work very hard. When they caught sight of the boss, Cory Simmonds, they'd work like hell, but as soon as he was out of sight they'd slack off. I remember I went to the bank at Cadomin to get my cheque cashed. They asked if anyone there knew me. I said I had a friend living there who knew me. The people at the bank said to get his signature on the cheque. My friend's bank account was in his wife's name and she was afraid to sign the cheque. She went with me to the bank and they told her it was okay. The next cheque I went to the store and cashed it."

"By the time deductions were taken off, my smallest cheque for two weeks was $3.62."

Pete decided he'd be better off at home hunting and fishing than working in the relief camp. So he quit and left for Foothills.

Pete explained that feelings were touchy during the early days of the depression. Men used to making their own way were out of work and unable to provide for their families. The mine officials on the other hand were sometimes accused of playing favorites and employing favored men.

" I went home and decided to go hunting. I went hunting and walked around the camp the long way."

Bill Duggan, one of the mine officials either saw Pete heading his way with a gun or was misinformed as to intent. At any rate the police were called.

"The Sterco agent doubled as a magistrate. I was taken to Sterco by the police and the doctor was called to examine me." Pete says he overheard a conversation that was similar to the following:
Doctor: "What are they trying to stick him with?"
Magistrate: "He allegedly threatened to shoot Duggan."
Pete, unable to contain himself shouted "What?"

"They offered to let me go if I went away to work on a farm. I refused and said I was going home. They took me to Edson and put me in a cell in the jail. My charge was for not working in the relief camp and supporting my family."

The following day the charge was dropped but Pete was in Edson. "I didn't have a dime on me. Sam Romano, a friend of mine there, said I could sleep at his house but they had a small house and kids, so I went to Stella's (a boarding house in Edson) and watched an all night poker game. The next day I got on the Coal Branch train. When the conductor asked me for my fare, I said, "See that mountie sitting over there. He brought me here. You ask him for my fare.""

Pete wasn't troubled again for the fare. He got to Coalspur "and it happened a speeder came along to get me from Coalspur to Coal Valley." Soon after Pete was called back to work in the mine.

"After we joined the U.M.W.A. we got a raise in wages and things began to get better and better. In the early days Cadomin, Foothills, Mercoal and Robb belonged to a Canadian Union, but Sterco and Coal Valley had a different union."

As his sons grew older, the boys accompanied the father on hunting and fishing trips. On one trip, Mike and his father ran into a bear with three cubs. Shells were rationed at the time. The three cubs ran up a tree and Pete says, "That bear came right after me. She stood on her hind legs and stared at me. Mike said, "Don't shoot." After awhile the bear got down on all fours and went away. I looked at Mike and he was white. I hardly slept that night and I dreamed of that bear for two or three months."

Pete said that when an animal was shot the whole camp often shared in the booty. The meat was often put in pails in the stream to keep cold.

He remembers when one fishing trip netted 640 rainbow trout. The boys and their father fished from noon to 11:00 p.m. "We took home what we could carry and buried the rest under the moss." By the time they got back for it the next evening the fish were rank. "We never did that again. We only caught what we could pack."

Mrs. Romaniuk canned fish and sometimes the family dried it for later use.

Mr. Romaniuk recalls the time he caught three bulltrout in one day, fish that had been eluding the best fishermen. "The first one cut my line on the bank, so I snared the other two." he said with complete aplomb.

Altogether Mr. Romaniuk spent four sessions in the hospital. Twice for hernia operations and once when carrying a plank, a large chunk of coal knocked him down resulting in two bones protruding from his arm. He spent 9 months in the University Hospital and two months at the Rehab Centre. This accident has resulted in compensation of $20. a month. Despite the impairment Mr. Romaniuk worked at Foothills till the mine closed in 1958. Many of the miners moved to Mercoal taking their homes with them.

He remembers his largest cheque as being $250.00 for two weeks, and his longest period of working when a fire broke out in the mines and the men fought the fire night and day.

Mr. and Mrs. Romaniuk now make their home in Edson. Several of their children billed as 'The Romaniuk Family' have gained some recognition as a western musical group.

. . . A Bear Came By and Walked off with Her Supper

Three members of 'The Romaniuk Family' comprise a western singing group. Edward Stanley Romaniuk and Mrs. Elsie Nettie Pysar started singing together as youngsters. When Mrs. Ann Zezel[29] joined them in 1964 they called themselves The Romaniuk Family.

THE ROMANIUK FAMILY BY EDDIE ROMANIUK

Ann was born on October 24, 1916, in the farming community of Chipman, Alberta. Our parents, Peter and Magdaline, and family of five children (Ann, John, Mike, Mary and Joe) moved from Chipman to the coal-mining community of Foothills, Alberta in 1927 where dad became a coal-miner. It was at Foothills that Elsie and Ed were born, in 1927 and 1930. Four more children were to be born here, Olga (who died when she was two weeks old) Peter, Rose and Deanne, making a total of ten living children. Foothills was a very pretty little place nestled among the hills in the foothills of the Rockies, about 60 miles southwest of Edson.

In 1933, dad bought our first radio and gramophone combination. This was the Golden Age of country music and Ann would copy all the songs that were being played of country artists. Mum bought a number of oldtime artists on the old 78's. It was at age nine, Elsie was eleven, that we began seriously to listen every evening to our idols, the original Carter Family. There was one particular program that we remember very well, 'Kernel Corn's' program from Sacramento,

---

[29] Anne's husband, Joe Zezel was the first white baby born on the Lovett Branch.

California. Elsie and I stayed up very late to listen to this 11:00 p.m. to midnight show, so we could copy and learn every Carter song. This was sometimes difficult to do because of static in the air and because several stations would very often come in at once, but because many of the songs were played over and over again, we were soon able to learn many of them. It was also at this time that Elsie and I learned to play the guitar. Ann bought a guitar in July, 1938 which she learned to play through the correspondence lessons that came with the instrument – all for $15.00. It had a very good sound and she still has the guitar to this day. Elsie and I learned to chord from Ann. We could hardly wait until we were dismissed from school each day so that we could come home to play the guitar and sing the Carter Family songs. We well remember the time that Elsie sent in a request for one of the Carter Family songs. How thrilled and excited we all were when the disc-jockey played her request and announced her name over the air saying that it came all the way from Foothills, Alberta, way up there in Canada. Little did we dream that one day we would meet Sara, Maybelle and A. P., to chat with them and even to sing along with Sara.

When I was about eleven, I bought my first guitar. It cost me only $5.00, but in those days it seemed more like $100. I saved up every cent I could get hold of for six months. Ann married in June, 1940 and took her guitar home with her, but when she saw how much I had missed the guitar (as I would walk two miles to her place at Reco or Mile 52 to play it) she allowed me to take her guitar home. When I bought my own guitar two years later, Ann still let us keep hers so Elsie and I could play together.

At our school the teacher would ask anyone who could sing, play an instrument, recite, etc. to take part in school programs. We progressed to performing at community functions, and then played at 'Smokers.' A Smoker was the coal miners' jargon for a social gathering on Saturday night highlighted by story-telling and partaking of many kegs of beer, followed by a fine lunch. Coal Branch people were very hospitable and social folk. Everyone knew everyone else and it was like one big, happy family. It was a fisherman's and hunter's paradise – it still is. There is fantastic scenery and one could go for thrilling hikes in the bush. About half a mile from town we dammed the Pembina River so that we could have our swimming pool. This was done each summer not only by school children but by the younger men who worked in the mine. Many a good time we had at the weiner roasts there as well.

This was excellent country too for berry picking, for miles around the coal-mining camps. Wild strawberries, blueberries, both low and high bush; huckleberries, raspberries, dewberries, low-bush cranberries, red and black currants and gooseberries. Whenever the huckleberry season was especially good we would be out in the bush for the better part of the day filling our buckets. It was not unusual for us to bring back from 75 to 100 pounds of this fruit from a single venture in the woods. After these were cleaned and washed, I thought nothing of using them to bake six pies for I was, and still am, very fond of cooking and baking. Of course the greater part of the berries were canned by mother for the winter. After a good season of berry-picking she would put up more than 50 half-gallons of this fruit. She didn't get to can many wild strawberries for as soon as we filled our pails and got home with them, we couldn't wait to smash them up, mix them up with sugar and eat them with bread.

We had no telephone, hardly any homes did. As I recall, the mine office, store and the mine officials were the only ones who had telephones. They were not dial phones, but old fashioned ones that you rang, and asked for a number.

We never had time to be bored for we had all sorts of chores to do around and outside the house before we were allowed to play. Some of these were packing water from wells, splitting wood and kindling; getting in the coal for stove and heater; cleaning out the chicken coop as we kept chickens; sweeping out boxcars into gunny sacks to get what little wheat there was to feed the chickens; emptying out slop-pails, emptying out ashes from the cookstove and heater, drying dishes, shopping for groceries.

In the summer when chores were done, there was softball and other games. Sometimes we would go for a walk and thought nothing of walking ten miles at a time. There were many fine streams to be fished, but I was not an avid fisherman. In the winter we would go skating on rivers or lakes; toboggan on many hills, ski, sleigh-ride, etc.

The older boys and men would go hunting for big game – such as moose, deer and elk which formed a good part of our diet. We used to walk two miles, in both winter and summer to our neighboring town of Coal Valley to see a movie once a week. This in spite of the fact that we were afraid of bears and wolves, as well as cougars. The bears especially were a nuisance as they used to frequent the camp in search of food. They would break into the local cookshack and get away with slabs of bacon, ham and other meat. Many a night we would be jolted out of sleep by the crack of rifle bullets, as men would fire at a bear.

I remember a neighbor who roasted a couple of chickens and set them in an open window to cool, when a bear came by and walked off with her supper. The black bear was the greatest pest but once in awhile the grizzly bear was seen in camp. There were brown and cinnamon bears around as well. Often, in the mornings we would look out our window and see moose feeding on willow.

Our summers were not always free to do with as we chose. For three consecutive summers mother had us attend catechism. This took up the greater part of our day as instruction began at 9:00 a.m. and ended at 4:00 p.m. with one hour off for lunch. We had to take along our lunch and walk two miles to Coal Valley where the lessons were taught. The session lasted six weeks each summer. The ultimate goal we were to attain was confirmation. I was 8, 9 and 10 years of age when I attended catechism.

For a couple of summers when I was 13 and 14 years, I was lucky to get a job in the local cookshack as flunkie. I was paid $15.00 a week which seemed like a great deal of money at the time. We had no days off. I say we, because a couple of my sisters were also flunkies. We had to get up at 5:00 a.m. and be at work at 6:00 a.m. We worked until 1:00 p.m. and then got a break of an hour and a half. We returned at 2:30 p.m. and finished work at 7:00 p.m. It was a very long day and we were really worn out at first, but in time we got used to it. I also had another job when I was 13 – this was janitor of the school. For this I earned $15. a month. With the money I saved I was able to buy myself a much better guitar, one for $30. Since I now had two guitars I was able to return Ann's guitar. With my earnings I was able to buy my first Carter 78's. I bought all those that were available, some 15 Bluebirds. That is when I became a record collector of Carter Family 78's.

I finished grade nine when I was 15 years old. Since there was no high school at Foothills, I had to leave home. I was bent on becoming a school teacher so I went to Edson to attend high school. My parents had bought a house and were renting the downstairs. I was to live in the two rooms upstairs, but my mother felt it was too lonely for me so she sent my younger brother Peter to keep me company.

Edson was only 60 miles from Foothills, but we only got home twice that first year – during Christmas and Easter vacation. No one in our family owned a car and the only way we could get back home was take the train which took 5½ hours to get there. The next year, Mother and two younger sisters moved to Edson. Peter quit school in grade 7 and went to work in Foothills. We lived downstairs which was much better. I had a great deal more time for my studies so that at the end of the year I won a scholarship for the highest standing in Grade XI.

I completed Grade XII in 1948. I went back to Foothills during the months of July and August and got a job on the 'outside' (of the mine.) I worked from 8 to 9½ hours, 6 days a week and was able to earn $400. I attended the University of Alberta and got a teacher's certificate. Nine summer sessions brought a Bachelor of Education Degree in 1966.

The mine at Foothills closed down in February of 1958 and Foothills became a ghost town in a few months. Elsie and her family moved to Edson on June 20, 1959. Ann and her family moved to Robb. Dad joined the rest of us in Edson. Dad and my brothers (except one) were never to work in the mines again and all got different jobs.

Selections that I have composed that relate to Foothills and the Coal Branch are: My Dear Old Foothills Homes;-My Alberta Rose;

My Rocky Mountain Home (Elsie the tune, I the words) and the Cadomin Mine Disaster from John McLaren's poem.

* * *

. . . It Hurt to See Them Pulling that Buick

GUENETTE – Paul Guenette had worked in the Yellowknife mine, so when he joined the army, the policy was not to send miners overseas. They looked at his record and sent him to Luscar in 1943. " I didn't even get my basic training finished, but I didn't get discharged till the war finished."

His wife Tanya (Tiny) says, "Coming from the prairies, I thought Luscar must be the end of the world. Coming up the Coal Branch on the railway, the train would stop so often, everyone would get off and pick berries. We were neighbours to Mrs. Kulyk there. Everything got so dirty at Luscar. When the wind came there must have been half an inch of dust on the sills. I looked out the window one day and saw a door of a boxcar go floating by. Keeping your house clean was a real chore because everything got so dirty. When I went there I had no washing facilities, so I asked a lady, Mrs. Tomich if she would do my laundry and wash my sheets. Later I found she had no facilities, had a large family and had so much work to do. I was so embarassed."

Paul saw the need for a trucking and transport outfit when the roads finally came through. He says, "Stan Kwasney was actually the first trucker on the Coal Branch."

I rolled 15 or 20 trucks. (Geunette)

Mercoal Mine, 1943

The couple moved to Mercoal and bought the cafe rooming house, with Paul working in the mine one day a week to stay on the payroll. George and Anne Trofimoff were part-owners of the cafe which they eventually sold to Mr. H. Goldstick. "Six months later it burned down."

In 1946-47 Paul bought his first truck. The need was there and he hoped to capitalize on it. Ernie Muldoon and Paul formed 'Paul & Ernies Transport.' The partnership lasted a year then the business be-

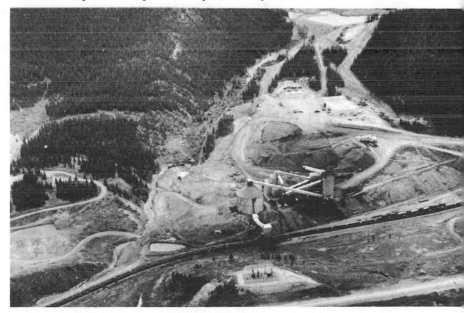

Luscar Coal Mine — The roads snake through the mountains at Luscar.

came known as 'Paul's Transport'. "I can remember in 1947 I must have loaded and unloaded five times with a load. The truck had a heavy box and every corner we went around the load shifted. This was two years before gravel was on the road and we'd keep a small truck full of gravel to meet the big truck and get us through the mudholes."

"Sometimes we'd take two or three days to get home with a load from Edmonton."

Tiny said, "It wouldn't pay to go back to the city with an empty load so I started buying beer bottles. It was a long time before I knew the kids would gather up the bottles at the back, and come and sell the same bottles to me all over again."

Many times Paul would try a hill, couldn't make it, back up and try again. Business flourished and Paul bought more trucks. The terrain was hard on the vehicles. "I paid $11,000. for two 'White' trucks in 1948 and traded them off eighteen months later for $2,000. a piece."

'I can remember Lloyd Mahon of Edson Motors coming up the Branch road to tow me out. He would make me get out of the cab in case the cable snapped. I must have rolled fifteen or twenty trucks on that road, but there was never much damage.'

Tiny says, 'I remember our first car was a Buick and the mud would be up to the doors. It hurt to see them pulling that car through those terrible roads."

Bans every year added to the troubles. "One spring there was a nine week ban on the roads."

Paul shrugs philosophically, "So when the roads started to get good, the mines closed, and the business flopped."

Mr. and Mrs. Guenette make their home in Edson.

* * *

... You Don't Dream About Girls when You're Hungry

PIETRO CHIESA came to Canada from Italy in 1908. He worked at Coppercliffe, Ontario; Michelle, Crowsnest Pass and in 1912 walked into the fledgling camp at Mountain Park. Here he was to remain for most of his life. At the age of 37 he made an important decision.

It was time to get married, so he went back to Italy and chose his bride, Julia. He left his now pregnant bride and returned to Mountain Park. Nino Vitalino Chiesa was born in 1922 in Udine, Italy. Mother and child left for Canada and Mountain Park the following year.

Regina was born in 1924, Alvio in 1926 and Pete in 1929. Complications of childbirth occurred and Julia died when Pete was but a baby of six weeks.

1938
First Row: Frank Martin, Jules Saver, Jack Gould, Nino Chiesa, Mike Polynik, Neil MacCauley, Joe Voytecheck, Lee Godby, Horrace Haddock.
Second Row: Jenny Natchuck, Liza Bishop, Virginia Chiesa, Peter Birchall, Alex Cavelli, Bobby Bracco.
Third Row: Lillian Gould, Mary Kwasney, Olive Berglund, Mr. Russel, Dyllis Griffith, Jean Nettleton, Agnes MacLeod, Rosa Madson, Mary Pavich.

Nino, Regina and Alvio were sent to a convent in St. Albert. In retrospect, Nino says, "That was a bad time of my life." From the freedom of roaming mountain valleys to the regimentation of convent life left an indelible impression on the young boy.

In 1932 the father married Maria in Italy by proxy and when she came to Mountain Park the family was united once again. Soon after Lucino was born.

Nino remembers when the community built the skating rink. Everyone pitched in, and Nino at ten years was in there along with the rest of them. He was sent for nails and in the process fell and broke his ribs and thereafter had to be content to supervise.

As a child he barely remembers Father Louis. "We always had a suit to go to church in. I know Father Louis had a lean-to half way between Cadomin and Mountain Park and Luscar, in case he got stuck with the weather."

Nino had a horse named Silver. "Everybody had horses, and the kids camped and fished in the mountains."

It was a carefree existence for kids. Nino remembers the beautiful big school he first attended, with ornately designed windows. (Thornton's Dove's Cottage). They built another school beside it eventually. His teachers were Miss Katie Arbuckle, Miss Dorothy Foster and Mr. Benny Farnham.

"We had lights from the town's inception, lots of fuel, and lots of credit."

In 1924 the mine went on strike for eight months. Nino remembers his father talking of that period. The single miners made raisin wine at Chiesa's with the mash to be made into moonshine. Word came that the police were on the way and everything was buried.

However the police went straight to the cache and Mr. Chiesa, Sr. was given the option of a $300.00 fine or six months in jail. Even with the prolonged out-of-work period the fine was collected from the miners and paid on Mr. Chiesa's behalf.

Nino says you followed orders and regulations in the mining camp. "If you got fired – that was it. You had to leave town."

However drinking wasn't considered a major misdemeanour. Nino says often the single miners went on prolonged drinking binges but they still lived in the company hotel, obtained company credit and still went back to work in the mine.

Hockey was an integral part of Nino's life. He remembers the Cadomin team coming to Mountain Park, sleeping in the train coaches overnight and then returning the next day. The train could be hired to go from one town to another on the Coal Branch for a fee of $125., later raised to $300.

"They used to charge $1.00 a head, so 125–300 people had to go watch the game, and they had many special trains. Where would you get 125–300 people out to watch a game today in places that size? You'd be lucky to get 30."

Quite often too the teams would pile into the caboose of a train. "If the railmen were in a good mood it was no problem."

Nino remembers an occasion when they weren't allowed in the caboose for some reason and all piled into an empty boxcar for the trip to Cadomin.

"The boys lit a fire on the floor of the boxcar because it was damn cold." By the time the freight reached Cadomin, the boxcar was filled with coughing smoke-racked players with the floor of the boxcar charred.

"We sure got hell over that!" says Nino in retrospect.

Nino was delivery boy for the Mercantile in his youth. "I'd have to get up at 6:00 a.m. three days a week to feed the horse 'Jerry' and pick up the freight from the train. I got $15.00 a week."

Nino decided to go to work in the mines and asked for a job in the tipple. He was brusquely told there was no opening in the tipple. "Come back when somebody dies!"

He went underground mining for 15 months and then decided to join the army. He saw action in England, North Africa and Italy. In Italy he was picked up and sent to a prisoner of war camp in Germany. Although never recalling hunger as a child he remembers half a dozen days of real hunger in the POW camp. "When you're hungry you never dream about girls."

Nino and his wife Jean remember the Sunday picnics the Yugoslavian club used to hold periodically near the Thornton Creek Draw. There was always plenty of beer and always a lamb would be barbecued.

They remember the dances which would invariably draw a large crowd. "There was always a fight after a dance," claims Jean.

A Madame Quoin used to visit Mountain Park with the latest fashions. She would set up in the store with the store taking a commission on garments sold. It was a great event with the women trying on clothes.

Their lives were regulated by the mine whistle with three short whistles signifying no work the following day, and one long whistle indicating there would be work. The whistle always sounded at 9:00 p.m. and would also serve as a curfew notifying all children under 16 years to be off the streets and to get home.

Nino had another whistle to live by in his youth. "When my dad whistled you could hear him all over Mountain Park, and we got home in a hurry."

When Nino went back to Mountain Park after his army stint he clerked in the store. In 1949 Nino and Jack Roome bought the store. Why, when the underground had already closed?

"There were still 108 men working on the strip mine."

But the strip operation also ceased. Mr. Chiesa, Sr. moved to work in the Cadomin mine. When it, too closed he bought the old Cadomin hospital and two houses and these were rebuilt into a home in Edson.

Mr. Chiesa, Sr. died in Edson. Nino and his family make their home there, too, where Nino owns the Buy-Rite Food Store.

* * *

. . . The Place was Lousy with Bedbugs

ALF FOSTER – by himself. I had my first view of the Coal Branch on the 14th of March 1929. We were a party of four going to Foothills looking for work in the mine there.

We left Edson at eight in the morning on a train made up of an engine, 25 boxcars, one coach and a caboose. The train was packed. We were not too impressed with what we saw from the train. It was a dreary boring trip and every station we stopped at, it seemed as though the train was glued to the rails.

We eventually arrived at Foothills at 3:00 in the afternoon. We were told the train had made a fast trip. We got off the train, parked our baggage at the store and walked over to Minehead which was just across the tracks. There we contacted the pit boss, a Welshman by the name of Deene, known to everybody as Red because he had red hair. His full name was Evant Gladstone Deene which gave me the idea his parents must have been very strong Liberals.

Well, it must have been our lucky day because we were told to start Monday morning. We left and went to get our mattresses which consisted of a long bag to be filled with straw from the barn. We then went to the bunkhouse at the top end of the camp.

We started work on Monday as miners and had to team up with two men. They must have weighed at least 250 pounds apiece. They looked at me kind of dubiously as I am small and weigh only 128 pounds. I realized right away that I had to pull my weight and prove I could keep up with them. I did just that to the extent that they told me I was OK. I worked with them for two weeks because the mine was closing down for the summer. Had we known that before we started we might have gone somewhere else, although the other three that started all quit within two days. I couldn't blame them because it was really damn hard work.

Coal Valley

— Godby

Anyway the Sunday before we left a bunch of us including Red Deene walked to Reco to a bootlegger where we all sat drinking moonshine. While there, Red told me there would be a job for me if I came back when the mine opened up in July. I may say I was very pleased. I worked in that mine until 1941 when I joined the army, except for one year in 1936 when I worked in the Imperial Hotel in Edson. That was where I met my wife, Nellie. Her father was well known on the Branch as he operated the train from Edson to Foothills for a number of years. His name was Hogger Brown. He died before we married.

I have never in my life met a finer lot of people than on the Branch. Morale was very high; there was an esprit de corp, all for one and one for all sort of thing. But that was common all over the Branch. It may have been because all the camps were what is known as closed camps, which means of course there were no roads to the outside so the camps were ruled by the companies. They did not take kindly to anyone ordering goods through the mail, but on the other hand they could not stop it either. That is not to say they didn't try.

I sincerely believe the Branch was the most cosmopolitan area in Canada at that time which goes to prove that different races can live together as one solid community. Speaking for Foothills we had Italians, Poles, Germans, Ukrainians, Serbians, English, Welsh, Scots, Irish, French and Belgians, and that is just a camp of 200 persons.

Nearly every Saturday night we walked to Coal Valley about two miles down the track. Sometimes after the bar closed we would go up to the Community Hall to watch the card games. Although there was a big depression on at that time, you would never know it by looking at the money on the table. Sometimes the ante was in the thousands of dollars.

There was a fellow at Foothills called Poker Joe. I can remember watching him play one night. He had an ace in the hole and two aces showing and that was his first three cards. It was stud poker they were playing, so of course he had to bet. He did not bet but instead threw in his hand, but that was the kind of player he was. Every Monday evening you could see him at the store sending a money order to some bank in Edmonton.

A man by the name of Bonny Brady was the landlord of the Coal Valley Hotel during most of the years I was at Foothills. He was a short stocky man and he operated a strict bar. The hotel had about 14 rooms upstairs.

Bonny left Coal Valley around 1938 and a fairly young fellow took over, I never got to know his name. Anyhow seven of us went down one Saturday night. We walked over to a table and ordered seven bottles of beer. This new guy came to the table with the bottles and seven glasses. I noticed him looking at me, then he said, "How old are you, sonny?" I said, "Come off it, don't make silly jokes." He said, "I'm sorry, I can't serve you. You will have to leave." Well, I didn't want to make a fuss so I started. We all left, then one of the boys went back and came out with two cases of beer which we took back to camp. The joke was on the bartender because I was only 38 (thirty-eight) years old.

At Coalspur, the junction point, the people had a pet moose. Anybody could pet it, even kiss it if they wanted to. Everybody loved that moose. One day some trigger happy bum killed it for meat. As far as I know, they never found out who did it. They figured it was somebody from outside who did not know it was a town pet.

211

If you should go to Coalspur you will probably see smoke coming out of the side of the hill. It is a coal seam that has been burning for more years than I can remember. It is not a rare thing. Once a coal seam starts to burn it is impossible to put it out.

The train after its run up to Lovett always returned and tied up at Coalspur until the next morning, when it returned early to Lovett for the trip back to Edson. There was to be no work the next day, so on that occasion some of the boys decided to go to Coalspur on the train to go to a dance. We arrived in Coalspur. As the dance would not start till that evening we booked a couple of rooms at the hotel, had something to eat and went to the bar where we stayed until 10:00 p.m. Naturally, we were not feeling any pain. Just after midnight while we were really enjoying ourselves a man came up from the station to say Foothills had phoned down to say there would be work the next morning. We walked back 13 miles, got to Foothills at 5:30 a.m. to go to work. We agreed on one thing. Never again.

A couple of years after I arrived at Foothills it was decided that it would be a good idea to form a soccer team. There were only ten Englishmen young enough to play the game and all of us had played in the Old Country.

But we had one big problem. It takes eleven men to make a soccer team so we had to find a goalkeeper; also a field to play on.

We solved the field problem with pick and shovels and the cooperation of the mine management. The mine manager at that time was William Duggan, a small built Welshman; so we had our field and started practice. A young Ukrainian fellow was interested in the game so became our goalkeeper, and proved to be alright.

Now we had to find teams to play. The only team on the Lovett Branch was at Sterco three miles down the line so we arranged a game with them. Our team lined up like this. Bill (goalkeeper) Alf Watkins and Bobby Kay, backs, Art Stevenson, centrehalf, Jack Hogg, right half, Bill Stead, left half, Owen Griffiths, Eddie Griffiths, Cliff Marshal, Alf Foster and Ivan Powell, forwards. We won that game 4 goals to 1. Sterco had a Scot playing back for them. He was beautiful to watch, his name was Dave Rankin. I saw him kick a ball 75 yards and it was never more or less than six inches off the ground.

Later we were in a Soccer Tournament involving Cadomin, Mountain Park and Foothills.

In the early thirties the workers at Mercoal went out on strike. It was a local trouble. At that time we all belonged to District 18 of the United Mine Workers of America. Foothills was on slack so we decided we would go to Mercoal to show them we supported them. We got there, and the ladies had a lunch ready for us, garlic flavored ham sandwiches.

We were to sleep in the Community Hall. The first night we had a good sleep. The next day we walked around and amused ourselves the best we knew how. It was boring. Around four in the afternoon we

Miners watch as train bearing Alberta Provincial Police and special police arrive to control strike action at Mercoal.

(Foster)

went to watch the train come in, only it was not the regular train. It was a special crammed full with Provincial Police. I don't know how many but my estimate was close to a hundred. They were armed and also carred night sticks. However they did not bother us, at least not then.

Night came again, which it generally does; we went to the hall to retire for the night. There were no lights as the power had been cut off. We went to sleep but not for long. Around two in the morning the police came and woke us up by poking us with those blasted night sticks. When we were all awake they warned us to be out of Mercoal by daylight. We were out at daylight. Whatever the grievance Mercoal was fighting for, they did not get any satisfaction. My opinion for what happened is that management panicked when we arrived and phoned or wired for the police.

At Foothills there was a two storey bunkhouse situated alongside the railroad tracks. I moved into it because it was close to the store and the washhouse. The place was made up of rooms (two men to a room) lined on each side top and bottom floor with a hallway from back to front and heated with steam pipes running through the halls. The place was lousy with bedbugs but I didn't care as they never bothered me.

The following spring when the mine closed down, I opened up my bag to pack my clothes and the three locks on the bag were plugged solid with bedbugs.

The management decided as soon as the mine closed down they would seal and fumigate the bunkhouse and leave it sealed until·

September. That fall when we moved back in a fellow by the name of Monconi chose an end room on the top floor. He wanted a cool room and hated bedbugs. The next morning we went down for breakfast and poor Monconi walked in, his face a mass of lumps. It seemed the only survivors had settled in Monconi's room.

We had a steam engineer first class by the name of Hicks who soon gained a reputation for a drink nicknamed 'Dynamite.' One night at a dance Hicks came and asked myself and a few others if we would like a drink. We went to his house not far from the Hall. Mr. Hicks gave me a waterglass full of greenish yellow liquid. It tasted good and I drank it all down. Like a sap I thought it was a soft drink and had another one. I do not recall being at the dance but apparently I was. That drink was the dynamite I had heard so much about.

One Christmas a bunch of us took off for Edmonton. The train usually got into Edson in the afternoon, and the train left for Edmonton about 2:00 a.m. As a rule we always booked rooms at the Edson Hotel, and also as a rule never used them except for one room. These trips involved liquor and hijinks.

A small colony of Metis people lived at Reco. We knew all of them and sometimes used to pay them a friendly visit, and have a few drinks of course. During depression days the law turned a blind eye to the Metis shooting game out of season. They could not be beaten when it came to making a meal of moose meat. It was delicious and very tender.

At Foothills our pro manager was a man named Walter Hammett. When I say pro manager it did not mean he was the total boss. He looked after everything that was connected with the office. He was a very religious man and was closely connected with the Anglican Church. Later in life he became an ordained minister. He was also a first World War veteran.

I joined the army in 1941 along with several others from Sterco. We had to go to Coalspur for a preliminary medical where we took the usual tests for diabetes. We had to report in Edmonton the following week which we did, where we took a stiff medical. There was also a few of the boys from other Branch points. The Second day we were there, they took us all in a truck to the McLeod Building for X-rays. One of the boys from Cadomin failed his X-ray exam because he had silicosis of the lungs. At that time the Compensation Board would not recognize it as a work hazard. They do now.

During the time Mr. Donald Ross and Mrs. Ross kept the store, we used to play a lot of bridge. One night we sat in the back of the store concentrating on our bridge when the door opened and a little girl came in. Don left the table to see what the girl wanted. The girl's mother had been in the store earlier in the evening and had bought a box of gramaphone needles. She sent the girl back to get another box instead of the one she brought back because there were only 199 needles in the box instead of 200. As you can see it takes all kinds of people to make a community.

The coal was broken up with a pick so it would go through the hopper and down the belt. (Sterco) (Nielsen)

Sterco Pit — 1927.

Coal outcropping at Sterco.

215

The Coal Branch starts at the junction of Bickerdike to go south west. You can see outcrops in the land and these outcrops continue all the way to both spurs. You will see old abandoned mines. Although they have largely been cleaned up, the scars remain.

Alf Foster – Edson

* * *

Dragline sits in the abandoned pit at Sterco — 1960.

Loading the train at Sterco.

Sterco Yard and Camp — 1928.

. . . Only Worked a Mile of Seam

NEILS NIELSEN was born in Denmark in 1890 and came to Canada in 1924 with the intention of becoming a farmer. He cleared land in the Legal area for a time and worked on B. C. steamships, but in the early part of 1926 found himself in Edmonton. He worked part time for Swift's for 25¢ an hour, but work was slack. Mr. Fred Metzel of Sterling Collieries asked if Neils and his friend would like to work at Sterco.

Wages were good. 55¢ an hour and 300 hours a month, even if there was no extra for overtime.

"There must have been 250 men working there at that time. We had two sittings in the cookhouse anyway. During the war we were down to about 80 employees but with better machinery we produced the same amount."

"The mine started in 1918, and from 1918 to when it closed in 1952 they only worked a mile of seam in all that time."

Neils loved the country. "It was not unusual to see a whole flock of moose. But I would shoot only one animal a year, usually on a Sunday because that was my day off. Years later after the road was in, hunters would come in by the dozen. I've seen moose hides piled higher than a table."

Neils said they bought a 1926 Pontiac Coupe in the summer of 1931 for $400.00. Neils had never driven so as the former owner had to go to Saskatoon, Neils and Ellen went along so Neils could learn to drive. "It took us four days to get back to Edmonton. Terrible windstorms and terrible roads. I never had the car in high gear all the way back."

Neils Nielsen stands on Rocky Point near Sterco. He says, "It was a fantastic view in the fall — to the west the mountains — to the north Swan Hills and on a clear day you could see Edson.

There were no roads in Sterco so the car was kept at Willis Garage in Edson for a rental of $3. a month. It stood so long between trips "it took ages to get it running again."

Neils said when the huckleberries on the Branch came out it was unbelievable. After the road was in, cars would be parked for miles with their occupants at the roadside picking and picking.

He remembers the camaraderie that existed between the railway men and the mining camps, and how the engineers would blow the whistle in such a way that warned all and sundry that the police were on the way.

Neils said many Frenchmen settled at Coal Valley and in earlier days he and Ellen would visit the camp to play bridge.

Later when the mines closed he remembers women on the Lovett branch staging a sit-down demonstration on the railway track in hopes the crews sent out to tear up the track would desist, but "it didn't do any good. The track was torn up anyway."

* * *

Mrs. Ellen Nielsen writes: I came to Montreal in 1928, had the liberty of vacation from my work. At last landed in Edmonton where I and my brother met Niels Nielsen, as at that time they were working in Sterco.

Mrs. Ellen Nielsen sits in her garden.

Two years after I went back to Copenhagen to my work and thirteen months after again went to Canada and married Niels. We arrived in Sterco and coming up over the hill, I asked, "Is this Sterco?" When confirmed I sat down on my hatbox and said "I think I should go back to Copenhagen to my weaving." However I made it up over the Hill. The place I was to live in for three years was a great disappointment. Thereafter, we got a home of our own. We made a big vegetable garden and flower garden that gave us a great pleasure, as we both are Danish and loved flowers. As years passed we found what kind of flowers liked to live at 4,700 feet altitude.

One year in late August Niels and I went out in the bush to pick those wonderful huckleberries when we met up with a Lady Bear. Some experience. My St. Bernard "Koter" had just growled beside me when Neils said, "Ellen, hold Koter." We were looked over very carefully before she moved. When she left, so did we. On our way back home looking down the valley, a big male bear strolled along picking berries. Koter and I did not go into the bush alone after that.

The Nature around the Coal Branch is something not easily forgotten. The wild animals, the different birds arrival every year to their houses Niels had put up for them. The bluebird would be there by date; the swallows after the first rainfall; the hummingbird when the flowers were in bloom. Such a delightful little thing to look at.

But as beautiful as it can be, to live that high can be just as unpleasant with temperatures 65 to 70 below. The weather can move just about from summer to winter, when the fog came in from the north – and overnight the peas about ready to be picked – all frozen!

Social life and entertainment amounted mostly to a bridge game – but then when we got the road into the Branch, life looked a bit better. We got a car in '48 and could get out and have visitors coming in.

219

In 1952 Sterco closed and we moved to Coal Valley. In 1957 Coal Valley also had come to an end and we came to Edmonton and found a home at 11905-69 Street – all bare ground. We brought three big spruce trees, a hedge of Mountain Ash, (native to Sterco) from the Coal Branch and pine from Hinton.

Two days after we moved in, the Edmonton Rehabilitation Society came to ask me if I would take the Weaving Department for six weeks as the lady they had wanted six weeks off. At last I said yes – but stayed 15 years – and designed the Alberta Tartan. Some of the handicapped became very good weavers.

* * *

A visit to the Nielsen home, beautifully landscaped, might catch Mr. Nielsen wearing a shirt in the Alberta Tartan, set off by matching Tartan chair head rests in the living room. Coffee and a delicious Danish cake will probably be served with a napkin in the Alberta

Mrs. Neilsen holds the Alberta Tartan designed and woven at the Edmonton Rehabilitation Society for the Handicapped. The design was adopted as the official Alberta Plaid or Tartan, March, 1961, registered, June, 1961.

Legend of the tartan is:

        Green for the forests
        Gold for our wheat and sunshine
        Blue for our lakes and the clear skies above
        Black for our oil and coal
        Pink for our floral emblem, the wild rose.

Alberta Government Photograph

Tartan. The house has lovely hand embroidered curtains made during the long evenings at Sterco. Mrs. Nielsen who obtained her handicraft knowledge at three centres of learning in Denmark may be working on her Cluny Lace, an art that is virtually non-existent in Canada. The lace is intricately woven with the aid of more than 60 wooden bobbins, the threads held in place in design by carefully placed straight pins. It looks altogether too complicated to learn. Asked if she had taught anyone the art, Mrs. Neilsen said no one had been interested in learning.

* * *

. . . *The First Thing He did was Shoot the Horse*

MIKE LUKACH works with heavy duty equipment in the construction of oil well reservoirs and tanks. He relaxed in the very nice living room of his home at 13803-88 St. in Edmonton and reminisced about the Coal Branch and his home at Robb.

"I was in my teens and ran with a group of guys older than me, I guess we were kind of wild."

"I worked at Mile 33 at Lakeside Coals chute loading, went on the strip at Mile 32, and was 'rope-riding' at Mercoal."

"There weren't very good roads and when the river was high we'd drive the tracks. I'll bet more cars drove the tracks up there than anywhere in the country. Can remember once when we drove the railroad to Coalspur to get some beer. There was a train coming and we just managed to reach a siding. I jumped out just before the train came. We were perfectly safe by this time but I just opened the car door and jumped. The guys doubled up laughing at me."

"I remember an engineer, Old Man McCaulay, used to pick kids up at Coalspur and take the gang to Mercoal to the dance. They managed to pack a lot of kids in that engine cab. The kids used to come back on the speeder or walk the eleven miles."

The kids up there were always up to something. At Cadomin they soaped the rails for a mile and the train spun and spun and couldn't get going. We tried it at Robb but it didn't work very well."

"I used to sit and listen to my mother and the older women talk. I guess in the twenties there was a strike and a bunch of scabs came to work in the mine. All the women, my mother too, got together and went down to the mine and called the scabs names and yelled at them and threw pepper in their eyes. They organized regular picket lines."

"I remember too when Cam Matthew's store was robbed at Coalspur. The R.C.M.P. took my fingerprints and Danny Poleszczuk's and some other guys. We didn't have anything to do with it."

Mike, wrongfully accused, swore vengeance.

221

This bull trout caught at Mystery Lake (between Jasper and Luscar and accessible only by horseback) actually measured 15″. Tied with some gutline and stepping a pace back Mike Lukach looks as if he had caught a monster specimen.

"I cut off the head of his registered rooster and strung it on the hen-house door, took the rooster and cooked it. He treasured that rooster and that's why I did it. We never did find out who broke in."

Mike talked of Jack the Frog, the bootlegger who became one of the Coal Branch's colorful legends.

"He ran a still out of Weald. About 16 or 17 miles. I got sugar once for him down at Edson; a hundred pound sack. He said, "Don't get it in my name." He paid me by giving me some moonshine. The good stuff. He had two or three different kinds and would say, "If those sons of bitches don't want to pay I'll put coal oil in it." I took it home and my dad took a drink of it and said, "bring more next time." Dad wouldn't go to the liquor store after that . . . said it was better than anything he could buy.

Coalspur — 1943

222

"The police tried to get Jack the Frog for a long time but no one would ever let on where he was. He used to live out in the bush with a negro woman. She was nice. She was blind but everyone said once she had heard a voice she would always remember who you were. Anyway the police finally got him. He was in camp once for something and had come in on his white horse. The police cut the horse loose, and the horse headed for home, straight to the still. Jack the Frog went to the Fort[30] for a while. When he got out he ordered parts for another still and sent them up the Branch under some of the section men's names. When he got back up the Branch the first thing he did was shoot the horse."[31]

Mike, wife and friends often fish now up the Coal Branch.

Several years ago, he and a friend Leonard Charleton made a trip to Muskiki Lake on horseback.

"You know we found old mine rails at Muskiki Lake? I'd sure like to know how they got there!"

Saddled with a Debenture Debt

John H. Finlay – I have no pictures and no records now of the time I spent working up in the Coal Branch.

I was the Coal Branch School Division official trustee and superintendent there from 1954 to 1959. The Sterco Mine closed out the year before I came. Mountain Park, Cadomin, Robb and Leyland were gone some years before that. Coal Valley, Luscar, Foothills and Mercoal closed down during my term, and I believe in that order, Mercoal closing in 1958.

While I was a trustee I recall the division being saddled with a debenture debt for the new school that had been built at Cadomin a year before the mine closed. I set up a trust fund in which I deposited any monies received from the sale of buildings and equipment and also any surpluses at the end of the year. When I left in 1959 the trust fund had built up sufficiently to wipe out the debenture debt and I was able to propose to the Edson School Board that they include Coal Branch in the Edson School Division, which they did since there was no debt to assume.

One other experience I might relate was several years before I worked in the Coal Branch. I believe it was the Labor Day weekend in 1947 when I accompanied the Vegreville Junior Baseball Team to Cadomin for a Provincial play-off series. I went along as the umpire. We arrived quite late in the evening, but the Legion was going strong and we were all taken down there, and then I was billetted at Wal Steen's. I know we had quite a party at his place on the Saturday night

---

[30] Fort Saskatchewan Gaol

[31] This story has been told to me in much the same way by three different former residents.

223

and on Sunday morning the pit boss and Wal took me down into the mine. It was the first and only coal mine that I have been in. I should remember the pit boss's name because he was killed the following year in the tragic flood and cave-in which closed the mine.

Jim McVeigh was our bus driver at Luscar while I was there and I believe he was one of their star hockey players when the Luscar Indians were the big team in intermediate hockey in Western Canada back in the 30's.

> J. H. Finlay,
> Associate Superintendent – Curriculum
> Edmonton Public Schools.

... *Fire All Those Russians*

Matt Zdunic of 12714–102 Street, Edmonton, spent 32 years of his life working as an underground miner on the Alberta Coal Branch. He was never injured but says, "I worked the 'safe' mines at Bryan, Lakeside and Mercoal which mined 'hard' coal. Cadomin, Luscar and Mountain Park had soft coal. Lots of men were buried from there. Soft coal, dust and gases. They choke you."

Matt was born in 1895 in Yugoslavia and left his native land in 1927, leaving behind his wife Rose and daughters Maunda, Mary and Katie. He would send for them soon, he reassured his family, but the 'soon' turned out to be 11 years later.

Coming to Canada to an uncle who farmed in Saskatchewan, he found times were hard and work was scarce so soon left to go further west.

He found employment with the Balkan Coal Co. at Robb. The company was owned by "about ten shareholders" all of European extraction. Orders were hard to come by and the group sold to Lakeside Coals, Limited.

Matt found that as often as not the mines would not be working, so supplemented his income by working on the extra gang at Embarass, or by peeling ties. In summer orders for coal were virtually non existent.

The young men boarded at the company minehouse and Matt remembers one instance where the men complained about the food. Company officials queried the cook, and when the cook explained he was doing his best, the company became incensed at the men and ordered them off the property. The men promptly set up tents a few hundred feet away on the railway right-of-way. Matt says, "the Farmer's Union heard about the dispute and sent up bacon, cereals, coffee and tea etc." to sustain the men. How long this situation would have gone on is a moot question, but fortunately the company received a big coal order and differences were resolved in a hurry.

Matt says the mine was sold and a dispute involving wages arose. The men belonged to the Canadian Union at the time. "Fire all those

Russians, they're just a bunch of communists," Matt overheard. The 'Russians' included all ten of the European shareholders. "They called everyone Russians – Yugoslavs, Poles, Serbs, Ukrainians," he continued.

"Did they fire you?" Matt was asked.

Dark brown eyes gleaming, Matt grinned, "No, no, but I wasn't a shareholder. They fired all of them who used to own the Balkan."

Work was periodically slack and men drifted from one camp to another seeking work. At one time a sign posted seven miles from Coalspur saved job-seekers a trip. It noted laconically that no jobs were available and men were not needed at Coal Valley.

Finally in 1938 Matt's family came from Yugoslavia. The family lived in Edmonton for a time and here son John was born in 1939.

Working on city ditches was not for Matt, so it was back to Robb, this time accompanied by the family. They rented one of the company log houses for $10. a month. "If you couldn't come up with the $10. they'd mark it on the books and let you stay anyway."

The rent was marked down against forthcoming wages.

Mrs. Zdunic says she enjoyed living there, but at first, "We didn't appreciate it. We thought it was the bush. Now I know how much I liked it. Nobody ever bothered you there. We used to have a cow and chickens."

The biggest cheque the Zdunics remember was a hundred dollars for two weeks, but proportionately bread was ten cents a loaf and the rent was cheap.

"And Jack the Frog's moonshine was $2.50 for 24 ounces," adds Matt.

A paper with a letterhead that reads Lakeside Coals, Limited, Producers of Minehead Coal and dated August 1, 1950 reads, "By the

We lived in this log house at Robb for 16 years. The house built by the company had beautiful hardwood floors.

Matt Zdunick

payment of $350. Mr. Matt Zdunic becomes the owner of log house No. 19, situated at Robb, mile 33." They have since sold the property.

Mr. and Mrs. Zdunic live comfortably in Edmonton, renting one side of a duplex they own. Matt receives $75. a month pension from the U.M.W.A., and pays $1.25 a month union dues. He delights in baiting son John with the fact that the income tax John pays comes back in the Zdunics old age pension. The couple are still active.

Matt says, "The doctor says don't sit in a rocking chair. Get out and walk."

* * *

. . . Combed the Hill Looking for Sausage

Violonda Giovinazzo remembers arriving in Luscar as a young child to find snow on the ground. In August!

"We just had light sweaters on. We had ridden up in the caboose from Edson. I don't know why the caboose I guess there was no coach at that time."

The father George Giovinazzo had already preceded his wife Maria Annuziata and had built a home near the railroad track in Luscar for his family. The couple had emigrated from Italy in 1906, worked in Toronto, Guelph and Port Arthur and moved west to Lethbridge in 1909. Here George worked till 1913 then spent ten years in the mine at Cardiff. This closed so in 1923 George moved and obtained work at Luscar.

Archbishop J. H. MacDonald of Edmonton comes to Luscar for the first communion class at Luscar — early twenties.

— Giovinazzo

226

Mrs. Maria Annuziato Giovinazzo gathers wood at Luscar, Alta. She has tied a length of cloth or rope around the wood before hoisting it on her head. Early twenties.

Luscar Colleries Ltd. miner drives a two wheeled cart full of rock from the mine to the dump, 1920's.   (Giovinazzo)

The boys in the family, Salvatori, Vincenso, Dominic, Albert and Antonio, and the girls Victoria and Violonda grew up in Luscar, while the parents thought of the daughter Rosa Maria they had left behind in Italy. By the time they were able to bring her to Canada she no longer wanted to come.

The Giovinazzos had a two story chicken house, and the children gathered eggs from the chickens on the first floor, while the mother used the top floor to hang and cure the home made varieties of sausage she was adept at making.

The house was two storeys too, and Violonda remembers the house shuddering while the fierce winds of Luscar tore through the valley. One year the top of the chicken house was blown 500 feet up the hill in the wind. The next day the Giovinazzos combed the hill looking for sausage, but none was to be found.

The children enjoyed sliding down the many hills on cardboard and tending to the goats the mother kept. All was not well. Maria, the mother suffered from dizzy spells and it was thought that the high altitude was a contributing cause, so in 1928 the family moved to Edmonton. The father bought a grocery store on Rice Street, and a nearby home. The house cost twenty five hundred dollars. It was the depression and despite valiant efforts the business went broke. Payments of $25. a month on the house could not be met so the entire family moved back to Luscar.

Ed Astley and Jim Giovinazzo, delivery boys for the Luscar Mercantile. On their way with a grocery order.

L. to R. – Fr. Landrigan, Tony Giovinazzo and Father Young, at Luscar.

Victoria and Tony Giovinazzo, Frank Rockwell, l., with a load of milk for Luscar residents. Milk was delivered from Edmonton and bottled at Luscar in the early twenties.

"We were never hungry but you had one pair of shoes. When they wore out you got another pair."

Violonda remembers only one strike and that was marked by her father coming home one morning with a pail of jam that had been given him by the mine union. The father avoided as much as he could the strike actions as he remembered too vividly the month he had spent in jail at Cardiff because of strike activities.

The children were encouraged in music as much as possible with fees paid to itinerant teachers by contribution to their room and board. A Ukrainian man taught Albert mandolin, Sam (Salvator) guitar, while Tommy Robinson taught Violonda the harp, Jim (Vincenzo) the violin and Mico (Dominic) the accordian.

Violonda remembers playing with a musical group at KD or Gebo as the mine three miles west of Luscar was first called, named after the man who found the seam.

The father built another house up the hill and the family grew up in a religious atmosphere. Mr. Giovinazzo did not encourage his sons to work in the mines, "One in the family is enough."

Visiting priests, and sisters of Our Lady of Charity of the Good Shepherd Convent were welcome guests. The Sisters would visit the mining villages convassing for funds to aid their work of caring for delinquent girls and orphans in the City of Edmonton.

Mr. R. J. Hughes was the teacher, says Violonda. He taught grades one through nine, then another room was added and another teacher, Miss Scott, came. Teachers lived on the second floor of the schoolhouse.

She remembers that Albert used to walk to Leyland to take lessons in morse code. Miko grew up to operate a butcher shop, part of the old cookhouse; Albert and Jim worked loading the box cars outside of the mine, while Sam worked in the mine, then left for Drinnan. Victoria and her friend Vivian Bartoff delivered milk to the houses; the milk brought in from Edmonton, then bottled in Luscar. Tony drove the water wagon. Violonda, feeling the influence of the visiting sisters, decided to enter the Good Shepherd Convent but after a year and a half decided she didn't have the disposition for the training so returned to Luscar.

The miners spent much of their time working at building a road from Luscar to Cadomin. Miko owned one of the first cars in Luscar.

She remembers too when Miko contracted typhoid fever and all his hair fell out. A nurse, Miss McKrimmon dropped in often to see to the patient.

Even in later years, doctors still had to work under inadequate conditions. At 29 years of age, in 1944, Violonda had to have her appendix removed. She had a spinal and watched instruments being sterilized in a boiler on the stove. After she was up and around she enjoyed meals with the surgeon, Dr. Epstein and his nurse in the kitchen hospital at Cadomin.

When the mine closed, the father, though elderly, still worked on the tipple. Violonda said her father never got over the closure and disbelieved till the end. Everything house, garage and greenhouse was torn down, board by board and brought into Edmonton. Much of it was utilized in the house built at 14334-106 Avenue where Violonda still lives.

* * *

. . . Fractures in Every Limb

Dr. & Mrs. H. Begg, 1930-1940, by Dr. Begg – Edmonton.

With the development of new pathways and pioneering flying to Northern Canada there was a natural attempt by intrepid bush pilots to fly anywhere not serviced by roads or only by infrequent slow trains.

One of these entrepreneurs was United Airlines based in Edson, and possibly financed by Princess Galitzine of Edson. The flyer was none other than the now famous Grant McConachie whose father was CN Superintendent at the time.

A clearing was made at Robb, Alberta which consisted of cutting out the trees on a strip just west of Robb. No attempt was made to level the ground.

On one occasion, Grant McConachie flew up with one passenger, Mr. Herdie McLeod. They loaded fuel and Herdie had a speeder take him to Mercoal as there were no roads at that time. However, on the take-off for return, Grant crashed with his plane. I, as the nearest doctor, was at Mercoal and the C.N. superintendent would not clear the transportation of Grant until he was seen by a doctor. I had to go to Robb by speeder and examine McConachie. He was not injured but his pride was hurt. He was upset at being held up until I got there, then went to Edson on a speeder supplied by the C.N.R.

The mechanics came up to ship the plane to Edson. One of them said the cause of the crash was that the pilot did not turn on the gas supply.

Not long after this incident a small plane crashed and landed upside down just west of the railway tracks at Bryan. The plane was not damaged too badly and the pilot was uninjured. I happened to be at Robb at the time and talked to the pilot and asked him what happened. He said that he had been flying in Eastern Canada and did not realize with altitude of 3,300 feet that with the rarer atmosphere he had started up all right but did not gun the engines hard enough to gain altitude. He caught the wheels of the plane on the fringe of trees at the east end of the runway. That was the last of the landings at Robb.

After World War II a young amateur flyer Ronnie Hall, a native of Cadomin, flew a plane around Cadomin. The wind was too strong and he did not risk landing the plane there.

However, another boy from Robb 34 gained his pilot's license and landed on the river flat north of Cadomin. The wind was usually too strong. Blowing down from the Mountain Park valley and joined by the Whitehorse Valley just two or three miles south of the town, placed Cadomin as it were in the stem of a funnel where the wind was concentrated and like a cyclone at times. It was not feasible to land or take-off unless the wind was light.

There is a landing field there used by the Forestry but only for helicopters.

The wind at Cadomin was something unbelievable at times. On one occasion, several boxcars were blown off the track when the train was crossways to the wind.

On another sad occasion a man working at Jock McKenna's place down on the flat north of town was killed by the wind. I was called down to see the man. The story goes that he heard the wind coming and went out to put the chickens in the chicken house. When the wind hit it strewed the chicken house like matchwood all down the field. Not a chicken could be seen nor were they ever found. The man was dead and he had fractures in every limb.

We lived in a log house third from the corner of the town square. The wind lifted the roof off a barn two houses south of our place and with saddles attached to the roof it sailed over Hugh Docherty's house and landed on our roof.

Mrs. Begg was in the house alone at the time and phoned me at the hospital to come up as she didn't know what was going to happen next.

* * *

GRETA JEFFERS – Mountain Park, the town built on the side of a hill in the mountains. It was quite the town. I was up there in the forties; my former husband was a railroader and used to go from Mountain Park to Luscar, and sometimes to Cadomin on the coal trains.

Many a time, I used to go with him. They even had me shoveling coal to the engine going up to Mountain Park once. There was just one store.

I used to see the men coming from the mine and you couldn't tell one from the other, they were so black. They were going to the washrooms.

A bunch of us women went through the mine once. I was so glad when we got out. There was one place we had to crawl on our hands and knees it was so small.

I remember one night after an Elk's stag, the men came to my place with beer and a guitar. It had been raining that night and there was mud all over the floor.

At station, May 23, 1944.

The busdriver, Mr. Philbrick in front of
the Summit.

Often when the train would just go to Cadomin and back all the
train crew would head for our place for a feed of bacon and eggs.

My husband's heart was bad so we moved to Prince Rupert and
he died in 1956.

I was up there sometimes afterward. It seems a shame there is nothing left but the grave yard. I wonder if it will ever open up again as
there is still lots of coal there. My daughter, Mrs. Nino (Jean) Chiesa
lives in Edson now. – Greta Jeffers, Box 68, RR5, Aldergrove, B.C.

* * *

Part of the train crew.

(Girardi)

... *Barrels of Pickles and Big Canada Cheeses*

A. MacKINNON–by himself. I was the first boy baby born in Cadomin, Alberta, the youngest son of John (Lucky) McKinnon, a Glace Bay miner who had two bothers killed at Hillcrest.

Dad came west from Nova Scotia to the Crows Nest bringing his small family then consisting of my brother Donald F. and Melba Florence

My mother originated in Ontario and moved with her parents to what was then known as the Territory of Alberta around the Lacombe area. She later went to the Crows Nest to work where she met my Dad and married him in Coleman, Alberta.

I originated in the year 1923, spring, the 6th of April in the beautiful area along the CNR spur that was known as the Coal Branch, and the Capital if there had been one would have been Cadomin at the base of the mountains.

Born to love the mountains which I still do, and to have been there to see all the wild animals there were, and to be able to scale the mountains was a sheer delight of which I never tired.

My life until I joined the navy was going to school in Cadomin, which I went to with regret. As a youth growing up in the mountains with all the hunting fishing and sports of all kinds, plus Jimmy Maddam's horses, I found it hard to attend school as well as I should have, but with all the distractions I still managed to get my Grade ten.

I remember the town of Coalspur when Old MacPhail was known as the 'Mayor' there. There are a lot of people who would claim to be Coal Branchers, I'm sure would not have been there at that time.

234

A. MacKinnon says "This was my home in Cadomin for 36 years. It was later turned into a post-office."

They came later when Mercoal started so big and after the highway got through in 1940.

Coglan's store at Coalspur. What a treat to go there where the barrels of pickles and big Canada cheeses and old fashioned hard candy in barrels stood around.

Oh yes, the Blue Flea Special, our own passenger from Metropolis Edson to Mountain Park, 76 miles in eight or ten hours; Pop Conrad the conductor – a tiring run by the time they got to Mountain Park.

I remember Fred Wald, the big rock miner. The kids always waited for him, his pockets full of coins. He would come out of the bar, a big

Mrs. L. F. MacKinnon, post-mistress, Cadomin, with her granddaughter.

man and so agile on his feet, would put on a display turning hand springs, etc. so the coins came out of his pockets and the children would scramble.

I remember Cadomin where men said good-bye to their wives and mothers when they left for work in the mornings or afternoon. They did not know whether they'd see them again that night after working the odds in that black, gas-filled (most of the time) pocket of coal east and west of the main shafts. But where it was a sort of challenge to work there and where no one would have changed for the world. The younger men talked of their conquests of the fairer sex while they worked deep down into the bowels of the earth; they talked of hunting, fishing, sports: hockey and baseball, soccer where Herman Varley was the goalie. Herman was a survivor of Hillcrest, lived at Cadomin for many years. This type of person was a backbone to our area.

The mine had disasters also, floods, gas and cave-ins although the cave-ins and the squeezes were really no big problem at Cadomin. The explosion at Luscar where so many were killed – the Zozaks, two brothers on one shift. I worked later with their father, Steve, who never really recovered from that one. A fine miner and gentleman, Steve Zozack . . . . the loss of two sons and a relative was a great blow.

The last shift of 1939 when James Maddams saved so many from the gas then was caught himself. I had been a close friend as I worked for him outside the mine when he had horses, packs, outfits, etc. He was a quite well known mountain sportsman, big game guide and outfitter with a full life ahead of him, yet at 29 years of age he was taken.

This was the first time really that death and what it meant got through to me. I suffered, and the whole Coal Branch mourned. The Miner's medal was placed with Maddams but it didn't seem to help much.

Then accidents such as Swanston going back to bury some tools and losing himself in the gas, and Bob Muir, the fireboss, forced to make the try to get him out, and himself going to the Edson cemetery.

The floods were terrible. I was in three of them, two in Cadomin and the last one in Coleman in 1964. That is floods inside the mine, where subterranean lakes broke in or water came from above. Where Jack MacLaren wrote the poem about Happy the Horse; the horse pulling the lads out of the panel. Myself and Lloyd Engley held onto the harness and were pulled out into the rock tunnel by sheer strength of this horse, while the mud filled into the top. The only two out of that Panel alive that night, and so many dead above, and such a terrible search.

I had left the mine to join the navy and sailed the seas for four years. After the war I went home and worked in the mine, then quit and went 'North to the Yukon' where I worked in the coal fields around Carmacks. I left the north and tried the oilfields around Peace River where I met my wife Marion employed by the Treasury Branch

236

of Alberta at Peace River, and who was born and raised at Hythe, Alberta.

We went to Whitehorse for a few months then home to Cadomin where my mother was running the post office which she had run since my father died in hospital in Edmonton in 1941.

I went back to the coal in Luscar and Mercoal; by that time Cadomin had closed down, but we still lived in Cadomin. My wife ran the post office when she took over from my mother who retired and went to Edmonton to live. She is still living in Central Park Lodge.

When the mines closed down on the Coal Branch, my wife and I moved to Hythe and are now on the farm with her brother. From here we both work out, my wife back with the Treasury Branch, and myself casual work.

Cadomin — after closure.

My brother Don is now an Engineer with Texaco Oil in Calgary, and my sister Melba is married to Bryson Smith, a minister in New York State in the U.S.

But I still dream of the Coal Branch and fun and living I did there as a youth growing up. I thank God that I had the opportunity to be there before the changes were made with seismograph etc. that we all believe destroyed the woods with so many trails that the game moved further back in the mountains.

A. MacKinnon
Box 274, Hythe, Alberta

Escape From Panel 8

HAPPY THE HORSE

written after the Cadomin mine disaster, June 14th, 1950 by a Cadomin miner – John McLaren

Twas afternoon on the fourteenth of June
When the men went down the East mine
They all looked so well
You could hardly tell
For five it would be the last time

The five all went where they were sent
to shoot coal away up on high
And little they knew of the storm that blew
Huge streams of rain from the sky

But over their head from a water shed
That had been built by man
Right into the seam with a steady stream
The surface water ran

The men below they didn't know
Of the danger from above
And they worked along with a joke and a song
And they probably sang of love

But as it must the barrier bust
That lay between them and death
It carried away huge rocks and clay
And like lightning stopped their breath.

The men below they didn't know
What made their eardrums hum
But they knew from signs of other times
And they all started off on the run

It was the displacements of air in the tunnels there
But this they knew it was something new
Something that might be their last

With a worried frown they kept on down
Till their way was blocked with coal
But with heroic will their hearts stood still
They eventually reached their goal

They started anew on a way to get through
And sometimes up to their waists
But they helped each other like men and brother
They sure played the game to the last

At last their prayer was answered there
They reached the bottom at last

Their heart was chilled for the place was near filled
With debris from the blast

But like heroes bold they all took hold
Of the lagging sides and top
And they all went ahead like bats from the dead
Till they reached the first safe spot

Of the haulage crew they were but two
Who were saved from death in the muck
By a horse's might from their awful plight
They were dragged from death by sheer pluck

The pluck of these two of the haulage crew
Availed them but little that time
For that awful muck their legs did suck
And pulled them right into the slime

But Happy the horse with tremendous force
Came charging along from chute seven
And each brave boy with his heart full of joy
Knew that 'Happy' was sent from Heaven

They both caught hold of the animal bold
And the horse with all his might
And the boys thought of a song
A song of praise that night

Of all the men who were listed then
They all came out but five
Who were left there still in the heart of hell
They never came out alive

For their bones have been found away under ground
They will never tell the story
Of how that night in their awful plight
God took them all Home to Glory.

* * *

Four stanzas of this poem have been set to music sung by the Romaniuk Family, recorded by Damon Productions and will be released in
1974–5 under the title The Cadomin Mine Disaster.

. . . Mixed the Punch in Washtubs

ALBERT PAULL – 16136–109th St. Edmonton was a Coal
Brancher for just two years and thinks he was able to work in the mine
because he played the saxaphone.

He was born in Broadview, Sask., Sept. 4, 1906 and grew up in
time to try for the scarce jobs of the depression years.

While working on a farm in the Duffield area he made a visit to Edmonton and here met Jim Packard. Jim had a contract for hauling coal at Coal Valley, and thought he might find 'Bert' work. After a few months at Coal Valley, Bert decided to join his brother Reginald who was working further up the line. So in February '34 he moved to Cadomin and stayed in a rooming house that was known as the 'Black Beetle', and ate at the company cookhouse.

Work was scarce but he feels he obtained employment because he could play E flat alto saxaphone. Bert worked for the Cadomin Coal Company Limited through the timber contractor R. A. Craig.

The superintendent, a Scotsman by the name of J. H. McMillan, fostered and conducted a 25-man symphony orchestra.

About ten of these musicians were subsidized wholly by the mine. The other members were miners and Bert says, "When McMillan called an orchestra practice you attended." There was no question. The miner informed his shift boss and went off to practice.

In this year of 1934, there was usually more time to practice than work.

Mr. Paull retains two wage slips – one dated Feb. 15, '34, shows 3 days at $4.45 for a total of $13.35 with 24.48 beside the name R. A. Craig for a total of $37.83. Deductions included .25¢ for sports; $3.00 for hospital, $3.50 for hotel, $23.50 for board and .50¢ for wash-house leaving him a net of $7.38.

The other dated Mar. 1, '34 shows 3 days for $13.35; 2 days for $8.90 for a total of $22.25. Sports took away .25¢; hotel, $2.00; board $16.80 leaving him a net of $3.20.

"They kept us on payroll I'm sure only because we could play instruments. There was the symphony and then there was the dance band section within the symphony. An excellent pianist by the name of Edwards played in both. Two Fraser boys played trumpet, and there was a fellow by the name of Frank Harvey. We held two or three concerts that winter. Bill Smith, a tenor, and Jack Stracken of Edmonton came in as added attractions. How those concerts were appreciated by people!"

Bert remembers fooling around with a trumpet at the rooming house one morning playing a bad parody of the 'Carnival of Venice.' The trumpet belonged to a quiet withdrawn fellow roomer by the name of Norman Fishwick. Norman stood it for as long as he could, then impatiently took the trumpet from Bert and raised it to his lips.

Forty years later Bert said reverently, "It was purely a golden trumpet . . . the tone. It was beautiful."

"It was Norman's turn for practice session that afternoon so I later sneaked the music to Edwards, the pianist. Edwards started to play and Norman joined in. So help me, you could see Edwards come alive. Everyone just froze and listened."

Mr. McMillan had walked in and stood under the balcony of the Cadomin Hall and listened, entranced.

In his broad Scotch he walked in and roared "My gawd, kin ya play like that oul the time?"

Norman looked up, blushed, and said nothing. Bert turned to the superintendent, "He plays like that all the time. He is a gold medalist."

McMillan looked at him and then at the self effacing trumpeter. "You'll play it to-night. That's an order."

Norman did and received encore after encore from an emotional audience.

Two other things stand out in memory during Albert Paull's short time in the mining town. One was the wind.

"When the wind came down the draw in the valley it could blow you off your feet. I remember clinging to the railing of the bridge going over to the cookhouse . . . really hanging on. If there were boxcars standing on the rail crosswise to the wind and if the side door was open they were blown off the siding. It's hard to believe, but it happened and not only once."

Another event he remembers was the giant reception given when the 'Luscar Indians' brought home the provincial hockey championship. Residents from Cadomin, Luscar and Mountain Park attended, Paull among them.

"Do you know they mixed the punch in washtubs? All kinds of it? What a night that was!"

The mining life was not for him, though. He came back to Edmonton in 1935, got married Feb. 19, 1938 and retired Sept. 30, '71 after 35 years with Taylor, Pearson and Carson.

* * *

. . . *Fred Says He was Sick*

AUSTIN JOSEPH HENDERSON left the farm at Colingdon, Alberta when he was 17 years old and went to work in Robb. It was 1927, and he considered himself fortunate when he got on at Lakeside Coals as a car-pusher, receiving wages of $4.45 a day.

Meals were eaten in the cookhouse, open at 7:00 a.m. daily. Albert La Bossiere was the cook and served mammoth meals. "But you made your own bucket lunch. Albert laid out cold meats, cold pork and beef slices, cheeses, fruits, pies, cookies, cakes . . . everything you could think of, and the men made their lunches. The idea was so they wouldn't complain about their dislikes in food. You made your lunch either before or after breakfast."

Joe soon graduated to rope rider and made $5.40 a day for an eight hour shift, six days a week. He worked there till 1928 and made his first move. As it turned out this was to be the first of many such moves, each time on a higher pay scale.

Luscar Coal Mine — Alberta Government Photo

"They were sinking two shafts at Cadomin and I got on as pump-man at $6. a day. The second day there was a man who went on shift at 8:00 a.m. fell down the shaft at noon and got killed. I forget his name. Johnny Braben was in charge of the pumps. At first I stayed with the men, the Black Beetle was one of the hotels . . . then I moved over to Gene Kilbride's. Kay Kilbride had four boarders, and we all worked on the shafts. A lot of the Shaft men were Scandinavians, Finns, Swedes. Would they go at it in the bars! They'd start a brawl that would clean the place out."

"They went down 1,000 feet on the shaft and hit bottom in October. On November 13, 1929 there was an explosion at five minutes to 12:00 noon. My watch was hanging on a nail and it stopped at that time. I got rolled about thirty feet with the concussion but didn't get hurt. Three men were killed, quite a few others burned. Very little damage was done. We had to do some retimbering, that's all.

The General Manager was J. H. MacMillan, Ed Copeland was Mine Manager, one of the pit bosses was Jim Hall . . . then there was Jack Roberts and Tom Carr. There must have been 800 people living in Cadomin at that time. I'd guess there were 250 men working in the mine. The shaft crew was around sixty."

Cadomin worked steadily all year round because they supplied the railroad with coal. When other mines closed for the summer men would seek work elsewhere. Coal Valley and Sterco would often hire extra men during the summer because they were strip mines.

About this time romance entered Joe Henderson's life. He attended a dance at the school in Robb and met Laurette La Bossiere, one of the cook's nine children.

The couple were married in Edmonton in 1931. She was 18, Joe 21. The couple went back to the farm at Collingdon up Athabasca way. In 1935 the family moved back to Robb. Joe found himself president of the mine union, served a term as secretary-treasurer, and was on the negotiating committee. From Robb they left for Mercoal. Joe was hurt here. "I got hit with the trip and was off work for a month. I dived into a manhole and that car came in after me."

At Mercoal work grew slack so the family moved on to Luscar in March of 1940. July 22, 1941 Joe joined the airforce. He was called back to the mines on industrial leave December, 1942 and was discharged October 14, 1943.

"At Luscar Jim Bush and I raised chinchillas," Joe said.

"In 1944 I wrote my Fire Boss papers; in 1945 I wrote my pit boss papers and then went to Mercoal as Pit Boss. I sold my chinchillas to Ray Bosetti when I left for Mercoal."

After a short stint in Mercoal Joe went to Mountain Park. Mrs. Henderson says "We had a huge house in Mountain Park, it had eight rooms and two fireplaces. The company repainted your house every year."

"Rent was $12. a month and $3. for fuel," added Joe.

Once again the Hendersons moved. This time to Cadomin where Joe was to be in charge of the Gregg River operation, about 11 miles out of Cadomin.

"I was getting $585. a month with house and everything free . . . free rent, free fuel and free electricity. The company provided the hospital, all I had taken off my cheque was $3. a month for medical expenses. That was big money."

"I remember driving out to Gregg River after a windstorm. The company supplied me with a jeep. The wind had blown a Mannix garage right across the road, so I had to drive around it."

"I told the cook at Gregg River to feed the railroad crews. They did our switching so it was a reciprocal thing.

Then I went to Cadomin as Senior Pit Boss in the Shaft Mine in 1947."

During this decade Joe trained the crews in safety. "I was Mine Rescue Superintendent at Mountain Park and Cadomin for the Workmen's Compensation Board."

Mrs. Henderson was busily raising her children. Their birthplaces almost tell the story of their moves; Patricia at Athabasca, Herb at Colingdon, Roly in Edmonton, Rosemarie at home in Robb with Dr. T. Moore in attendance, Lloyd at Edmonton, and Dawn at Mountain Park in the hospital. Mrs. Henderson says "I canned everything. Vegetables, the fish Joe caught and the meat he shot. Every few weeks we'd send out to the Alberta Trading Co. for groceries because everything was so high priced there. I never liked the Coal Branch too much."

Payday was every second Friday, and Joe recalls many a poker player would head for a house on the hill to play the weekend away.

"They'd start Friday night, play all night, all Saturday, all through the next night to Sunday. I fired very few men, maybe half a dozen in eight years. If you didn't like the way a man was working you just made it tough for them and they'd quit."

How?

"Oh, you'd take them off the coal and put them timbering. For drinking, I'd say, "Turn your lamp in. Three days at home!" At $25. a day this can hurt. Sure they drank. There was always a handful who missed a couple of days after payweek. They could stay at home two days without a doctor's certificate. Can remember one old fellow who was a pretty good drinker and was off after nearly every payweek. One day he showed up with a note that read:

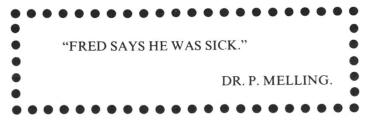

"FRED SAYS HE WAS SICK."

DR. P. MELLING.

"I told Fred he could just go home for another couple of days. He was sick all right. Sick from losing another two days pay. Everybody I caught coming off shift early, I'd dock an hour. But if you've got good men and they're producing, you don't ride them."

Layoff lists were posted in the lamp-room effective on such and such a date, but Cadomin worked steady. "Every six weeks the men were rotated so that everyone got about four turns a year in the pillars where the really big money was made."

Joe said Cadomin was shut down about July, 1952. "The bank manager told me there were many people who had $20,000. in the bank. But these people had worked through the depression steadily. They were making up to $25. a day in the thirties when other people were lucky to make a dollar at other jobs.

"I think Harold Riley was the General Manager when they shut down, then there was Norm Clybourne and Jimmy Docherty. From there I went to Luscar and worked till the end of March, 1953 and the next day started to work for the Provincial Government as Assistant Instructor of Civil Defence."

The Hendersons live in Oliver Place, in Edmonton, their twelfth move during their marriage. Joe is now Assistant Emergency Planning Officer for the Department of Health and Social Development. It's a job that entails driving thousands of miles annually. Due to retire soon, the doctor advises him to take it easy. "That pace is not doing your heart any good."

* * *

. . . *Never Did Find a Trace of George*

H. LLOYD DOUGLAS - by himself. To start with my name is H. Lloyd Douglas, born in Calgary, 1916. My parents came from Quebec and Manitoba to the Crows Nest area of Alberta.

My dad, Stuart Douglas Sr. worked in the mines until he enlisted in the 89th battalion out of Calgary and went overseas in the First World War.

After his return from overseas and a sojourn in Sherness in Southern Alberta we moved to Cadomin in approximately 1921. My Dad was engaged as a driver boss with the Cadomin Coal Co. until his retirement, 1948-49. Two brothers and two sisters comprised our family.

I worked in the mine at Cadomin for my uncle, R. A. Craig in the lumbering business, after taking my schooling at Cadomin. I enlisted in the airforce in the Second World War and saw service overseas in the old country and the far east.

Hunting trip, 1923 near Mountain Park. L. to R. Stewart Douglas, George Taggart, Jack MacMillan, Mr. Clements, Dick Craig.

245

Returning to Cadomin I decided to get my ticket in the mine and ended up with my pit boss ticket, when the bottom fell out of the mining industry.

In 1951 I left Cadomin and came to Edmonton where I am presently employed as a steam engineer for the Government of Alberta.

One incident I recall was the case of George Panek. It seems the crowd George travelled with made him a patsy for supplying the liquor and then kicked him out. Finally one night he decided to rectify things with a twenty-two calibre rifle. One man and wife he caught at home in bed, and wounded the wife. He later shot her brother (who was crippled for life) and another chap in the arm.

The following morning the local R.C.M.P. arrived up at R. A. Craigs lumber camp on the White Horse Creek. They inquired from my cousin and I who were working there at that time if we had seen George, because you could go through that way to Miette Hot Springs by trail.

I thought this was quite amusing at the time and I could not just see a man who thought he had committed murder waking us up to tell us he was going through.

Of course, there were no roads up the branch in those days and they brought up more police and tracking dogs, but never did find a trace of George. Everyone's sympathy seemed to be with George.

The climax of this just happened three or four years back when a former Cadomin resident on a return fishing trip, stumbled on a skeleton off the trail leading to the Little McKenzie creek east of Cadomin, which proved to be George's. He had apparently committed suicide. – H. L. Douglas, R.R. 6, Site 18, Edmonton, Alberta.

Mine horses at Cadomin. You can barely see the leather head coverings the horses were required to wear for protection.

H. L. Douglas

. . . Gave us Two Rooms, Cozy Indeed

VICTOR BAICH — It was in spring of 1939 when I landed on the Coal Branch; Luscar, Alberta was the town. At that time two men were killed through gas in the mine. I do not know their names. I was selling Fuller Brush at the time. My first customer was Mrs. Defossey; she was so nice. In fact all the people at the Coal Branch were very friendly. Mrs. Wm. Kulyk was the second customer, and naturally with the people treating me so well, prompted me to settle there.

That fall I got a job in the mine and became a Coal Brancher, which I was never sorry for or about. The same fall I got married to Miss Annie Leah Croteau of Edson. We had no place to stay, so got permission to fix up the old church, by pulling it along to the new church, which gave us two rooms, cozy indeed. I was so proud and happy. We stayed there till the spring of 1940, then bought Mr. Blair's house on Moonshine Hill. Oh yes, our districts were named. There was that district, also Aristocratic Hill, Shack Town and the Giovinazzo Hill.

Mr. and Mrs. Pat Mahoney were our close neighbours, and they were very good neighbours too. Also we had Mr. and Mrs. Bill Shipka, Mr. and Mrs. Bill Thomas; The Davies, below us, Mrs. and Mrs. Die Davis to the north; Mr. and Mrs. Clarence Peet, Mr. and Mrs. Tom Reese, Mr. and Mrs. Bob Weale etc. Well, many people lived in that area.

My first job was timber packer, later on I became pipe fitter helper to Bill Croft. Soon I became Fire Boss, later on Pit Boss. We all know (at least us Coal Branchers) the demand for coal. We had one mine

Spring of 1942, Vic and Francis Baich — road leading to Mountain Park.

247

After the explosion — No. 5 Mine Firehouse, June 21, 1944. Luscar.　　　　(Baich)

and developed five mines during the war period; two underground and three open pits.

For recreation we had a good hockey team as well as a baseball team. Mr. Bartoff was the manager, played ball and was very good. Mr. Bartoff managed the Luscar Hotel, owned by Mr. Archie Mitchell, which included feeding and boarding at least one hundred and fifty men who worked in the mines. They were mostly single men. In fact I got initiated into mining life by working in that cookhouse. My first task was washing dishes. I remember so well my first week on the job. Mr. Phil Morris came to me and asked me to do his lunch bucket better – apparently I was not doing it properly. He died a few years later and is buried in the Glenwood Cemetery at Edson. Often we visit the cemetary, one reason is because my wife's parents are buried there as well, and of course we visit Mr. Morris's grave too.

Our hockey team was the Luscar Indians and they played in the Allan Cup. Ironically we played Nanaimo Clippers in 1943, with the Clippers beating us. Now we live in Nanaimo and still have the Clippers except they are Jr. A. hockey. The Luscar Indians were coached by Duke Keats of Edmonton, and C. Bartoff was the goal tender.

The Luscarites were very sports minded and that takes us to Ice Carnivals. That was something to see – we used to fill the arena to the rafters – very successful. We hired top notch fancy skaters to teach our children how to skate, then all the town would get together and put on an ice carnival. This went on for years.

Then in 1947 Leduc oil well blew in, and from then on the coal industry went down, while oil went up. The mine closed down. We moved out prior to that time. It was January 20, 1952 when I moved to Daysland, Alberta, which is 87 miles south-east of Edmonton. We stayed there for ten years, then moved to Calgary, where I took on a position as General Manager of the Calgary Diagnostic Laboratories and X-ray. Then we moved to the west coast. We chose Vancouver

LUSCAR COALS LIMITED
INDIVIDUAL PAY SHEET

No. 513

NAME _V. Baich_

OCCUPATION _Fireboss_   PERIOD ENDING

DEC 14 1946

DEDUCTIONS				CONTRACT		COMPANY		
				No.	Hours	Hours	Rate	AMOUNT
Supplies								
Smithing			Sunday					
Rent			Monday			ϒ		
Light	4	55	Tuesday			ϒ		
Water			Wednesday			ϒ		
Coal			Thursday			ϒ		
Wash-house			Friday			ϒ		
Cash			Saturday					
Doctor	1	80	Sunday					
Library		50	Monday			ϒ		
School Tax			Tuesday			ϒ		
Union			Wednesday			ϒ		
Insurance		50	Thursday			ϒ		
Income Tax	13	85	Friday			ϒ		
Dom. U. Insurance			Saturday					
War Savings	12	00						
			TOTAL Company				102	00
Board			TOTAL Contract					
S. & A. Fund	1	00						
			Due - - - - - - - - - - - - - - -				102	00
TOTAL	34	20	Less Deductions - - - - - - - - - - -				34	20
			Net - - - - - - - - - - - - - - - -				67	80

Island, Nanaimo, B.C. This is the Canadian California. We enjoy it immensely.

Victor Baich,
950 Capilano Place
Nanaimo, B.C.

249

... 'Gay' Ladies Would Come in on the Train

MRS. EDITH HICKS – by herself. In 1922 . . . I had never been among miners in my life till my brother – Frederick G. Chapell, Police Magistrate and Justice of the Peace in Cadomin met me, a widow, and my two young sons in Calgary.

Their father, a grand man, was a war casualty, 1914–18, came home and died with TB in a Chesterfield Sanitorium.

My brother asked me if the rooming house over the store in Cadomin would be too rough a job for me to look after. It was rough alright. Mr. Tom Burnett owned the store and my brother, Fred, managed it for him. With a great deal of thought I took the job.

There was a shack on the hillside called 'The Police Station' but my brother often tried the prisoners in my rooms over the store for his convenience. I found it interesting. Later on Fred and Const. Mc-Elroy asked me if I would act as Matron re a woman prisoner, Edna? She had come to Cadomin to hide through stealing money in Drum-heller and stayed with a miner in a Cadomin shack. Well, this man went to buy a lady's hairnet at the store, and that gave Fred the clue to pass on to McElroy.

McElroy, myself and Edna left for the court in Edmonton. I saw her safely in the cell and left to get an appointment with the late Dr. G. Gray for an operation I had to have later for a cyst (internal) and appendicitis.

Mrs. Edith Hicks — 1923 stands in front of the rooming house over T. Burnett's store.

McElroy had a wire waiting for him to get back quick to Mountain Park, there was a serious shooting there, so he said goodbye and got on a boxcar right away.

I was five weeks in the Misericordia Hospital. After I got back, Arthur E. Hicks of Portland, U.S. who was one of the roomers started helping me put coal in the big heaters and take the ashes out. This led to friendship, kindness and love.

My brother foolishly gave up his police position and took the managing of the new hotel (the old one had burned down) much to his regret later and mine. Fred asked me if I could clean those rooms over the hotel (as well as my own) till the janitor arrived from Edmonton.

I loved him too much to refuse and took that job; rough it was and then some. 'Gay' ladies would come in on the train and keep out of sight till I went back to my rooms over the store, then into bed they went to make their haul. Word would come over to me early the next morning and I'd have to get them out. They would try a sob story on me, when it didn't work, they didn't like me any more.

Saturday nights were enjoyable. We enjoyed the dances till the wee hours and the dresses were beautiful. The 'Masons' opened up while we lived there. My dress was black net all covered in black sequins . . . one hundred dollars, in 1922!

I married Arthur Hicks, my second kind and loving husband of 47 years. We were married in Cadomin on March 28th, 1923 by the late Dr. Langfeldt of Edmonton. There were no conveyances to take us to Mr. Bill Locke's home where Mrs. Locke provided us with a lovely supper for close friends. Mr. Locke was running the hotel at that time and a wire came through that the strike was over - all the people went wild. We had been married in Locke's living room and wanted a quiet ceremony. With the strike being over, Bill Locke wouldn't hear of it. We walked by two's over to the Community Hall where most of the people joined in the dance.

Mr. Locke sent big big kegs of beer to the 'shacks' where the roughest of miners batched to keep them away from the dance and fighting.

The roomers treated me more like a sister and were exceptionally generous with wedding gifts to us.

On December 1st, 1923 there was the big fire. This snap of me was taken the day of the big fire. I had just finished all the rooms and was sweeping the wooden sidewalk outside when the late Fred Faulkner shouted, "Hello, Edith" and snapped the picture. The new butcher shop of Burns was opened that day by the late Mr. Fred Henson and his wife Mary. Fortunately they were not in line of the bush fire that got out of hand and swept the rooming house and store. It was terrible. We picked up what we could in our homes and with our children made straight for the washouse, like refugees and stayed there all night.

We four slept on the floor of my brother's place till some miners were leaving, and they sold us their tent which Arthur made into a shack for us. There were no houses to be bought or rented at that time.

There were only 14 of us who had insurance. I grabbed my Hudson seal coat but we lost everything including all our wedding gifts. It was a great loss. Mrs. Benner (later Coupland) a good friend of mine ran the post office which was at the back of the store. Her son Karl Benner writes to me from New Zealand. He and his brother went to school with my boys who are now Cyril Shaw, president of the C.A.A. and past president of the A.M.A. My youngest son F. Kenneth Shaw is a staff inspector of the Edmonton Police Force.

My husband worked at the hotel to help Fred, but in 1925 we decided to leave Cadomin. Arthur was from a farm all his life and didn't like picking rock.

* * *

... Paid All of a Nickel Admission

NICK and ANNIE BLYZNIUK by their daughter Mickey.

Nick and Annie came to Luscar around 1924. Prior to this Nick worked in the mines at Crows Nest Pass and Nordegg. As an immigrant from Europe and a soldier in the Austrian army, he experienced many hardships and was classed an alien upon entry to Canada.

Annie Eleniak was born at Chipman, Alberta. Her uncle, with another man, were the very first Ukrainians to come to Canada.

Nick met Annie at the Calgary Stampede, so the story goes, where he literally 'roped' her in the gaiety of it all. They came to Luscar where three children were born to them. William, now living in Edmonton, married Lorraine Weib and have two girls; Minnie (Mickie) living in Red Deer, married Charles Makofka and have three children, Julie living in Kelowna, B.C. married Morrise Haw and have two boys.

Annie and Nick moved to Edmonton around 1950. She died in 1957, he in 1967.

There was much talent in the small community of Luscar. I recall the Davies' who were Welsh, and like so many of that nationality had excellent voices. During the Second World War, they were instrumental in putting on concerts to raise money for the Red Cross. One such production was Alice in Wonderland, another had a gypsy theme (I still have my costume and tambourine.)

The Mitchell's opened their home to the girls in the community for weekly sessions of knitting afghans for the Red Cross. A Mrs. Duncan Hamilton organized girls into the first C.G.I.T. group there.

There were regular Sunday night movies, no second class type either, where children paid all of a nickel admission. The regulation

Class of 1938 — Luscar.

(Shipka)

size indoor rink was well used by children and adults to say nothing of the nationally known Luscar Indians hockey team.

Most of the town sent someone from the family to wait for the Richmonds to open up the post-office wicket, a social event in itself every Monday, Wednesday and Friday evenings. Can anyone who attended school there ever forget R. J. Hughes who ruled with an iron

Luscar Hotel.

East End of Luscar.

Building the cleaning plant at Luscar   (Shipka)

New Luscar Lookout Tower   (Shipka)

Mt. Luscar   (Shipka)

hand and a wicked shot with chalk, but would often interrupt teaching to drift into lengthy discussions of anything from the evil of taking aspirin to his summer trip to Yellowstone Park.

Competition between Luscar, Cadomin and Mountain Park for champion basketball team or field events was fierce.

Will anyone forget, too, the horror of the mine whistle blasting away to indicate a mine accident.

As I moved out into the world and met people my own age from all over Alberta, I realized how fortunate we really were to have grown up in a town such as Luscar.

Mickey Makofka.

* * *

. . . *Three Possibilities for the Unskilled*

A. PILICHOWSKY by his daughter Rosie Bova – My father Alexandra (Sandy) Pilichowsky (Sandy was a nickname given to my father by a Scotsman) emigrated from the Province of Bukovina, West Ukraine and arrived in Canada in 1911. He settled for a time in Saskatchewan then worked in various coal mines . . . Michele, Edmonton, Brule, Mountain Park, Coalspur and finally coming to Luscar around 1921, moving to Edmonton in 1953. He died of a coronary thrombosis in February, 1957. In Stenen, Sask. he met and married my mother Maria Kurulok in June, 1919. My father and my mother's father were from the same district in West Ukraine. My mother was born in Quebec City, Quebec in June, 1903, where her parents disembarked. Shortly after my mother's birth they continued onward to Saskatchewan where her father homesteaded. In Edmonton, in April, 1959, my mom died of cancer.

Luscar from the road at the Lookout tower.

256

The mining crew at Luscar Collieries Ltd. Early thirties.

In Luscar my parents lived across the small creek from the sulphur spring.

My dad said that when he emigrated to Canada there were three possibilities of earning a living for the unskilled and often illiterate immigrant . . . homesteading, railroading or coalmining. He did not wish to farm and chose mining over railroading as the wages were somewhat higher and there was no travelling involved.

During the depression years when the mines were working one day or less per week, my father sent my mother and my two older brothers and sister to live with her father in Saskatchewan, for almost a year and a half as the little wages he received did not support them all.

Luscar Power House and No. 1 Mine Hoist   (Shipka)

I should like to mention something of Mr. R. J. Hughes' generosity and concern for the continued education of my brother George who was a bright student. During the terrible depression years my brother left school to work in the Luscar Mines. Mr. Hughes begged my father to insist George complete his Grade 12. My father left the decision to my brother who opted for the coalmines.

During Grades 7 to 9 every Friday movies were shown by Mr. Hughes, the school principal. Mr. and Mrs. Hughes retired in Creston, B.C. where they both died. I understand that Mr. Hughes left his estate to the Salvation Army.

Both my brothers served in the Second World War. My brother, George was a gunner on bomber airplanes in the RCAF and brother Bill joined the Navy. My brother Bill was injured when his ship was sunk and my brother George's airplane was shot down.

DATE Oct 19th 32

LUSCAR SKATING AND CURLING RINK

CERTIFICATE No 138

SHARE CERTIFICATE

THIS IS TO CERTIFY that S. Pilichowski **is the owner of** 5 **shares of the above rink, shares of no fixed value. Each share represents one day's work donated to rink or a five dollar subscription to rink.**

The holder of any share or shares will be entitled to one vote per share at all general meetings.

Certificates not transferable except with the consent of the committee.

SEC.-TREAS. J.O. Bush PRESIDENT A. N. Scott

Transfer:

Date .... To .... Sig. Sec.-Treas. ....

Date .... To .... Sig. Sec.-Treas. ....

Date .... To .... Sig. Sec.-Treas. ....

Date .... To .... Sig. Sec.-Treas. ....

Date .... To .... Sig. Sec.-Treas. ....

Date .... To .... Sig. Sec.-Treas. ....

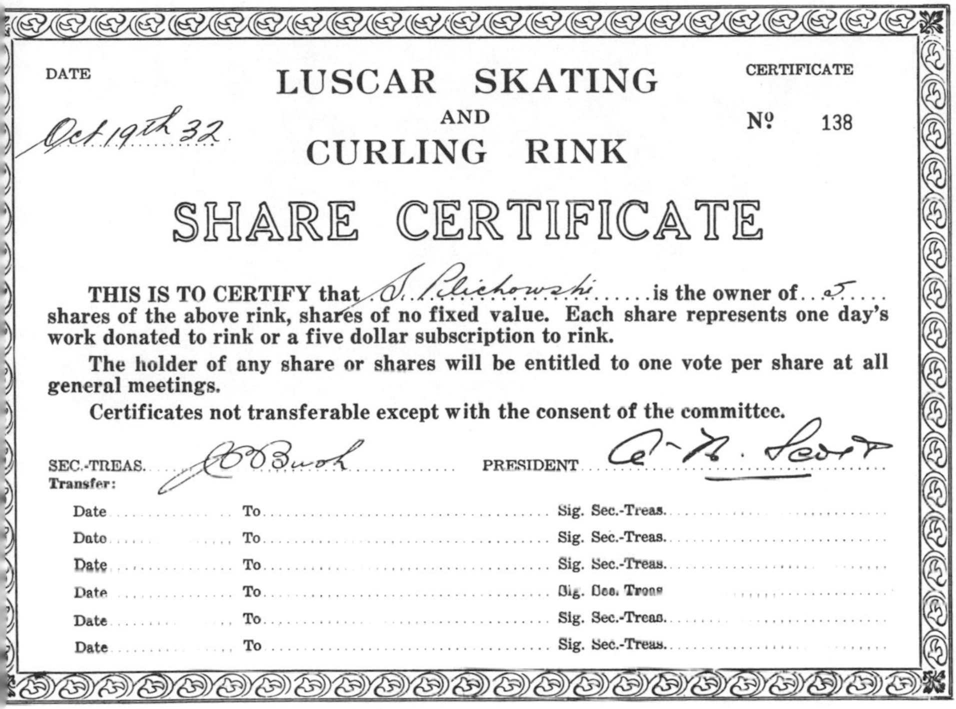

I remember my father saying something about living in tents in Luscar when the mine first opened up. My father was once trapped in a cave-in in January, 1942 and nearly lost his life.

My parents had five children, George Pilichowsky now of Edson; Mrs. Nellie Daniels, Victoria; Bill, Vancouver; Mrs. Patsy Kemp, Golden, B.C. and myself, Mrs. Rose Bovo of Edmonton.

* * *

. . . A Ranger Rode 30 Miles

SILVINO BARUZZINI by himself. I was born March 4, 1927 in Mountain Park and lived there till the underground mine closed in 1948.

My father, John, came from Italy and settled in Mountain Park in 1921 after working in the Crows Nest Pass and other mines.

He went back to Italy in 1922 and got married. My sister Mary was born there in Italy, and they came back to Mountain Park.

My dad worked in the mines till he lost his eyesight in 1944. They left Mountain Park in 1950 and moved to Luscar where my two brothers worked on the strip mine till that mine closed down and then they moved to Edmonton.

Mountain Park Grizzlies
Pete Chiesa, Secondo Baruzzini, Mike Pavich, Eddy Bracko, Mike Black, Able Black, Roy Gould, Cliff Parker, Bill Robertson, Bud Fleck, Isadore Baruzzini.

My dad died in 1957 about four months after my brother Secondo was killed in Canmore, Alberta at the age of 26 when he became entangled in the gears of a power shovel he was operating for Mannix Construction. They are both buried in Edmonton.

My mother went back to Italy in 1961 and died six weeks later of cancer and was buried there. At the time of her death I was on a hunting trip near the headwaters of the Brazeau River, near the Brazeau Lake, with four Americans. A forest ranger rode 30 miles from the White Goat River to notify me that my mother had died.

Barbara Baruzzini and Louise Swick taken at Whitehorse Falls about 5 miles from the Park on the way to Cadomin.

All our family was born in Mountain Park outside of my oldest sister Mary. Her husband Robert Watson died in June, 1973 and she lives in Edmonton.

Next is Zita, married to Donald Gilchrest and she is in Ottawa. Then there is myself, then Dora, now Mrs. Art Bredo. Isidor, a truck driver for C.P. Transport; Loretta (Mrs. Milton Morrison); Caroline, Mrs. George McNally, and they all live in Edmonton.

We used to meet the train every Monday, Wednesday and Friday as kids, then go for a three mile walk and think nothing of it. We would often swim in the pond behind Miner's Roof in the summer, though it was no higher than your knees.

Lucio Faccinutti and friends bag their quota of mountain sheep.

Mountain Park

261

I started work underground at the age of 17 and worked till the mine closed. I remember the Summit – sitting there drinking milkshakes and playing pool in the basement. There was a room in the back and we played blackjack . . . you name it. Of course this was after we had all started to work for a living.

What we used to do is gamble all night, start out Friday night and gamble all through Saturday and Sunday and get home in time for work Monday. We'd shoot crap – go over to the hotel for breakfast, and then go back and keep on gambling.

I got married to a girl from Edmonton and went to work in the mines in Nordegg till they closed down in 1955. I worked on construction projects for a couple of years then started with the Alberta Liquor Control Board and am still there, Oct. 1, 1973.

The things I remember best are when I was going to school. We lived about one mile from school and walked there and back every day, and it didn't seem to bother us at that time.

The skating rink was about 100 yards from our house so we went skating every night or sleigh riding. The thing I really miss about living in Mountain Park is the nice scenery.

I spent three weeks up the Branch this year with my sons, John and Robert. We stayed in Cadomin at Barbara McMillan's house. Her husband was fire boss at Mountain Park; I used to work for him.

We've been going up there fishing, hiking, shooting and drinking for the last six years. This year we got close to a hundred Rainbow, Speckled trout, Eastern Brook in the three weeks we were there. We fished the McLeod, Cardinal River, Ruby Creek, Flapjack Creek, Luscar Creek and others.

I can remember going to Nordegg from Mountain Park by horseback – 81 miles as the crow flies.

I like living in Edmonton but for some reason whenever a few of us get together from the Coal Branch it seems we all have something in common and it's hard to change.

Silvino Baruzzini
13328 Fort Rd.
Edmonton, Alberta.

. . . Train Backed Up All the Way to Mountain Park

TERESA GIRARDI (nee Ciciarelli) by herself — As I Remember the Coal Branch.

I was eight years old when I first saw the Coal Branch. At that time there was only Mountain Park – no Cadomin, Luscar, Sterco or Robb.

262

It was in 1917–18 that we left Blairmore in the Crow's Nest Pass to go to Mountain Park. My father had left the Crows Nest Pass to take a foreman's job as switch back, and round table builder for the railroad engines to turn around at Mountain Park and go back to Edson.

When father sent for us after he had a house for the family, mother, myself, three sisters and baby brother left Blairmore and started out to our new home.

The train trip was really something to remember. From Blairmore to Edmonton where dad met us was not too bad, but from Edson to Mountain Park was terrible. It took one day and one night to go from Edson to Mountain Park. The train, it must be a museum coach now – old wooden coach, wooden slat seats, coal oil lamps nailed to brackets on coach walls, and an old wood and coal stove for heat. If you wanted air in the coach, the brakeman would come along with a long handled stick with a hook on the end to open the vent in top of the coach. I won't forget that as I still have the scar from one of the vent windows which was jerked too hard, fell out and crashed down and the glass cut my arm.

Well we finally arrived and I can still see the two rows of houses, one two storey house and a one storey – one after the other all painted white and trimmed in green. We got settled and mother asked dad where the water tap was; he said the water man comes two times a week and you get it in these two barrels.

Well things went along ok – and I was settled in the school, a one room school house with long desks and bench which seated four children to each desk. The classroom was heated by a big potbellied stove stuck in the centre of the room, but I guess I got my start in the 3 R's.

There were no churches at that time, but I remember Father Louis saying mass in our front room early in the morning and the friends and neighbors coming to mass. We didn't have mass regular in those

days, just whenever Father Louis made it to Mountain Park. He walked hundreds of miles in his lifetime to bring God to all the people from Edson to Mountain Park. He was called the Saint of the Coal Branch. He treated everyone alike and was revered by everyone too.

I also remember that one day in 1918 there was a picnic to be held at Coalspur. There was a special train to take the miners and their families, so everyone packed a lunch and the train was packed. Everything was going along ok when all of a sudden the train stopped. There had been a rock slide up ahead, and the track was covered, so all the men got off the train to clear track. By the time the track was cleared it was too late to make it to Coalspur, so the train backed all the way back to Mountain Park and we had our picnic on the train.

Well we didn't stay at Mountain Park very long – two years, as the climate was too high for mother. Dad went to Edson and got work with the CN as boiler maker's helper. Part of my family is still there, that is two brothers and one sister as mother and dad have both passed away.

I took all my schooling in Edson, right through Grade 12.

While I was on holiday at the Coal Branch I first met my husband, and after a short courtship we were married in Edson in 1927. After our marriage we made our home at Luscar where my husband was employed as miner. We built a nice comfortable home at Luscar and it wasn't long before we had our first child. Our three children were born at Luscar.

We enjoyed our seven years at Luscar, and then my husband decided to go back to Cadomin, his old stamping grounds, and we built a home there. The children left, and Dad and I stayed on at Cadomin. We enjoyed curling, horseback riding, hunting and fishing. I guess if we hadn't had the mine disaster, and the work got slack and slacker until the mine closed down we would still be there. We loved the Coal Branch and when I talk about the Coal Branch I still call it home.

When the mines closed down and we had to leave, it was a feeling too hard to describe – like losing a good true friend. I think perhaps you understand.

I am now living at Creston, B.C.

Teresa Girardi, Box 895
Creston, B.C.

Mountain Park Closure

by W. Tommy Gates – U.M.W.A. Mountain Park Local Union, Sec. Treas.

UNDERGROUND – How well I remember the shut down of underground operations on April 9th, 1949. This was Saturday pay day and all underground employees received a notice in their pay envelopes

MOUNTAIN PARK COALS LIMITED
INDIVIDUAL PAY SHEET   No. *317*

NAME .... *W Gates*

OCCUPATION .... *Carp*   PERIOD *17-31-1/49*

DEDUCTIONS			Date	Contract		COMPANY			A	I	8	M
				Hours	Rate	Hours	Rate	Amount				
			S				11⁰⁵					
			M									
			T									
			W									
Income Tax	1	91	T									
Dom. U. Insurance		54	F									
Smithing			S									
Labor												
Supplies			S									
Cash			M									
Coal	6	20	T									
Rent			W									
Light	5	=	T									
Light Tax			F									
Water			S									
Arrears			TOTALS			9¾		104 95				
Wash-house		50	Overtime									
Doctor	2	,										
Club		50										
Arena												
Union												
Life Insurance												
Room												
Board												
Sw.												
			Gross Earnings – – – – – – –									
			Deductions – – – – – – –			16	95					
TOTAL			Net Earnings – – – – – – –			88	⁼					

advising them that their services were no longer required. They were
also advised to come back Monday morning the 11th to get out their
tools.

The shut down came very suddenly. We had no inkling of it until
less than a week before it happened. We had had a strike of two

The library at Mountain Park.

months duration the previous year and most of the workmen had hardly recovered from the effects of that strike.

All laid off workmen had to come to me at the Union Office to get their transfer cards and many of them were in dire circumstances. Mountain Park being the first to close down the government had made no provision for moving them out as they did in later mine closures.

However, somehow, some way they managed to overcome their difficulties and on meeting many of them in later years it was not such a disaster as it appeared to be at that time.

STRIP MINE CLOSURE

The strip mine operation closed down the following year 1950 on the 22nd of June. It was not such a shock as the closing of the underground. The mine operation during the winter had been very unproductive and the most of us could see the writing on the wall.

The major problem on this occasion was the June 21st flood which washed out both the highway and the railway. We were isolated for about a month then the railway resumed operation, the highway was made passable by the company a short time later.

The shock of both these shutdowns was softened somewhat by the ability of Luscar Coals to absorb quite a number of the laid off employees, but the relief was of short duration as Luscar itself closed down about four years later.

DISPOSAL OF COMMUNITY EFFECTS

I believe Mountain Park was the only town on the Coal Branch to make an effort to dispose of community effects consisting of a modern

X-Ray machine and much other valuable equipment necessary for the operation of a small hospital.

We had also the arena equipment consisting mostly of curling stones and other items necessary for winter sports. We also had some cash on hand left over from payroll deductions for community projects.

The Mine Manager, Mr. Don McKinnon and company accountant, Mr. Vic Riendeau worked out a plan whereby in conjunction with the local union we would sell these assets and divide the proceeds among those workers who were still on the payroll at the time of the strip mine closure.

The plan was that when all sales were completed, the money collected, the total sum would be divided by the total number of years of service by all employees and each employee would receive so much for each year of service.

I think it worked out around $2.50 per year, therefore an employee with ten years service would receive $25.00. It was much better than just walking out and leaving it.

I understand some people who had been forced to leave earlier were disgruntled because they did not share in the division of this money; but had we tried to locate them all and include them in the jackpot there would have been nothing for anyone.

MOUNTAIN PARK SERVICE MEN Ivan Donkin; George Bryson, Harry Dawes; Henry Forgie; Sandy MacLeod; Pete Lintross; Coventry Fleck; Thomas Fleck; Robert Fleck; John Fleck; James Fleck; Robert Todd; George Oakley; George Barnes; Bill Stevenson; Tom Stevenson; Harry Savage; Bill Martin; Bob Watson; Jim Watson; Bill Shirey; Tom Davies; Mel Price; Nino Chiesa; Gus Snyder; Paul Chomin; Stan Kwasney; Bill Harrison; Dunc McLeod; Laughlin Cook; Tom Gates.

I am sure all of the service men mentioned here and others that I may have missed have never forgotten the tireless efforts of the Mountain Park Knitting Club on their behalf – the many parcels of cigarettes and other items we received during the war years and the wonderful welcome reception we received at the end of the war.

I do not remember the names of all the ladies who participated in this effort but it was organized and directed by Mrs. Walter Talbot. We will have to extend our appreciation through her. Thank you Mrs. Talbot and all of the above mentioned ladies.

Signed on behalf of Mountain Park Servicemen.

W. Gates (Tommy) 13507–70 St.
Edmonton, Alta.

... Demolition Crew Arrived in the Spring

WILFRED (TOMMY) GATES — I was born at River Hebert, N.S. on July 25, 1904 and grew up and went to school there. I was christened Wilfred, but because of a resemblance to my grandfather soon acquired the nickname of Tommy. That nickname has followed me all my life. Very few people know otherwise.

Because of economic conditions I had to leave school at the age of fifteen in 1919 and went to work underground. I left Nova Scotia in 1925 and came west on a harvest excursion train in August of that year. The harvest trains were a yearly event until the last one in 1927.

After the harvest I went to work at Saunders in the Nordegg area and stayed until spring, then went out to Vancouver and found employment on a construction job. The next few years I worked on various construction jobs and at mines in the Crows Nest Pass and Drumheller areas. I was at Wayne in the Drumheller district when the depression started. It kept gradually getting worse until by 1935, work was nonexistent. Family allowances, unemployment insurance and welfare benefits so common now were years in the future at that time.

Conditions being what they were, three of us, Jim Davies, Jack Peebles and myself decided to look elsewhere. We boarded a freight train at Drumheller and struck out for the goldfields of Northern Ontario. Riding the freights was the accepted method of travel in those days; very few people could afford railway or bus fare. This was the middle of May and still quite cold at night. As for sleeping accomodation we bedded down in a straw stack near the rails. They were quite numerous on the prairies before the combines appeared.

We got as far as Winnipeg and learned that the Ontario mines were all closing down, so we headed west again. I had known Mr. Pascoe the Mine Manager at Mountain Park, at Saunders ten years previously, so decided to try my luck there. Jack and Jim had nowhere else to go so they came along as well.

We had less than fifteen dollars when we left Drumheller, so money was pretty scarce by this time. We arrived at Mountain Park, May 22nd at about 9:00 p.m. We were tired, dirty, hungry and broke. Our first objective was to find the washouse and get cleaned up. This accomplished we took a walk to the power plant where we soon got acquainted with the four firemen on duty, particularly Mr. Bill Shirey.

About the first thing he asked was, "Are you hungry? When did you eat last?"

On being assured that we were indeed hungry he advised us to wait for him at the washouse until he came off shift and he would take care of that problem. We did that and went home with him at midnight

268

where Mrs. Shirey cooked up a wonderful meal of bacon and eggs. This was followed by a generous helping of Bill's home brew. Many former residents of Mountain Park can testify as to the potency of this liquid refreshment. By this time we had played a few games of crib, we had become very well acquainted. Bill was a very ardent crib player.

We spent the rest of the night at the washouse going to the office at 8:00 a.m. and being told to come back at 4:00 p.m. We met two old friends coming off the night shift, Eilvio Tona and Rod McDougal. Needless to say we did not miss any more meals, they took care of that. We went back to the office at 4:00 p.m. and met Mr. Pascoe, General Manager and Mr. Dutton, pit boss. The outcome of that meeting was the three of us were hired.

I worked at Mountain Park until June, 1940 when I joined the Armed Forces, South Alberta Regiment. Jim Davies died that year leaving his wife Grace and two children, Bill and Marion. Bill and Marion are both married now. Bill is employed by the Provincial Government and is living in West Edmonton with his wife and three children; Marion lives at Schuler with her husband Doug Robins and family of four boys. Doug is employed by North Canadian Oil Ltd.

I married Grace Davies in May, 1941 and went overseas the following month. I had transferred to the Royal Canadian Engineers, 3rd Div. and remained with them for the duration of my military service returning home in 1945.

Grace had moved to Edmonton and worked at the Macdonald Hotel while I was away. However I went back to Mountain Park in Jan. 1946 and the family moved up shortly after that. I was employed as Mine Carpenter until they shut down in 1950. After the mine closure I was kept on as Caretaker with various duties associated with plant disposal.

Two other families remained at Mountain Park during the winter of 1950-51. Mr. Angus Crawford and family (Forest Ranger) and Mr. Archie Emblau and family, unemployed miner. However they both moved to Cadomin and Luscar respectively in 1951.

The first year after the mine closure was a busy one. The first job was to put a fence around the strip mines, East and West sides. For fenceposts, the blacksmith cut small rails into six foot lengths and welded a hook on each post about three feet above ground level. There was an abundance of old steel cable laying around which we hung on the hooks; a single strand was sufficient. The purpose of the fence was to prevent wild animals and stray horses from wandering into the pits which soon filled with water. This job was done while we still had a small work force.

Another major job was making and attaching shutters to the windows and doors on all company buildings, hotel, houses, barn, office,

269

garage etc. There were many other smaller jobs that had to be done before winter set in.

By this time the company had advertised for sale all equipment that they were not taking to Luscar, and prospective buyers were beginning to come in. I had a direct line to Luscar and was in touch with the office at all times. This was absolutely necessary in order to relay and receive information in regard to heavy equipment such as mine hoists, electric motors, power plant equipment, etc.

Before the work crew left we had moved into an official's house. These houses were quite large, four bedrooms, kitchen, living room and bathroom, a large basement and furnace. We had about twenty tons of coal put into the basement so there was no shortage of fuel and also had room for the car.

It was a very busy time for Grace as we had arranged with the company to provide catering services for their customers. She is an excellent cook and seems to thrive on hard work. The job would not have been possible without her. We usually knew in advance when customers were coming.

The water line had frozen by mid September. After that I hauled water from the river at the office bridge using the company jeep and a stone boat. I also kept the Emblau family supplied with water as they had no means of hauling their own. The official houses were serviced by septic tank.

All housework had to be done by hand as we were without electric power. Grace still had her old wash board.

By this time it was hunting season and we had many visitors, friends from the Sangudo, Mayerthorpe area, ex-Coal Branch residents and others. Game seemed to be plentiful as the most of them got something, usually an elk. After the hunting season was over it became quiet and I had time to do some work for myself. I had bought the snow shed over the outside Mine track (about ¾ of a mile in length); the trestle bridge over the McLeod River and some smaller buildings. The bridge was constructed of square timber 10″ × 10″ and 9″ × 12″ hanging up to forty-four feet in length, plus bracing and decking material. It was all fir timber. I hired my stepson Bill Davies to help demolish the bridge. That was during the summer of 1951. I sold the timber on the Coal Branch, one carload to Bryan Mt. Collieries at Robb, Mile 32. They were constructing a trestle at that time.

Back to the fall of 1950. I was working all my spare time demolishing the snow shed. The company had sold all their buildings by this time to the Adby Demolition Co. of Edmonton, but they were unable to do demolition work until the following spring. They had also sold the power house boilers to the Northwest Brewing Co. in late November. A working crew of thirteen were coming up immediately to get them out. This was more work for Grace as they were to board with us. For sleeping accomodation the company provided beds and bed clothing. I set the beds up in the Mine Office and provided heat with a large pot bellied heater taken from the Library. It was quite comfortable with ample supplies of fuel and water. This crew boarded with us for more than two months just going out for the Christmas holidays. They were a cheerful bunch and we enjoyed their stay.

We thought Christmas would be a quiet affair but it was just the opposite. The house was full, the two families still in town, the station agent and his family and a number from Cadomin and Luscar. I distinctly remember the Hermans and Hendersons.

The rest of the winter passed quietly. I had time for my own work. The demolition crew arrived in the early spring. They had their own living accomodation, cook house, etc. so we did not see too much of them.

We still had a lot of buyers coming all through 1951. By the end of the year most of the major items had been sold. We still had a lot of visitors, mostly farmers. I had a lot of corrugated iron from the snow shed and they were buying it as fast as I could tear it down, and using it mostly for implement sheds. Lumber was also still in short supply and easily sold.

Time passed quickly. The second winter came and went. I still had a lot of work to do and did not get it all cleared up until September, 1952. By this time the demolition company was about finished and most of the coal company material had been disposed of.

I came out to Edmonton in early October and bought a small acreage with a house just partially completed. I had shipped in two carloads of lumber, therefore an acreage was a necessity. I completed the house and eventually disposed of the lumber, and then went to work for a large house construction company. I stayed on that job for just about nine years, then had to give it up because of a health problem. I finished my working years on a caretaking job and am now semi-retired. We are still living in our original home in the Delwood area, North Edmonton. T. Gates.

. . . *This Kid Running the Store'*

ARTHUR WILLIAM LEONARD, born in Edmonton, May 6, 1909 started his merchandising career early. Safeway opened its first store in Edmonton in 1928, and he worked there. In 1929 he went to Luscar to work for Walter Knight at the Luscar Mercantile.

Residents of Luscar were overjoyed to have him. Not because he was a personable young man, but because he could play clarinet, and the Luscar Collieries Silver Band desperately needed someone for the woodwind section so they could enter the competition at the Edmonton Exhibition. The band was comprised of a goodly number of

Welshmen who were employed by the mine for the dual purpose of working in the mine and playing in the band . . . "neither was I as talented as the Welsh ones but they needed me in the worst way." said Art.

Art tired of the limited social life available in the mining camp so came back to Edmonton and worked at the 95th St. and 114th Ave. Safeway. Mr. Harry Maddison was divisional manager for Safeway for Northern Alberta and Arts says, "I married the boss's daughter." Iris Ruth Maddison was a stenographer for Safeway, and the couple married June 27, 1933. Soon after Art was transferred to Wilkie, Saskatchewan as manager. The following year Art received a phone call from his old employer Walter Knight, "I've just bought the Mountain Park Mercantile. Do you want to run it?"

The offer was good. $140. a month plus living quarters in comparison to his present $27 a week gross. They decided to go, but as Iris was due to have her first child, she would remain behind. Soon after Art left, Iris was taken to hospital in the covered wagon kept warm by a coal and wood heater and provided courtesy of the doctor. Here on Dec. 28, Dennis Arthur was born, with the maternity charges of $68. being paid in cash, much to the delight of the hospital sisters who were hurdling the depression era of non or slow payments.

The baby had contracted impetigo in hospital so Iris stayed with her mother-in-law Mrs. Jessie Florence Leonard in Edmonton for a time till it cleared. The trio left for the two day journey to Mountain Park – overnight in Edson and the slow ride to the Park.

Iris was pleased with the spacious living quarters above the large building that was the Mountain Park Mercantile. The building had been a project of an unsuccessful co-operative venture and was owned by the mine, and rented to Mr. Knight.

Bill Laughton, Jim Docherty, Art Leonard, Em Wagner, Tom Seaton, Ellio Bello. Early staff of the Mountain Park Mercantile.

Interior of the Mountain Park Mercantile Bill Laughton, butcher, Tom Seaton, groceries clerks Ellio Bello, Em Wagner.

At the falls down by Craigs Camp. Agnes Farley and Iris Leonard, 1935.

Iris arrived February 5th and that first night went to bed in a building surrounded by deep drifts of snow. She awoke to a building surrounded by water. A chinook had visited the area through the night, and she asked her husband when the next train left for the city.

"It flooded every time there was a chinook, and it stopped bothering me, but that first week – no way did I want to live on an island."

Art was having problems too. Most of the staff were far senior in years and here was this manager, 'this kid running the store.' However it wasn't long before cordiality existed with the staff, then Maude

273

Beardsly, bookkeeper; Tom Seaton, manager of the grocery department; Jim Docherty drygoods; the butcher, Bill Laughton and Len Dickhout, errand and delivery boy.

The supply situation could be difficult with trains only three days a week. Heated rail cars were unavailable on the branch line so canned goods had to be purchased in the fall before danger of freezing along the line. Art ordered to fill a box car and stored all in the huge basement. Chinooks and springtime brought another problem; the basement flooded and paper goods floated about.

Because of the ordering procedures and supply, there was always a shortage of green stuff. "Turnips and carrots were great, but lettuce and celery were hard to come by."

Art soon learned to order vast quantities of snuff. "Miners weren't allowed to smoke in the mine and they chewed a helluva lot of snuff."

Miners had charge accounts at the mercantile but if as sometimes happened there was no snuff available they could pay for it at the confectionery run by Bill Kitch or the cafe run by Suie and Tuie.

In later years, "We had $10,000 or $12,000 on the books any day of the year, but we had power of attorney and could deduct it off their pay cheques. However, inevitably you got involved with people's problems. A miner would come in and say, "I just sent the wife to hospital. Could you let it go this payday?" Sometimes you wouldn't do things in a very business like manner. In the early days, sometimes the deductions would eat up the gross.

The Leonards soon found themselves caught up in an active social life. Bridge was a popular game and the library a social centre that saw many games played, while bridge clubs abounded.

Art played socially with Joe Dutton, the Mine Manager, Tom Davis, Sec. U.M.W.A. and Charlie Brown who was office manager prior to Vic Riendeau's time. Any activity on the coal branch was done in a fiercely competitive spirit and bridge was no exception. The four played bridge for years "despite radically different views. Two bucks was a lot of money in that time – would you believe that at least once a week we'd ask for a decision on a particular hand?"

The queries were mailed off to Eli Culbertson in New York, (an early bridge authority), and the quartet would impatiently wait for an answer.

Visitors to the Park sometimes found that an overnight stay developed into a much longer period. A delegation of O.O.R.P. ladies had their short visit elongated to ten days when the railroad washed out. Billeted at various homes, hostesses found that the food situation could become a strain. Art at the time found the situation quite delightful. When someone would come in and order hamburger he was for the first time able to say, "You'll take liver because that's all there is."

This was the flapper era and hairstyles for women were short. For Iris a haircut meant an eight mile walk to Cadomin to the hairdresser.

"We used to enjoy it. We'd walk the tracks to get there, and catch the train back."

"You banked by mail to Edson and in later years you could go to the dentist in Cadomin."

The school, hotel, Leonard's suite and the official's houses had running water and indoor plumbing, but the Leonards found painting 'at least once a year' a necessity because of the coal dust.

"The cleaning plant created a lot of coal dust and coal didn't seem to burn without a greasy film covering everything."

In all sports, Mrs. Leonard says, "They played to the letter of the law. If you curled, were stuck in a snowdrift and were five minutes late, you lost."

An inter-town competition would often see a race of the young men from a point in the town to the top of Mt. Harris and back. "Because of the thin altitude it was quite a feat."

Hockey was fiercely competitive too. "If Luscar or Cadomin had a final game with an outside team, they'd contrive to have the game played on Mountain Park ice as a neutral area. You'd see Calgary players for instance, rush up the ice once and because of the high altitude their tongues were hanging out. I really didn't think that was too fair," reminisced Art.

Patricia Anne was born December 16, 1937 at the Leonard suite with Dr. P. Melling, the mine doctor and a nurse, Agnes Farley in attendance. By this time Iris said, "I loved the doctor, I loved the nurse, I loved Mountain Park and wouldn't have left for anything."

Mary Anne was born October 4, 1939 with the same doctor and a Miss Ford in attendance.

Because of the high altitude Dr. Melling advised that children should be taken out of the Park periodically, so every summer Iris would pack up the family and take them to Seba Beach for the summer.

While there were roads of a sort between the camps, there was none 'out' to Edson. So residents would ship their car by rail from Coalspur to Edson for a fee of $76.00 This in proportion to salaries was extremely costly so Leonards and John Bulet, the Pit Boss in the mine came to an agreement whereby one would ship his car out, the other would arrange to take holidays immediately after, and use the car 'out' while the other would use the car remaining.

Christianity was really practiced. "Congregations were small so everybody worked for everybody's church."

In 1945, Walter Knight's son Hugh, arrived at the Park. Art couldn't quite see how two men could manage one store so approached Walter Knight with "I'd like to own a store of my own, but haven't got the money. Would you help?"

Knight agreed and as it turned out the move was fortuitous for the Leonards, as the mines closed in '49 and '50.

275

After researching several stores Art Leonard became the owner of the Buy-Rite Store in Edson.

Here Bryan was born, March 19th, 1952 followed by Bruce who was born July 4, 1954.

In June of 1966 Bruce was playing with friends at an abandoned sand pit in Tollerton when the sand caved in. Chief Constable John Macdonald at Edson was busy directing traffic at Glenwood Cemetery for the funeral of James C. Ross[32] when news of the accident came. Jim, a friend of the chief, had died suddenly of a heart attack while racing his daughters up a hill on a camping trip near Rocky Mountain House. Now John left the cemetery and rushed to Tollerton, a short distance away, but found that it was too late to save the son of another friend.

Art Leonard became president of Alberta Grocers Wholesale in 1960 which then had a membership of 37 stores. In 1970 he retired from that position because one had to be an active retailer to retain the position and Art had sold the business to a long-time friend and employee, Nino Chiesa, and had ostensibly retired.

However the Board of Alberta Grocers had asked Art Leonard to research a good insurance plan for employees which he did. Then someone was needed to look after the plan, so Art, presumably retired, travels 23,000 miles a year visiting 185 member stores as Manager of C.B.T. Consultants (Alberta) Ltd.

The Leonards live at 63 Rosewood Drive in Sherwood Park, sharing a home with their daughter Pat, now Mrs. Terence Curry and visit daughter 'Mickey' whose husband Dr. John Utendale is on staff of Washington State College. Son Dennis is president of Leonard, Hurst and Miller in Edmonton and Bryan is an employee of Jean Joints.

* * *

. . . Mule Had More Experience Than I Did

CLAUDE ROOSEVELT HELLEKSON was born in South Dakota in 1904. In 1910 the Hellekson family was part of the surge of American migrants to Canada and they came to Holden, Alta. The spring of 1913 the family moved to Edson and Claude's father took up a homestead 5½ miles north of Edson. The mother objected to filing a homestead before the snow was out and she proved right. The land was muskeg. The family moved by covered wagon to a claim at Hattonford. Here the Beaver Meadow School in the Poison Creek District was closed for lack of funds. Because of the children the family moved to McLeod Valley in 1917, then to Derby and then to Mahaska in 1920.

[32] My husband

Claude at 18, decided it was time he left the farm so headed for the mine at Mountain Park in 1922. Here he almost immediately ran into two miners who knew the family. The tow-headed youth was advised, "Go back home. This is a rough place, no place for you to work."

Claude, young and naive though he was, fell in love with the mountains and decided to stay.

He said he made his first mistake right away. "Ray Mustard was the guide there and offered me a job. I thought that would be fine but the next morning Bill Robinson said, "Come to work (in the mine) at midnight. So I did and I've been sorry ever since."

The second night of his employment there was a cave-in, "and I was so scared. Kelly Eccleson and Jack Appleton had advised that if anything went wrong to go up. So I went down. Someone was shouting, "Where's that blonde kid?" They found me, "What the bloody hell are you doing? Go up."

"I had never seen a man hurt before, and here was Peterson the fireboss, his head and body flattened. Frenchy (he was a good hockey player) was laying beside him and his leg was pinned under the same debris. They said, "Are you going to be sick?" I said, "No, no. We got them free, and when we lifted Peterson's body it was like pulp, as if there were no bones in him." The C-West entry was abandoned then.

After that beginning, 'Blondie' as Claude was soon called, learned more about mining with the aid of the older miners who delighted in the initiation.

NO ROAD painted in red on a wide plank and nailed across an entry signified there was gas in the tunnel that hadn't been cleaned out. The 'braddish' man funneled the entrances with burlap to regulate the air. Air is drawn out of a mine and the fan house blows fresh air into a mine. Claude was told to head for the mine Rescue Car near the entrance where there was facilities to help if he ever ran into gas, "as the gas came up on you quick and easy."

The miners decided that 'Blondie' should visit an abandoned mine shaft. Thinking this all was part of the learning process Blondie agreed.

"That abandoned shaft was the most gruesome thing I've ever seen. Men's droppings . . . any organic matter, had mould inches high."

Claude decided he would like to be a driver and approached the pit boss with his request.

"Ever handle a horse before, Blondie?" Claude was asked. "Oh, yes."

"How about a mule?"

"Nope – never seen a mule." Claude replied but quite sure within himself that there really wasn't all that much of a difference.

"Okay, work on Level 4 to-day."

Claude went down to Level 4, was briefed quickly, and was told to walk between the mule and the track.

"If you walk on the other side of him that mule will squeeze you up against that tunnel wall, stand there and bray."

Claude set his lunchbucket aside and went to work. He figured he was doing just fine. Then came lunchbreak, and Claude went for his lunch bucket, but it was empty.

"What's the matter Blondie?" the men asked quietly, chewing on their lunches.

Claude explained in bewilderment that his lunch was gone.

The men enjoyed his discomforture, but after some chuckling they gave Claude a bit of lunch each had saved. He was informed that the mule could get into any lunchbucket left about and it was to be carefully hidden if he wanted to eat his lunch before the mule did. "That mule can open any lunchbucket."

The men asked Claude to get another car ready shortly before the shifts end. Despite all his exhortations Claude couldn't get the mule to move. The men watched in amusement and finally Claude gave up. "That mule had more experience than I did. He knew exactly what time was quitting time. At the end of the week he wouldn't go back to the stall, but started up, just like he knew that mine regulations stated he had to go out in the air every week."

Claude stayed in the Mountain Park annex paying $51. a month for board and room. As rope rider's helper he made $6.88 a day and as a spike team driver $8.01 a day.

"At Mountain Park you walked up to the bar and stood up and drank. Tex Byers had his barber chair in the middle of it, to one side there was a flute table and on the other a snooker table. They gambled upstairs of the Chinaman's, but I didn't gamble. There were a lot of stills out of Mountain Park and Cadomin. The nearest policeman to Mountain Park was McElroy and he was stationed at Coalspur. McElroy would give anyone a very good chance to get away."

"Can remember once when Tom Roome, a kid I used to run with said, "Let's go down and see what McElroy is up to. He's meeting the train. McElroy deputized some fellow standing near him and when the train came in, a big well dressed fellow stepped off carrying two big suitcases. McElroy said, "Would you open your suitcases please?" He did after a bit, and there was two suitcases plumb full of whiskey laid out just like sardines."

"Mountain Park was a rugged little town. Kids raised in a mining town, they learn to talk tough. The kids used to hitch their sleighs to the waterwagon, but when one of them got hurt the company made a new regulation that it wasn't to be done anymore. You should have heard their language, when the waterwagon driver told them to lay off"

Claude heard that Hood's who owned a store at Leyland wanted someone to learn to run the store and eventually work their way up to managing. Claude went to Cadomin, but by the time he got there, another young man had obtained the position so Claude applied for work in the Cadomin mine.

Shortly after starting as a timber helper, he was waiting for some timbers when a man in riding britches approached. "What the hell do you think you're doing?" the man asked. Claude, sitting down, explained he was waiting for some timbers. The foreman in exasperation told him he had been talking to McMillan the Mine Superintendent and that if he ever came across him again, not to just sit there for christ's sake, but work!

Claude says his first experience with the Cadomin wind was while he was visiting Hoods at the Leyland store. They urged him to stay overnight, but Claude started off for Cadomin, about a mile away. Fighting the wind, he gave up about a third of the way and returned to the store to spend the night. "That's the first time I've ever seen chunks of coal and stone flying in the air."

Cadomin residents when in close proximity to the river perched their privies near the river's edge. The next day a resident told Claude that he looked out his window during the height of the storm and saw a "Whole row of out-houses two-stepping down the river."

"In springtime they laid us all off."

Claude spent the bulk of his lifetime farming, trapping and received his A guiding license. Many of his trips have been from points out of Mountain Park and the Coal Branch.

At 70 years of age, and exhuming energy and a stature many a younger man would envy, Claude says he made his last trip last year, 1973, "Now I'd rather take their picture than shoot them."

However a coyote ready for skinning hung outside his home in the Mahaska district. A widower, he talks of his son Leslie Claude, a flight-sergeant killed overseas, a daughter who died of a kidney transplant and his other two daughters, Mrs. Bob Bradford and Mrs. Orville Armstrong, Edson area residents.

* * *

... I Would Never Marry a Miner

CARL FRANCESCKI by his family – Carl Franceski came to Canada at the age of 16 with an older brother. They first worked around Medicine Hat on the railroad, but didn't care for the hot dusty prairie, so went to Mountain Park in 1918. His brother went back to Italy so he was alone in this new country and never did go back, even for a visit. His whole life revolved around horses, hunting and fishing, and when he eventually married, his family may have just edged out Lady, Silver, and many more horses. He was a good man, never said

Jack Roome, Cherega and Carl Franceski
enjoy a hunting trip.　　　　　　　　　Carl Franceski　　　　　　　　(Koskoski)

too much, and we feel he left part of himself at Mountain Park when we finally had to leave in 1942 because of his health and the health of his daughter, Margaret.

Mary Lenteris came to Mountain Park in 1926 with her parents. They stayed only a short while and finished their years in Vancouver. Mary and Carl were married in December, 1927 at home as it was such a severe winter they couldn't heat the church; very deep snow and so cold the train froze and was very late coming.

Margaret was born in April, 1929 at home as all the babies were then. They left Mountain Park for a couple of years and Jean was born in January, 1931 at Drinnan (now Hinton) then the family moved back to Mountain Park where Johnny was born in March, 1939. The mother, Mary, daughters Margaret Gaetz and Jean Koskoski now reside in Lethbridge while Johnny lives in Chilliwack, B.C. Carl passed away in Lethbridge in 1963 leaving five grandchildren.

Jean remembers: I was young but I still remember war being declared in September, 1939 and my uncle Peter Lenteris, who lived in Mountain Park then, with two of his friends rushing to join the army. I used to write long letters to him often. They were on the first boat going to England and they all came home again.

The war touched us a bit in Mountain Park. Even though my Dad was a naturalized Canadian he was still declared an alien during the war and was kept watch on by the RCMP although never intimidated. They did make him sell his gun though, so his mining partner bought it till after the war.

280

I only remember one mine disaster while we were there. The tipple whistle blew very loud one summer day while we were at school. Everyone knew this meant an accident. School was let out and everyone gathered at the mine. I still remember thinking, "It's not my dad 'cause nothing will ever happen to him." I guess I wasn't too sure what it was, because Mom says I questioned her about death. I think it was shortly after this that I made up my mind I would never marry a miner.

Going to school was fun then. At Christmas time the whole school participated in the concert and when we had a winter carnival most of the school had skating parts and we practiced during school hours. At the beginning of each school year we had a picnic in the 'Bush';

Left to Right — Dora Baruzzini, Fay Molloy, Eva Dimick, June Lancaster, Anne Terplovoy, Barbara Malloy, Eileen Chapman, Eliza Bishop.

Eileen Chapman and Avis Bentley in front of background scenery at a winter ice carnival.

that's when Margaret tore the ligaments in one knee, being chased (probably by some boys) and caught her foot in a hole. She was brought home on a chair made by hands of the older boys. She was off school for a month.

I never knew what 'separate school' meant till we moved to Lethbridge. At Mountain Park we went to our own church but we all went to the same school and I feel the children got along much better that way. Father McGowan was the priest who came up for christening, weddings and to teach us at Sunday School. He made such an impression on me, I still remember his smiling face and teasing ways. He could get the worst boy to do what he wanted.

One of the greatest pleasures was Dad taking us out to pick and cut down our own Christmas tree. There was always lots of snow but I don't remember it being too cold. He also used to take us to get fresh water, with a stone boat and horse. Water was delivered once a week and then later twice a week.

I even had my own pony. Babe was born from pure black parents and as far as could be determined, black from the generation below, but she was a beautiful Palomino with a white face. My saddest day was leaving her as I never did get a chance to ride her when she was old enough.

* * *

Mom remembers: Jean was very ill when she was three years old. We thought she had the measles. After not showing any improvement two days later, the doctor was called and he diagnosed it as a gall bladder attack. She was on a partial diet till eleven years old when she had a severe attack and Dr. Peter Melling sent Jean and I to Edmonton where she was operated on for gall stones at the Royal Alex Hospital. Many years later in Lethbridge a doctor remembered the case as it was medical history at that time for an 11-year-old child.

I believe it was the winter of 1920 that we had such a severe snow storm the horses were caught out in the mountains. The snow was very deep so the men went on snow shoes pulling toboggans of hay to feed the horses, as they were starving standing there snowbound. These animals were a part of the mens' lives and there was no way they were going to lose them even if they died in the attempt. The horses were about eight miles from town and it took the men all day and all night to go and come back, but they saved all the animals and no one was hurt.

I don't remember much about the moonshine still that was found in the mountains, just that there was one there for awhile.

There were very few cars in Mountain Park as there really wasn't many places to go. Roads were very bad. After the outbreak of war roads were improved and we started seeing more cars up there. At that time a new car could be bought for $1,000.

Carl and I found a baby deer one rainy day when coming home on horseback. He carried it on the horse for nineteen miles. It only lasted for about a month. A friend had taken it to Edmonton for a zoo or whatever they had then.

There wasn't too much excitement in the town so when the train came in Monday, Wednesday and Friday, there seemed to be a crowd to see who came, then everyone collected at the Post Office and visited till the mail was sorted. The train left Tuesday, Thursday and Saturday.

We did our shopping in the local grocery store but once in a while we bought direct from the Alberta Trading Co. in Edmonton. This was bulk buying and shipped in via train, which was still cheaper than at the store. The men also bought their hay for the horses by the ton. Every corral was piled high with hay for the winter. The horses always came in for the winter unless they were caught in a sudden blizzard as I have already stated.

Some of the winters were bad and some not too bad. When the snow got deep and the wind howled, the men used to go to the mine in groups, with one man breaking trail and the rest following in his footsteps. This especially at night as it was so dark a man could fall or wander off and not be missed till too late.

The men hunted deer, moose, elk, mountain sheep and goats. The game laws were not as strict then as now, but the animals were shot for food. We preserved the meat in crocks, sliced thin, salt, pepper and oil, or in the winter just chunks hung in an outside building. What we couldn't use for ourselves was always shared with friends. Nothing was wasted; the same applied to all the fish that were caught.

One summer Carl had a bad leg so he went with his horse and pack horse which was also lame, to the Miette Hot Springs, cross country. He was never bothered with that leg again. I'm not too sure about the horse. Carl seemed to have a built-in compass as he never got turned around in the mountains.

* * *

Margaret remembers: Whenever a newly married couple came back from their honeymoon all the kids gathered at their place and made terrible noise with tin cans, whistles, anything, until they came out and threw nickels or candy. Sometimes we were sent down to the confectionery and each one was allowed one five cent item. These chivarees were great fun.

We used to have fun when we went picking huckleberries. One time a black bear just lay in the bushes watching us till we left. Another time a black bear just walked by one of the ladies as she was picking, didn't bother with her at all. The dogs used to go crazy but we were never attacked by any of them.

I believe it was the spring of 1940, April, that the dog and I went looking for Lady as she was due to foal and the snow was still very deep. We found her and the foal up on a hill but couldn't get them down so had to go home and get dad and mom. Everyone helped

Mr. Suie — Mountain Park.

break the trail and the rest of the horses in the same area followed us home. No casualties.

I thought it was great fun to go to Suies Chop Suey place for his home made chop suey. Mom would send me down and I would sit near his stove while he cooked it fresh. Gee it still makes my mouth water. I never seemed to think of him as Chinese. We had one Negro family there for awhile and we were very good friends with the daughter. Those days there didn't seem to be any prejudice in race or religion. In fact I didn't run into this sort of thing till we came to the city.

* * *

. . . The Women Got Suspended Sentences

MIKE KRYPAN by himself – I was born August 19, 1899 in Austro-Hungary, Empaci State of Croatia. I was conscripted in the Yugoslav Army and served for eighteen months, then suspended on sick leave for six months. Before my sick leave was over, the war ended and I' was honorably discharged.

I hoped to emigrate to the U.S.A. but I could not get an affidavit so tried for Canada. My uncle was in Kenaston, Saskatchewan and sent me an affidavit, ticket and $50 for expenses. I arrived in Kenaston in April 1924. (Mike left behind his wife Theresa, a boy who had died ten days after his birth in 1919, and the other who was to die at age ten from pneumonia, Frances born in 1921 and John who was born in 1923.)

284

I was paid $30 a month plus board and room but in October my uncle said he could not afford to pay me wages anymore. A man told me that I could make $10 a day in a mine so I decided to go looking for a coal mine.

I arrived in Edmonton, November 2nd but no one was looking for miners so I was shipped to a sawmill west of Edson at Hargwen. Four of us arrived together. The second day I got frozen tocs and was not able to wear shoes. I wrapped my feet in rags and worked like that. Ten days after four of us got laid off. The company took us to Hargwen. The section foreman told us the passenger train did not stop there but the freight would stop and pick up a boxcar for East or Edson. The boxcars were sealed so we broke the seal on one and got in. We arrived in Edson and the next day went to the bank to cash our chequcs but the cheques were no good. I was delegated to Robb to see if there were jobs for the four of us. I was told, "not even for one." When I got back to Edson my colleague was gone to work someplace for the CNR. I packed up my stuff and got back to Robb and waited for work. I stayed at the company bunkhouse and ate in the kitchen. Board was $1.25 a day but I ate only twice a day and in this way saved 25¢. I was eating on credit (in December the Balkan Coal Co. decided to put him on the payroll, probably because he was now indebted by two months.)

I was told to get ready to go to work. My job was rope-rider, twelve hours a day and 50¢ an hour.

At the Balkan Coal Co. at that time there was John Minerich, Mike Dimich, Frank Krsnarich, George Beilaick, Peter Stanich, Tony Lukach, Pete Berich, Nick Paripovich, Mike Lisica, Mane Marjan, Paul Mileusnich (Miller), Joe Soich, Dan Vidakovich, John Stimac, Ed Zemyrsky, John Yasensky, Alex Novak, Paul Mirsky, Peter Baretsky, John Kwasney and others.

I learned that Mane Marjan, Joe Soich, John Stimac and Alex Susnar were expelled from University back home for disorder or advocating nationality.

There was a Jock Smith living with his wife and kids in something like a roothouse. I understand that was built to store explosives when the railway was built. Smith made moonshine and one day a miner from Mile 32 got drunk and started to go home. He got to the railway track and fell between the rails. A freight was coming through the tunnel and the engineer noticed something but by the time he noticed it was a man he was not able to stop. The cowcatcher on the train dragged him for some distance. They took the man to Edson Hospital and when he came to he asked, "How is Walter in the mine?" He did not know what had happened.

The Balkan Coal Co. was organized by a man that had emigrated to the U.S.A. before the First World War and then emigrated to Canada.

By February I was laid off and told there would be no work until October so I packed up and moved to Edmonton. I arrived in Edmonton, March, 1925. The only job I was able to find was with a shipment of men to work in the bush at Jasper Park. I believe the company's name was Owens and Ogden some 18 miles up the Athabaska River. My job was to cut dry timber. Wages were $60 a month plus board. In May the camp was closed and the company paymaster gave each man $10 cash and a cheque for wages. We had our belongings loaded but walked to Jasper. Next day we lined up at the bank to cash cheques. The bank announced that they had no more cash. I believe the company did not have enough money in the bank.

We went to Edson but had no success in cashing the cheques. I had worked two months for $10. In Edson I got a job stocking coal. Some days I could make five to six dollars, some times three dollars, depending on how many cars I could get to load. At the end of June the job was finished, so hearing there was highway work in Princeton, B.C. went there. Then I worked at Golden, B.C. The following year 1926, the work was finished. We had made $5.25 a day plus room and board. I proceeded to Kimberly, B.C. and was told if I wanted a job I would have to buy one for $50 or $100 depending on the job. Also every month a bottle of whiskey would have to be purchased for the shift boss. We left and went to fight fire at Nelson, B.C. In two weeks we were replaced by Chinamen. In Nelson we got paid but my colleague lost all of his money overnight on poker in August, 1926.

We went back to the Coal Branch and waited for work. In September we got a job at Mile 32, and worked till February, 1927. Then D. Davies the manager told all of us to go because the kitchen and mine would be closed till August. I moved to Mercoal and got a job in the coal mine, $5.40 per day, eight hours a day, company work. I was after the pit boss, Bob Robinson, and the manager Andrew Miller, later chief inspector, to get contract work but was not able to do so. In September I quit and got a job at Mile 33, Robb. In 1927 the Balkan Coal Co. sold property to Mr. McBain and we worked steady. Before this there was no organized union because the shareholders were in majority. After McBain we organized the Mine Workers of Canada. I was told this Union was supported by the Communist Party. On one occasion we were out on strike for a short time but the grievance was settled.

In 1930 there was trouble at Mercoal. The majority of men joined the Mineworkers of Canada but the company favoured the United Mine Workers of America. The local union was asked to send miners to Mercoal to protest and picket. One day we were on the ridge facing south to the mine entrance. Some RCMP were escorting some men, about ten or twelve to work. We were shouting Scabs go back. One man by the name of Peter Maticevich and another in a brown leather coat jumped down between the police and the scabs. A commotion started and we thundered "Hura-Hura" and started pushing, fist fighting, throwing rocks. Even some of our men got hurt. How we got separated I do not know but they did not start work for some time. One day we got news for Coalspur. Two passenger cars arrived with RCMP and Alberta Police and Special Police. They sent a section man from Coalspur to go ahead of the train because some body was told the Communists set dynamite on the railway. We were told to go home to our camps. In a few days the police started to round up the suspects. They arrested Pete Meticevich, Jack Tomicich, Tony Botrkof and Louis Matonvich. Meticevich and Tomicich were deported and Matonovich and Botrkof served prison and were released. Funny thing is, Matonovich was not in this last push, but someone else was wearing his brown leather coat. If Matonovich told who was wearing his coat he only would put another man in the same spot. The company and U.M.W. of A. won and started to produce but not for long. The company was bankrupt and after, H. McLeod organized a new company and started to produce at Mercoal.

In 1931 a fellow by the name of Tom Robson got fired at Robb, Mile 33. We were after the company to give him his job back but the company would not agree so we went on strike. We were not able to picket because it was company property and the mine was protected by the Provincial Police. They brought scabs in who were escorted to camp. We organized the women and they went one morning on the bridge that was leading over the ravine to mine entrance. The scabs were escorted by the police to work. A woman shouted "Scabs, go home, do not take bread from us and our children." They proceeded with the police escort between the women. Women started to throw salt and pepper in the men's faces so they returned back. The next day they got better protection and went to work. The women got a summons to appear in court. Court was in the school at Mile 33

Early "libbers" picket the mineworkers at Robb. L. to R. Mrs. Romanoff, Mrs. Boretsky, Mrs. Koncar, Mrs. Kwasney, Mrs. Lukach, Mrs. Mandriuk, Mrs. Beggan, Mrs. Yosensky, Mrs. Werzun. In the background males are l to r, Nick Gnatovich, John Blazevich, (killed at Mountain Park,) Sam Sarich and Matt Butalo, 1931.

287

Robb. Beside the women all the miners were present and lot of sympathizers. When court was opened, one woman, Mrs. Werson said that she had a baby at home and nobody to look after it. The RCMP came to me and told me to go to Wersons home and watch the baby. When court was over the women got suspended sentences.

The single men were ordered off of company property and we settled on government land in tents. Sometimes the temperature was 45 degrees below. Some of the old timers did not come out on strike. Miners they hired from outside worked on flat seams and were not too successful in working the angle 35–40 degrees up the hill. Food was donated by the Unions and Locals and Alberta farmers. We were on strike till March then we got word to go look for a job somewhere else because the Union could see the strike was lost.

I went to Mercoal and stayed with a bachelor friend. One day I got a telephone call from Mr. Bill Foster, the Mine Manager, through the store. He asked me to come back and work. I went but not for long. The scabs gave me a hard time so I left and moved back to Mercoal. I got a job at the mine there working just one or two days a week. I realized I could not go back home so I brought my wife and kids to Canada.

Our daughter Frances was born in 1921. She married in 1939 and lives with her family of four children in Richmond, B.C. John was born in 1923 and now has four children. Nick was born in Mercoal in 1935 and is a mining engineer with two children. Helen was born in 1944 and is a Lab Technician.

When the family got to Canada I thought things would get better but every year things seemed to get worse. I started borrowing and living on credit. In 1934 miners started to apply for relief. Somebody told me that I could not apply or my wife and children would be deported. I was made a British Subject in 1930, so my wife automatically became a British Subject by my citizenship. The RCMP sent for us and asked some questions. He told me, "It is not your fault you are not working. Don't be worried about deportation."

I got relief for my family. $17.50 a month but I had to work on the highway to work this off. In 1939 we started to work a little better. In 1941 the McLeod River Hard Coal Co. was sold to another company and we started to work steadily.

When the Second World War started one day all foreigners, even if they were British Subjects had to be registered and we went to Coalspur and had our fingerprints taken. Two RCMP were in charge. I had a twenty-two special and the police took it to keep until the war was over. I said, "I do not want the gun any more. You can have it." One of the police asked what shape the gun was in and I said in good condition. "Do you want to sell it?" I said he could have it for nothing but he would not and gave me five dollars and a bill of sale.

1929 at Robb — a strike of short duration. Single men were required to move off camp limits so set up tents near the railroad right of way.
Seated L. to R. — Louis Prpich, Red Vojnovich, John Sarich, Mike Kepson, Matt Butala
Very Back: Matt Zdunich, Dan Pesyt, George Bulaich.
Back L. to R. Eli Knezovich, Harry Chmara, Joe Prpich, Joe Henderson, Martin Turak, John Sckulich, George Skorep, Sam Sarich, Philip Bulaich.

The other policeman was looking at my citizenship papers and he said, "Look here. His mother and father were citizens of Austro-Hungary. Who can tell if he doesn't have German blood in him!"

I was really disappointed and said, "My mother and grand-mother never saw Germany in their life. Your name sounds more Germanic than mine." He said, "Shut up or I'll put you where you belong."

I had to report every month to the RCMP at Coalspur, 18 miles away.

One day I was in the Mercoal Store. Mr. T. Conger asked me how I was. I said, "Like sh--." I explained. He said, "Do not worry, they are looking for enemies where none exist." Mr. Conger was an officer in the First World War. Where he wrote a letter to, I don't know but nobody bothered me after that.

Mike said the registration had a profound effect on him. "I never felt the same after that."

Despite his bitterness he was one of a committee who sold war bonds, in Mercoal. There was one Italian, one Pole, two Yugoslavs, one Irishman and a Ukrainian on the committee. "Our commission was a quarter of one percent."

In 1949 Mike suffered a broken cartilage of his knee cap in the Mercoal mine, and later it was found he had a light silicosis of the lung.

Born in August, 1899 Mike looks now serenely on a long and varied life. He is a keen conversationalist. Mr. and Mrs. Krypan live at 11023-122 St., Edmonton.

. . . Life was Beautiful There

MARILYN REDLINGER by herself – Both my grandparents came from Europe and both settled on the Coal Branch. My father's folks John and Mary Zelenak first settled at Weald and later moved to Coalspur. My mother's folks, Mr. and Mrs. Tony Lukach settled in Robb and remained there after most folk had moved and all the mines had closed.

My parents, Mary and John Zelenak, Jr. met, fell in love and married and remained in Robb until they moved to Drayton Valley in 1961. Although I was born in Edson, my parents were living at Robb and moved to Mercoal three years later. At that time I had one sister Linda, three years older than myself. Six years later another girl Shiela came along. Funny thing I remember father called all three of us Sonny.

My father built a house in the south west part of town. We had the regular sheds which consisted of coal and wood, and of course that dear old house out back.

Life was beautiful there. I had a very happy childhood with loads of things to do. Times were fun of fishing, exploring old mines, having picnics and living without a TV. The radio, playing games and cards played a big part in life.

A big thing was visiting family on Sundays and holidays. A real treat was to visit my grandparents in Robb, Tony and Helena Lukach. There was a big house and garden and six wonderful aunts and uncles that played with us by the hour. Grandpa took us to the local store for candy. A man called Humdadee ran the store.

I went to school in Mercoal and recall some good teachers. After grade five the mine was closed and the children rode a bus to Cadomin. Grade nine took a bus the other way to Robb. My father was a mine electrician which was why we were one of the last families to leave. My father, John Zelenak Jr. ran the generator or light plant for the remaining people.

I remember hearing my mother and father talking of Japan not needing any more coal. I was very scared. I wondered where we would go and what we would do. Perhaps the whole town was thinking the same thing, a lot must have been scared. Especially the older men that knew really nothing but coal mining.

I do remember the hotel burning in Mercoal. It was in the middle of the night. We could see the flames from our place, they were very high. My dad went down, it was something to do with the power, as he went to all fires.

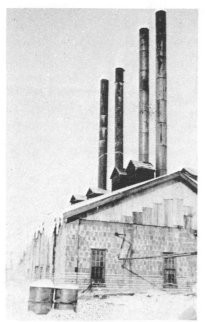

Power house at Mercoal, 1927.

Mercoal, taken about 1954, just as I remember it.

Photo — Redlinger

Mercoal Mine in heyday.

I remember waking in the morning and my mother putting wood in the stove to start the fire. She would add coal later and when it was warm everyone would get up. The floor was real cold on the feet and we shivered for a little while.

Every summer my husband, myself and now my son go up fishing and camping, as do my parents and a lot of people from there. We have met all kinds of people there, people all across Canada and from the States. They all love it there as I do. There's a feeling one can't describe, maybe of peace or just freedom. But it is a good feeling and I love it there and really wish it had never shut down. – Marilyn Redlinger – Edmonton

. . . *Bedsheets Turned Yellow From Disuse*

JOHN KAPTEYN – Born May 21, 1899 in Lekkerkerk, Holland, John Kapteyn was the second oldest of fifteen children. Three died in infancy.

John had to leave school at the age of ten to help on his father's dairy farm. Money was scarce, and it took a lot of food to satisfy the appetites of the ever-growing family. Eggs sold at three cents each that winter, and even these seemed beyond his father's resources. John says, "He was an excellent dairy famer, but a rotten businessman."

His mother died four years later, leaving a new-born babe of six days. The bemused father was left with twelve children.

Help was immediately on the way. Six sisters and sisters-in-law of the dairy farmer came. Each took one of the younger children. They cared for the children for a period of one and a half years. Then the father, feeling he could cope once again, returned the family to one fold.

During that period of time, John while haying with his father was struck in the left eye with a fork tine. The eye, untended by a doctor, lost most of its seeing power.

At 16, John joined the army under Holland's 'lottery system'. He hoped in this way to obtain an education. But because of the eye, John was discharged six weeks later.

Helping on his father's farm and obtaining whatever farm employment he could, John brooded on the fact that he would have to remain a farm laborer all his life. Inwardly he admitted that he detested it.

Canada needed immigrants. Farm laborers. He saw his way out to a new life in a new country. Finally March 11, 1924 he disembarked from the Saxonia and along with others was sent to the Winnipeg immigration office.

Part of the group, John among them, was sent to the area near Dome Creek, B.C. Here they worked for a month in the sawmill. It took this long to learn that few if any wages would be forthcoming. The group notified authorities, and were sent to Edmonton. From this point they were dispersed to farms in the Provost area.

After harvest, John put in a short stint laying ties for track on the railroad. A co-worker suggested, "Hey, Dutchy. Let's go to work on the Coal Branch."

A typical shack in hills of Mercoal. Skidded logs out of the hills were used to build shacks.

John Kapteyn — 1946.

The two made their way to Edson. Here it was necessary to stay overnight to catch the thrice weekly passenger train to the mines. Work was unobtainable in Luscar and Cadomin so the two continued to Mercoal. The mine in Mercoal was operated by the Saunders Ridge Coal Co. They booked into the Mercoal Hotel, built by Wes McKinnon, the owner of Burns Mountain Lumber Co. Mr. McKinnon then sold the thirteen room hotel with small beer parlour to a trio, Thomas Mellon, Edwin D. Conger and J. Paulson.

John settled down for the night, little aware of the significance that this hotel would place in his life.

Early the next morning, John was roused by a knock at the door. He opened the door to a little Japanese who identified himself as Tommy Tomoto. Johns knowledge of English was as poor as Tommy's but finally the Japanese cook made him understand that they

Pete Dobrich, Roger Conger and Mike Smilanich, busy barbecuing four lambs at Mercoal.

294

needed a dishwasher at the mine cookhouse. The job was John's if he wanted it; $60 a month – room and board.

He soon became a part of the busy activity in the long log cookhouse which could seat 100 men at a time. He made a good friend of the little Japanese cook who had wed a Scots woman as short in stature as himself. The couple lived in a room built back of the kitchen, while John bunked in the dormitory above the eating quarters.

John, a strapping six feet tall and well muscled was soon promoted to bull-cook, a job he held for three years. The long kitchen range sported three ovens. Two forty gallon steel barrels were connected to the firebox. As bullcook, it was part of John's job to keep the two barrels full of water for dishwashing and cooking. Then there was a third barrel for cold water.

This was no small job. It meant hitching a team of the mine horses to a sleigh loaded with a wooden tank that held up to 300 gallons. Then it was off to Mercoal Creek, a stream which ran through the townsite and into the McLeod River.

In summer the sleigh was replaced with a wagon. In winter there were problems. A bucket of water was scooped from the creek and poured into the top of the wooden tank. When the tank became too congested with ice, it would be off to the mine power house where it was de-iced with exhaust steam. Many times he would wrap a rag around the valve at the bottom of the tank, set the rag on fire to melt the ice in the tap until it ran freely once more.

Soon he found he could pick up some extra money by hauling water to nearby homes.

His expertise with the team of horses was noted and he was approached with the offer of an additional job.

A perennial problem was to get someone to empty the human excreta which piled up in the wooden toilets situated baldly behind all the buildings.

John, young and strong decided to take on the job after his own duties as bull-cook were finished for the day.

Hitching the horses, this time to a dump wagon, John was amazed to find he had made $45.00 that first night. This at a period of time when miners not under contract work made $5.40 top wages per shift.

This was big money! So started a career that made 'big money' but was to leave a stigmatic blight that he would not be allowed to forget. Decades later his children smarted under the taunts of 'Crap-can Kapteyn'. While not one wanted the job they never allowed the future successful businessman to forget how he got his start.

However this didn't bother the young man. Everywhere he looked he saw money to be made. He was not above capitalizing on the situation either. No one really went around measuring the piles of excreta in the toilets. Soon he had this work down to a science. He built a giant T-stand of two by fours which he placed at the back of the toilets. Then the toilet was tipped to an angle, a few shovels full of excreta extracted into the dump wagon, and the toilet shoved forward again. The job could be stretched to many more visits if he wasn't too diligent about it all. Just skim a little off the top of the frozen mounds.

When there was an extra job, he took it, and tried to squeeze in six hours of sleeping time. He was carefully accumulating a small nest egg.

Around him the life in the mining town ebbed and flowed. Because of the virtual isolation of the camps the men had to create their own amusement and practical jokes were a commonplace.

At this time the chief mechanic at the mine was a man named Herdman McLeod, sometimes known as Hurdy and often called Peg Leg. Peg Leg sometimes drove his victims to distraction but his pranks were a constant diversion to the residents.

One day Peg Leg sold John a raincoat that not only proved to be warm, but was completely rubberized. John felt that for $10 he had made an excellent buy. He happily wore the coat during the drizzling rainy spell that followed.

Sitting atop the waterwagon peacefully driving towards the cookhouse he noticed the General Superintendent, Mr. Andrew Miller, striding towards him. As he came nearer, John noticed the official's facial muscles agitating to the extent that his mustache quivered. John, still a young man and nervous in the face of authority could not understand what was wrong. When Mr. Miller could find his voice he roared, "Where in hell did you get that coat!"

John hurriedly took the coat off. When he accosted Hurdy McLeod and told him the story, that venerable gentlemen listened with glee. He happily refunded John his $10.

The mine whistle was very much part of the lives of the people in the town.

It blew in the morning to mark a shift beginning and again to mark the shift's end.

Residents waited each evening at 9:00 p.m. If the hour passed without three long whistles penetrating the valley, men prepared to work the next day.

Coal contracts were slow, and in some years more often than not, the 9:00 whistle disconsolately sounded the message, "No work to-morrow. No work to-morrow. No work to-morrow."

Short toots signalled a fire in town. One day residents were puzzled to hear the mine whistle blowing. It was an early Sunday morning. The whistles were not short and staccato, so that meant no fire – long mournful blasts that went on and on. They dressed and left their homes. The story was soon known.

A man of Ukrainian extraction and over 60 years old was a cook in a bush camp some 12 miles out of Mercoal. The previous evening he had attended a wedding in the town and walked the trail back to camp. Workers at the bush camp became alarmed when he was not on hand to cook breakfast. One of the workers hurried into town to notify the mine officials.

The long mournful whistles were being used in the hope that the man, if he had become lost in the densely wooded area, would get his bearings.

A search party was formed and within several hours the cook was found walking along the trail. Apart from being tired and cold he was fine. The whistles had indeed helped his sense of direction. Shivering and cold, the cook carried a full, unopened bottle of whiskey.

When asked why he had not drunk some of it he indignantly replied in Ukrainian, "No, no. If you'd found my carcass in the spring, everyone would have said, no wonder the old buzzard got lost. He was drunk."

* * *

Ever alert to making a dime John Kapteyn tried all sorts of ventures. Coyotes were a nuisance at the dumpground. The accountant at the mine, Bill Rawley, suggested John buy a sow ready to litter. He reasoned that the pigs would eat the refuse and lessen the coyote nuisance.

John agreed and Mr. Rawley made arrangements for a sow to be expressed from Edson.

The newly bred sow was penned. The gestation period of three months, three weeks and three days quickly passed and the sow bore a splendid litter. John kept his eye on them and they grew to good sized weaners.

One night Hurdy McLeod showed up at the cookhouse and asked the Japanese cook to roast the young porker he was carrying.

However Tomoto knew of John's venture and also knew that no meat ever appeared in the town before Friday when the refrigerated car came up from Edson.

He adamantly refused to cook the little pig. John noticed one of the litter missing and having heard of the incident accosted McLeod. Hurdy cheerfully admitted to the theft and paid up. There had been a poker party and the roast pork much enjoyed. Three times a pig disappeared and three times McLeod serenely made good. In retrospect, John says, "Never lost a dime on him, but sometimes he sure got your goat."

The McGillveray Coal Co. at Coleman which had vested interest in Mercoal sent up a surveyor several times a year to estimate coal extraction. The surveyor, Bill Hall, was a happily married man and returned to Coleman after a Mercoal visit. Mrs. Hall, unpacking, was more than surprised to find a suitcase full of ladies lingerie. After a stream of verbal abuse a small note was found at the bottom of the case attesting to Mr. Hall's virtue. Hurdy, the prankster, disclaimed all knowledge of the event. As he generally made good on his own ideas, it was generally acknowledged the culprit must have been someone else. That same unknown must also have been responsible for a clothesline that had been stripped during the evening of Hall's visit.

A fellow countryman, Pete Boersma, told John of a boxing card that was to be held in Cadomin featuring 'Kid Holland'. The two felt they should offer support to the fighting Hollander, so hopped the freight for transportation.

Just out of Leyland, the train jerked to a stop. The two friends sat patiently in the boxcar waiting for the train to move. When it did not, they decided to walk the short distance to Cadomin. Coming towards the engine, they came across the train crew who were busily disengaging rock from the overhanging banks. With a grunt of satisfaction they managed to dislodge a good-sized boulder which tumbled down gathering other debris and effectively blocked the track.

Now the auxiliary unit would have to be sent out from Edson to clear the track. This would take several hours or even longer. Certainly long enough for all the crew to see the fight in Cadomin.

John Kapteyn grinned in retrospect. "It was a good fight, but our fighter, Kid Holland, turned out to be a mulatto."

John obtained a contract for stuccoing houses and soon was so busy he hired a man to help him paying him the goodly sum of $1.00 per hour.

His sidelines became a full-time occupation. He worked in the mine for nine months; long enough to obtain his miner's ticket. Then it was contracting with the coal company for mine props. However work in the mines was slow. During the summer months people didn't buy coal. The main market was Winnipeg and Vancouver, and summer often saw the mines working "maybe two days a week."

While the slack periods created a hardship for miners, they didn't bother John too much. He was usually too busy anyway. He contracted with the mine company to haul away the 'slack' from the domestic coal. This was shipped to the cement plant at Marlboro.

John, still smarting from his lack of education began taking night classes under the tutelage of a Mercoal teacher, Louis Burger. John leaned towards mathematics.

Two of the miners told John of a young woman who had come to Canada to a sister because her parents had both died in Germany. The sister lived in Edmonton. The miners arranged a meeting. They met – John, and Martha Weder. On December 29, 1927, Martha celebrated not only her 29th birthday, but her marriage to John Kapteyn in an Edmonton Lutheran Church ceremony.

John worked, studied and saved. He eyed the hotel partnership of Thomas Mellon, Edwin D. Conger and J. Paulson that didn't seem to be working out too smoothly; John took an option on the hotel in the spring of 1930. Then on September 22, 1930, despite the fact that mines were not operating and business was poor, John bought the hotel for the sum of $15,000.

He took a deep breath, paid his total savings of seven and a half thousand as a down payment and fervently hoped that things would improve economically. He also started taking correspondence courses in hotel management. The hotel had thirteen rooms and a small beverage room with eight tables. On good nights each table was surrounded by six chairs and more chairs added when necessary. Bottled beer was packed in barrels and shipped from Edmonton.

He and Martha lived in a small house near the hotel. James Heinz, the firstborn arrived October 15th, 1928 with the mine doctor in attendance. On March 31, 1930 a sister, Gloria Helen joined Jimmy. A baby girl, Norma Delores died at the age of six weeks in 1931 and Norman John came May 8th, 1932.

1933 was a bad year for all. The mine hoisted coal for only 62 days in all of 1933.

Bedsheets turned yellow from disuse in the hotel bedrooms. Help was paid off and John ran the hotel by himself. Consistently, feeling the binding effect of his nationalistic religious childhood he offered a free nights lodging to all clergymen of whatever denomination. At the end of 1933 his books showed $183.50 total for room rent.

Beer sales were poor too. In June of 1933 he was using quarter kegs and the month's turnover was $310.

A few miners came, drank, and when bladders were full went out the front door and around to the side to the 'air-conditioned' toilets.

But beer sales shouldn't be that poor even in these dire times, John pondered.

It was rumored that the mine was going bankrupt. John had extended a 20-year ground lease when he purchased the hotel. The mine owned the ground rights and residents paid $1.00 a month to build their homes on the land. The word was that if the business leases could be broken, new management would come in and start anew. It was a very real fear. So real that John and Mr. Conger who owned

the Mercoal Mercantile and also had retained a $2,000 interest in the hotel wondered about rumors of arson. A co-op business had gone bankrupt, and the building, now abandoned stood between the hotel and the mercantile. The two men pondered that if the building became afire, it could be a real hazard to both the store and the hotel. It would not be the first time that a convenient fire had solved a problem. Quietly, they bid on the building, hoisted it on skids and hauled it away.

John then heard of "Frenchy" who had suddenly set up operations near the hotel, selling moonshine at low cost. It was rumored he had a 'still' here, one there. It was hurting. John Kapteyn took his problems to Edmonton.

Here he presented his problems to Robert Noble, Vice-president of the Alberta Hotel Association.

Mr. Noble contacted the Liquor Control Board and told the fire commissioner's office of the threat of arson.

Police promptly arrived in Mercoal and arrested the moonshiner Frenchie. They also found a coil (used in making moonshine) at the home of W. Brooks, an employee of the mine. Mr. Brooks was arrested too, and the pair put in jail at Fort Saskatchewan.

Mercoal residents were up in arms. W. Brooks was a good honest citizen and had not sold moonshine. They felt that an arrest had been made on circumstantial evidence only. Feelings were not too favorable towards John Kapteyn, the instigator of these events.

Miners who were in sorry circumstances themselves because of the lack of work pooled their resources and finally raised the fine of $250 towards Brooks release.

The money was entrusted to a man named Stenhouse. Time passed and the ill-fated Brooks did not come back. Finally contacts were made and it was discovered Brooks was still in jail. The fine money had not been turned in. Enraged residents contacted authorities. So Stenhouse and Brooks exchanged places. Stenhouse became the prisoner and Brooks returned home. "Brooks never sold a drop." mused John Kapteyn.

The thirties. Relief camps were spotted throughout the country. Between Mile 12 and 13, men camped and worked building trails and dirt roads between the mining camps, with horses and wheelbarrows.

The United Mine Workers of America were entrenched on the Lovett Branch. They came down to Mercoal to picket the poorly organized Canadian union.

Young Jimmy Kapteyn was five years old and taken to Edson where he was terrified on viewing his first car.

John Kapteyn ruled his hotel with an iron hand. While the hotheaded miners could slap each other around to their hearts content, it immediately became John's business if they used one of his 'Hotel'

300

glasses or 'Hotel' chairs. He promptly laid complaints if it involved any hotel property.

For years the hotel office served also as a courthouse. First Magistrate Chris Pattinson, then Magistrate Jock Thomson would journey up from Edson to pronounce sentence. The Scot's 'Thir-r-r-ty dollars or thi-r-r-ty days' was a common sentence. John Kapteyn would often not only lay the complaint, but also pay the sentence fine. He reasoned that it was poor business to lose a customer. The man would pay him back when able and all would go well till the next fight that involved hotel property.

A special box soon became a routine part of hotel business. In between paydays, a cheque could be written, and the cheque put into the box. It would be held till the next payday and if not redeemed for cash, would be deposited. If there was not enough money in the account John would prosecute. It was good business. The cheque writer would receive the cash and go happily off into the beer parlour. When payday came along, a steady stream of miners would visit John's office, redeem the cheques for the amount written and simply tear them up.

Life in the mining town droned on with Peg Leg McLeod still enlivening the conversation with his antics. The man's sense of humour could entrap almost anyone.

Bill Cook, a maintenance man in the mines was heading 'out' to Edmonton for a vacation. Peg Leg chanced to meet him on the bridge behind the cookhouse and asked where the man was going all dandied up in his best. Bill said he was off to Edmonton. Peg Leg said, "Aw, you haven't got the money." Bill proudly showed him the bills, whereupon Peg Leg quickly reached out a hand and lop-sidedly but swiftly took off with the money. He ran to the hotel and hid out. Bill Cook futilely searched for him, but of course no one had seen Peg Leg. Bill Cook missed his train, which was the object of the theft, and had to wait two days for another.

* * *

Peg Leg prevailed upon a fellow miner to shoot a moose. Peg Leg sent it 'collect' to a dentist in Coleman. That worthy sent Peg Leg a present in return freight collect. A vicious looking bulldog with gory colored circles painted around his eyes and all over his body. Peg Leg kept the dog and months later the paint finally wore off.

* * *

Emmil Ivicich bought two cows because no fresh milk was procureable except by train. He pastured them near a ridge not far from a cluster of homes inhabited by miners of Italian extraction. The cows proved their worth providing Emmil's children with milk and there was enough left to sell to a neighbor or two.

One evening Emmil found one of his cows lurching dazedly around the make-shift pasture. The cow looked sick and Emmil sorrowfully shot the animal.

The next day the second cow was in like condition. Emmil came home for his gun. A neighbour prevailed upon him not to shoot the animal just yet. The neighbor scouted the area and found the cow drinking the next day from a low lying ditch. The Italians poured out the residue from their wine-making into the ditch and the cow was lapping it up. Quite simply the animal was looped. Fencing off the area restored the cow to sobriety. However poor Emmil was kidded about the incident for years. Anytime he drank in the bar to any extent he was mocked with, "He's drunk. Take him out and shoot him."

The hotel was the central core of the town. Kapteyn had a steady tapman now by the name of John Varadi. Varadi had his own orchestra and suggested that when the hotel was renovated the basement be made suitable for a dance hall. It was a small hall but everyone looked forward to the dance.

The night of the dance drew a good crowd. When the dance was in full swing, culprits threw stink bombs through the small basement windows. The dance unfortunately broke up in a hurry. Kapteyn declared it a lost cause and thereafter rented the space only for union meetings or community events, of a quieter nature.

Business had gradually improved. War was imminent.

John, thinking of the ravages of war in Europe and remembering how his wife's parents had lost everything in a war said to Martha, "Your people lost everything. We have the money now, so we'll buy a car and you a fur coat, so we'll have something, whatever happens."

Dealing through a Cadomin man, arrangements were made to purchase a car.

Delivery was to be made in Edmonton. John and Martha took the train to the city and the transaction was made – a Master Deluxe Ford for $1,067.25.

John had never driven so the day was spent with John behind the wheel up and back Portage Avenue (now Kingsway Avenue), mastering the intricacies of driving.

With only that experience, the next day the Kapteyns left for Los Angeles. Martha, her heart in her mouth, refused to sit in the front seat for the first three days, feeling greater safety in the back seat.

John had urged her to keep a sharp lookout so she sat in the back seat shouting mightily at John behind the steering wheel.

On their return, the car was shipped by rail from Edson to Coalspur to the road, such as it was.

When John got in the car at Coalspur it refused to start. A mechanic knew the trouble instantly. The carburetor had been adjusted at Seattle to sea level. The mechanic readjusted it to cope with the higher altitude and it started readily.

The Ford was used when possible. Many times because of the poor road conditions it was impossible. John recalls the time the car got stuck in the mud at Mile 13 between Cadomin and Mercoal and there it sat for six weeks.

John found that inadvertently he had become a taxi-driver. Because there were so few automobiles in the town residents who had to make the 18-mile trip to Cadomin would ask John to drive them.

Many times a miner, bolstered by the beer John sold earlier would pound on his door and ask for taxi service.

"We'll give you ten dollars."

"Go away, I'm tired."

"Come on, we have to get back. We'll give you twenty dollars."

Ever aware of a way to earn more money he would sleepily get up and make the trip hoping to pick up some Mercoal miners stranded in Cadomin. John began to foist more and more of these trips on to his bar tapman, John Varadi.

Business was good. The mines were operating steadily. John decided it was time to expand. Tradesmen came from Edson; George Koebel and crew for the plumbing and heating; Alex Davidge, carpentry, Gus Kneteman, masonry.

Canadian Collieries Dunsmuir Ltd. became the owners of the mine at Mercoal, in 1940.

Contracts were excellent and everyone was prospering. John opted for a 1500 square foot beverage room with a walk-in cooler. He built eight more rooms above the beverage room. Business improved so rapidly that no sooner was that finished than he increased the beverage room again to a total of 3,000 square feet.

More rooms – more customers. Up to this time the law had been pretty lenient with Mercoal. Because of the isolation of the camps on the Coal Branch, as long as they held p-r-e-t-t-y well within the limits they were left more or less on their own. For example Sunday theatre was held regularly decades before the rest of the province. Show night was always Wednesday and Sunday.

By 1940 roads of a sort pretty well connected the mining towns. Cars still travelled in groups of two or three to aid each other when getting stuck, but still had to be shipped in and out by rail to Edson.

The Alberta Liquor Control Board insisted that John build a cafe. Business was so prosperous he had no trouble getting financing . . . from the banks . . . the brewery. He muses, "When you're making money, there's nothing to getting more money – when you need it in the worst way – no way you can find it."

He called back the Edson tradesmen. Sometimes they had to wait some time to be paid off for earlier work and John was grateful. He planned with a flourish – a seating capacity for thirty on the horseshoe counter, six booths for six, and four booths for four – a total seating capacity of 82. Chrome – lots of it and the first neon light on the Coal Branch which proudly proclaimed Hotel & Cafe. More rooms, now a total of forty. The hotel sat flush to the railroad and more than one traveller was delighted to find and use the modern facilities.

Miners made exceptionally good wages, lived hard, drank hard and spent freely.

Miners always knew they were going to work, but the question of whether they would come back up and out was always variable. The work was dangerous, and many lived as if each day would be his last.

With wartime production at full swing, labor was scarce, and there were jobs for all as a travelling hobo found to his sorrow.

He had hopped the freight to the Coal Branch in error. Police picked the man up and put him to work in the mines, whereafter he was always known as Boxcar Mike.

Poker and blackjack were a favourite pastime. Booze provided by the owner of whatever house was having a game at the time, was paid for by silver picked up off the table. As the drinking progressed the tab for the drinks became higher and higher depending on whatever scruples the host of the night may have had or not had.

At one of these games a hard working miner by the name of John Shoroko had a lucky streak and worked his stake up to a pile of bills. He went to the Mercoal hotel beer parlour and talked of his luck. He would go to see his wife in Poland. He hadn't seen her in 24 years.

John Varadi, the tapman asked, "How much did you win?"

"I don't know, all of this." He waved a pile of bills. "Let's count it."

The town of Mercoal.

The two men counted the bills which amounted to $3,600.00. A small fortune.

"Look," the tapman urged. "We'll put this in an envelope, witnessed by two others and put it in the hotel safe. Then you'll get to see your wife for sure."

Shoroko shook his head. "I'm a big boy. I can look after my own money."

The tapman shrugged and returned to his taps. It was none of his affair, really.

Early the next morning, the waitress from the hotel cafe came to John Kapteyn seated in his office.

"John Shoroko is here asking for breakfast on credit. He says he has no money."

Kapteyn shrugged. He'd heard that Shoroko had returned to the blackjack game after the beer parlour had closed, and lost all.

"Feed him." he said laconically.

Beer became rationed. The ratio was based on the previous year's business which was three kegs an hour. When nine kegs were finished on a Saturday evening, the beer parlour was closed up.

During the day John opened the bar for a few hours, then closed for a few hours. Some afternoons he simply quit serving. He split cases, selling six bottles to a bag per customer and suddenly gained a whole new flock of customers. Wives and non-drinkers suddenly seemed to have developed a thirst.

The Coalspur Hotel, a converted bunkhouse reaped the overflow. Customers came, seven miles by rail, or 4½ miles by the shortcut. Some on foot. Bootlegging flourished. Boxcars were loaded in Edmonton with the liquor. One Christmas the car unloaded at Mountain Park, Luscar, Cadomin, but there was none for Mercoal.

John notified the mine, the union, and phone calls were made to Edmonton. Beer was dispatched in double quick time.

John had hired a Chinese chef, who in turn hired three Chinese cooks and a flunky. John had told Ken Wong, his chef, that he could take time off when he wanted but to always make sure he had a replacement.

Mr. Wong followed the race circuit, and when racing season came along, mysteriously a capable chinese chef would step off the train. Ken Wong got on the next train and was gone for three months. The system worked admirably for both employer and employees.

The Chinese dishes were soon a specialty favorite of the hotel.

John kept up his correspondence courses and could be seen pouring over books like Wenzel's Menu Maker - Managerial Control.

He used every method to promote business and when Red Thomson shot an outsize cougar the animal was brought into the beverage room and left on display. It was good for trade, and the animal marked a prosperous few days for beer sales.

305

The Kapteyn children now helped to man the tills in the cafe, and on show nights the whole family was at work.

Help was hard to get and when two of his waitresses got into a hair-pulling fisticuff over a good looking electricians helper, John sat stoically at the counter till the shift was over. Then he diplomatically switched the shifts around so the two women would not have to work with each other.

He still acted as bouncer of his own hotel. One evening, an unknown well educated man, said to be a remittance man, created a disturbance in the beer parlour.

John, secretly envying the man's Eton accent asked him to quiet down or leave. "Always did detest a drunk, and still do." John says.

The man haughtily drew himself erect. "I've been ejected from Asian bars, Africa, and the best beverage rooms on the continent. But never by a man who had a start like you."

John stolidly looked at the man. He'd heard this over and over again during the years.

"I probably stunk at the time. Now I've go a 40-room hotel a beverage room and a cafe that seats 82 people . . . and it's all paid for . . . now get out!"

By 1947, John Kapteyn felt the need of a long holiday. Although the hotel was to be left for his children, he felt the same end could be achieved by a partial ownership. The hotel was solid, financially.

In June of 1947 he sold a half interest in the company called Mercoal Hotel Co. Ltd. John held the bulk of the shares, his wife the rest, except for one share held by the lawyer. One half of the company was sold to Mr. Charlie Young for $55,000, with a down payment of $35,000 in cash paid. It was said that Archie McGavin of the well-known bread company had staked Young to the tune of $25,000. However . . .

Breathing a sigh of relief, the Kapteyns tried to book passage for Holland, but in this year, bookings were hard to come by. While waiting for a booking the Kapteyns spent July of that year in Jasper and at Miette Hot Springs, relaxing and unwinding from the years of toil.

They came to Edmonton, registered at the Royal George Hotel, and John Kapteyn put in a discreet call to an agent of a steamship line. There was always a way if you looked for it. After an evening of wining and dining, John explained they were most anxious to obtain a booking. The two men shook hands on it with the agent receiving a $20 bill and a $5 bill in the handclasp. Whether this had any bearing, at any rate soon after bookings were obtained and passage made to Sweden, then by boat and train to Holland.

The two enjoyed their visit in Europe and came back to Edmonton in November. It was in time, to John's sorrow, to attend the funeral of John's long-time business associate, Edwin D. Conger.

The couple returned to Mercoal.

The new partner said business was dropping off. The clientele had become rougher and tougher.

John sat back for a few days and watched what was happening. He concluded that Charlie had let the clientele get the better of him by catering to the younger rougher element.

"You are going to lose the license if this rowdiness keeps up." he told the Youngs. If the license was lost the hotel would be a bust.

He decided he'd better get back into the business. A cheque was written for $35,000. and returned to Charlie Young. The license was now reinstated in his name and John started on a wholesale clean-up. He'd never been concerned about popularity, he was concerned with running a good business. Good for him. The rougher element kept customers away. He gave notice to fifteen room occupants to clear out. They'd be better off in mining dormitory quarters, and the hotel would be better off without them. At least as permanent residents. He once again started lodging complaints, but now cases were heard in the courthouse at Edson.

With the discovery of oil at Leduc, John knew that the mining town's days were numbered. He decided to sell.

The sale of the Mercoal Hotel was finalized August 15, 1952. He sold the business to Andy Lesyk and James Askew of Edmonton for the sum of $100,000.

Part of the purchase price was paid in property; a $20,000 home of Askew's on 57th Street and $55,000. evaluation placed on a dairy farm of Andy Lesyks.

Sixty three acres of the dairy farm was south of 137th avenue in Edmonton, east of 127th Street. Three parcels were north of 137th avenue and were located in the Municipal District of Sturgeon. These parcels, thought to be 19 acres turned out to be 23 acres when consolidated several years later.

The farm was leased at the time and John and Martha settled down in a house in the Highlands district.

The lessee wanted 'out' to farm on his own, so the Kapteyns moved to the old home on the dairy farm.

John put up a sign – John Kapteyn – 122nd Street. Their mail was received in the West Edmonton post-office located in a grocery store.

John decided to grow potatoes on the land, and even here luck was with him.

He remembers a week in 1957 when potatoes were in short supply. He and a hired hand transported more than 1,000 sacks that week to wholesalers, hotels and cafes at $3.00 a sack. He wouldn't accept an order less than 25 sacks of the netted gems. The following week the price dropped to $2.25 per sack. It didn't matter, he was sold out.

The Kapteyns had by this time lived on the farm growing potatoes and other products for four years.

The City of Edmonton was experiencing growing pains and Fekete Construction Co. Ltd. approached John Kapteyn with a view to buying the property south of 137th Avenue. Fekete took an option on the property in the fall of 1957 and started building the new sub-division of Kensington. John sold the property for $85,000 and no way would John release the title till it was paid in full.

Martha's arthritis was getting worse. The house on the farm had not full amenities and John decided it was time to move. He approached the Fekete company with a view to selling the 23 acres north of 137th Avenue.

Mr. Fekete was fully aware of the value of land, but the area north was not yet part of the city and not zoned for residential housing. When approached he simply told John that his money was tied up in housing.

John said, "I don't need any money. All I need is a house." Feeling slightly ashamed of himself John asked $30,000 for the 23 acres. The company didn't think the sum was untoward so the bulk of the purchase price was made in the form of a new house for Mr. and Mrs. Kapteyn at 13507-125th Street.

Once again, John and Martha headed for Europe while the three bedroom house with double car garage was being constructed.

Martha died August 26th, 1966 having suffered with rheumatoid arthritis for painful years.

Son James lives at 125 Fairway Blvd. River View Heights in New Brunswick and is a Maritime Zone manager for General Motors. Daughter Gloria lives in Los Angeles, and is married to a printer, Howard DeMoore of 3725 Bentley Avenue, Apt. 9, son Norman, an employee of AGT lives with his family at 13608-111th Street in Edmonton.

John Kapteyn married a widow, Mrs. Jo-anne Van Hemert in January, 1970. The couple live amicably apart. Mr. Kapteyn lives an active life – gardening, is a member of the Senior Citizens Lion's Centre, calls bingo for a fraternal lodge and still curls. A visitor to his home may well receive a variety of cookies or special cheese biscuits 'baked with butter' because margarine doesn't give a true flavour. "Always used butter at the hotel."

"Now if you'll excuse me, I'm making a chicken casserole for supper. My grandson, Grant, lives with me now." said John Kapteyn.

. . . A Slip of a Girl, Asking for This Tremendous Loan

MRS. ROBERT SPANACH, 11019-111th Ave., Edmonton, was born to George and Mary Pankovich on April 15, 1926 in Raduc, Lik, Yugoslavia. She was named Amelia.

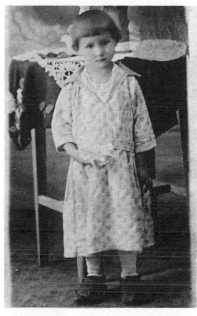

Amelia arrived in Canada at a tender age. (Spanach)

Amelia's father borrowed fare money from friends and arrived in Canada in March, 1927. His fare was paid to Winnipeg, but once there he decided to go further West. Arriving in Edmonton, he got a job in the bush at Smith, Alberta through the immigration office. This lasted for several months, and then he was put to work on the subway being built on 109th Street.

After a few months George decided there was better money to be made in the mines so headed for Mercoal. He obtained a job with the Saunders Ridge Coal Co. and stayed in the company bunkhouse. His wages were $4.20 a day. By saving diligently he was able to bring his wife and child to Mercoal in 1931.

Amelia remembers her first years in Canada as very unhappy. Unable to speak a word of English she was taunted and teased by her playmates. This country was so cold and had so much snow!

Mrs. Pankovich was a lonely woman. There were two bachelors and only one other family who could speak Yugoslavian. The other woman of her race, Mrs. Mary Zdunich was much older, and bedridden much of the time. Mary was indignant to find that her husband had renovated 'a chicken coop', for living quarters. Be that as it may, the two rooms were comfortable and were leased at only one dollar a month.

The depression years had set in and work was sparse. Annie Pankovich was born September, 1932 and the delivery was made with the help of neighbors. Amelia remembers huddling in a corner, trying to help and despairing. She says today, "Poverty exposes children to so many frightening things. To live in a town without hospital facilities . . . when someone got sick you just panicked. It's the worst thing about living in an isolated place."

Amelia endured the feeling that she was the only outcast in the school, and suffered the calls of 'bohunk' from her classmates. This feeling hung on throughout her school years.

"While I was growing up I suffered. At times I hated to go to school."

From 1931 to 1939 work was spasmodic. Mr. Pankovich remembers there was a period of six months when there was no work at all.

But because of the poverty and the isolation there developed a great empathy between the people. "Everyone shared . . . tragedy or happiness." says Amelia. "A child with a bad asthmatic condition had to go to the Mayo Clinic. Everyone dug down and came up with something, and she was sent."

Michael Pankovich was born February 22, 1935, but this time Amelia was spared the torment of fear. Dr. Begg, the mine doctor was in attendance.

Preparing for a wedding at Mercoal. Cooking was done in the tent and guests catered to in the house. Pictured are Mrs. Mary Pankovich, Mrs. Manda Zastankovich and her son.

The local gathering place for the miners was Art's poolhall and men talked of fishing and hunting . . . whether there would be work to-morrow.

The Pankovich family now owned a cow and chickens and grew a vegetable garden every summer. The Pankovich children enjoyed the chickens but developed an antipathy towards moosemeat that was to stay with them for the rest of their lives. They became so suspicious their mother was putting something over on them, that even when she purchased beef at the store, the three children would sometimes not touch it for fear it was moose.

Although Amelia had enjoyed the concerts at school, and the school activities she wasn't allowed to take part in the skating, or the sporting activities of her peers. The European attitude prevailed in her home that a girl should be at home learning to cook and sew and helping with the housework. A girl was wasting her time at sports!

There was no high school at the time, and Amelia felt relief when she had gone as far as she could go – Grade 8. By this time she had developed into a pretty girl with her flashing dark eyes a most attractive feature.

One day she was sent to the Mercoal Mercantile, and purchased some supplies for her mother. She noticed a young stranger in the store who turned out to be Bob Spanach.

Bob was of Yugoslavian descent too. He had come to Canada at the age of 17 with the aid of an uncle who worked in the immigration department.

He had come against his family's wishes, and once in Canada was lonely and wept bitter tears when no one was within hearing range. He was stubborn, too and would not go back.

Bob had come to Canada in 1928 and secured work as a miner in Luscar. He liked the bush, saw opportunity there, and began to supply the mine with mine props as a sideline. When work was slack he did the cutting himself, and when the mines worked, hired a couple of men for the bush.

Timber work increased and gradually bigger orders came his way. He cut mine props near the KD mine and at Trapper Creek. He started cutting near Steeper and eventually established a planer mill there. The mine contracts grew and he opened more camps, hired more men and quit the mine to go into fulltime timber contracting.

But this day he was in the Mercoal Mercantile impatiently killing time because his vehicle had broken down; he was waiting for it to be fixed . . . when in walked Amelia.

He was instantly attracted to the young girl. When she.left Bob quizzed the store clerk. When he found that she too, was Yugoslavian that did it. In no time at all he was knocking at the Pankovich door inquiring if there was milk or fresh eggs for sale.

On August 25, 1941 they were married. Bob was twenty-nine years old, Amelia just fifteen and a half.

The couple moved into a two-roomed bachelor shack, and added rooms as the children came. Their first born, a girl, came in 1942 and died three years later.

George Robert was born February 10th, 1944 and Diane; November 14th, 1945. Amelia insisted on coming to Edmonton for the births, and as her husband was financially an up-coming man, this was no problem.

Bob was a busy man. Business had prospered to the extent where he was supplying Luscar, Mountain Park and the Mercoal mines.

In 1941 Mercoal started to boom along with the economy. Because her husband was so busy, and one winter employed close to 200 men in the various camps, Amelia found herself caught up in a network of a hundred different chores. Many times she found herself in the position of a landlady, putting an employee up overnight and feeding him until he went out to camp.

Mr. and Mrs. Bob Spanach on their wedding day. He was 29, she 15½.

Bob was away much of the time so she would find herself meeting the train to get the freight, groceries, repairs for vehicles, axes and saws, and trundle them home on a sleigh. In winter the freight train always seemed to be late, and if you weren't there to claim, freight mysteriously disappeared. Then there were letters to be mailed, money orders to be purchased, if not for her husband, then for the men in the camps.

The post-office was in the store as was the phone. Amelia was called on to make the phone calls in connection with business, and on one occassion remembers waiting from 9:00 a.m. till 2:00 p.m. to get her call through. The line was perpetually busy.

Amelia was happily busy, too, with the children and all the other activities.

With the building boom of the forties, Bob's operation came into its own, and Bob was kept hopping to keep orders filled. The only other moderately big timber operator on the branch was R. A. Craig. Mr. Craig supplied for the Cadomin mine and shipped a great deal of timber out of province, some as far away as the Northwestern United States. The two men worked independently without conflict, each operating in different areas, producing everything from railroad ties to dressed lumber. Both were similar in another respect in that neither ever formed a company, but operated strongly from day to day. It is said that Mr. Craig supplied the Cadomin Coal Co. for twenty-seven years on the basis of a verbal agreement.[33]

Bob gave lumber to the Mercoal Legion to build on a 'pay when you can basis'; the same with the B.P.O. Elks Hall. He built the Mercoal Cafe in 1944 where lunches for the men could be packed. It had an adjoining coffee shop and rooms upstairs. He supplied lumber for the new theatre . . . and people began to expand and spruce up their homes. It was a prosperous time for everyone. Bob had purchased more heavy equipment to aid his work in outlying camps. He obtained the GM dealership and built Mercoal Motors.

One morning in October Bob headed for an outlying camp, but his vehicle became stuck and he couldn't get through. He was not far from his planer mill at Steeper, just a mile out of Mercoal, so headed back and started to work the planer.

It is believed his sleeve got caught in the machinery and he was pulled into the works and badly crushed. Emergency aid was given and then the race to an Edmonton hospital began. He died in the ambulance enroute. Bob Spanach died October 25, 1949 and was buried in Glenwood Cemetery at Edson. The impact of his death was felt throughout the town, and that term the high school year book cover featured a memorium to Robert Spanach.

Amelia at 23 years of age was left a widow with two children. The next four years Amelia varied from 'carrying on' to 'cracking up.' Bob, like many a man, had made no will and much of his business was carried "in his head." The estate was held in probate by the public trustee until things could be straightened out. Interests at Wabamun were discovered among others.

While people were kind, the locusts also descended. Efforts to secure the Spanach contracts were made, and Amelia involved her whole family in the operation – her father, brother, close friends – and in between ran first to Edmonton, then to the Mayo Clinic then back to Edmonton for help with her ever tightening nerves. She was advised to sell. An unnamed man from Edmonton and his son arrived in Mercoal and offered a "ridiculous" price for the business. Amelia decided the only thing to do to settle the estate would be to buy her children's shares out and carry on.

The mine at Cadomin closed in 1952. Mr. Craig moved from Wampus Creek to Antler Creek.

The Mercoal mine was fair enough. As long as Amelia could supply the contract was to be hers, and they would help financially if she could swing the operation.

In the fall of '73 when this interview took place, Amelia, still a strikingly handsome woman laughed . . . "When I think of it now . . . there I was, just a slip of a young girl in her twenties, with a Grade eight education, knowing nothing from nothing, and standing in the bank at Edson asking for this tremendous loan."

[33] David Lake

313

Despite the incongruity of the situation, the loan was given. Amelia started anew as the Spanach Lumber Co. Mercoal Motors became Coal Branch Motors. Amelia ran the business but on a much smaller scale than her husband. The contract was there but whereas "Bob could produce 200,000 I would produce 20,000. While I was making a comfortable living, I never really made money." Amelia admits the coal company was fair, "but I also had to dance to their tune."

Northwestern Pulp and Power Limited came into the picture in 1956. The Hinton based company began to obtain large timber leases which included many parts of the Coal Branch. "Things started to get rough for the smaller lumber operators. I was mainly dependent on the mines but it eventually became almost impossible for the smaller operators to continue," she continued.

R. A. Craig at 65 years of age chose this time to retire. Amelia, still somewhat secure with the contract from Canadian Colleries (Dunsmuir) Ltd. continued on. In 1959 the Mercoal mine closed.

For the miners the change was drastic. They had been accustomed to paying in the vicinity of $40 a month for a four roomed house, and found that in other points of the province this rental was considered ridiculously low and was not even considered.

But even as families moved out there were those who continued to cling and hope. There was talk of reopening the mine on a strip mining basis only. Thirty to forty families remained on the strength of this thread of talk and it became an actuality – for a very short time.

Friends at the mine kindly but mistakenly, told Amelia that her equipment for the stripping process was hopelessly antiquated. Amelia considered. This was her home, and if new heavy equipment was needed, then she would take the plunge.

She did and the strip-mining operation lasted three weeks! Amelia says serenely, "I've been in trouble ever since."

In retrospect Amelia says, "I would have done well if the mines had not closed. We stayed till the last possible minute then had to move because school was starting. We came to Edmonton in September of 1959."

"So here was I, with new equipment – it was lose everything or the alternative – try and find work. Again I dragged the whole family into it."

Amelia was tempted to learn to operate the heavy equipment, "but my father wouldn't let me."

In her search for work she presented herself at various points, and burly contractors would look at the young woman and ask in surprise, "Whose equipment is it?"

Amelia in her husky voice would say softly, "Well, it's mine."

In 1973 Amelia still operates on a small scale. Her relatives still work, but hold other jobs too.

314

Son George Robert Spanach played tackle with the Eskimos, went on to Montreal then Vancouver where he injured his knee and ended that career. He lives in Edmonton, as does his sister Diane, now Mrs. Radmanovich.

Amelia lives in a comfortable home with her parents, and they all think nostalgically of the Coal Branch where "people were genuinely interested in each other."

The Spanach home still stands in Mercoal, one of a handful that are used as summer homes.

* * *

. . . The Wind was Too Much

MINA GOURLEY by herself – August, 1929, George A. Gourley bid on the position of CNR agent at Leyland and got it, so we prepared to move from Edson.

We had 200 spring chickens. George made crates for them and our furniture. The dining room chairs were securely hung in crates to prevent scratching. One crate had been about one inch too wide and had to be remodelled before it would go through the door. The CNR provided a boxcar and we had it full. On arrival at Leyland there was a strong desire to burn down the old station before moving in. The living quarters had been calsomined dark rose maybe ten years previously. It was filthy. The wall between the living quarters and office, waiting room and freight shed was dried out V-joint. You could see through the cracks and the noise was bad at train times. A few months later the B & B men came and reinforced the wall and painted throughout. This made it a pleasant place to be; the mountain air was lovely.

After being there a few months we had to sell the chickens. The CNR and the forestry both had objections to chicken houses being on their property.

We had good neighbors living in cars – Bud Wendt, Bert Woodcock, CN operators, Gerald Hurst and family lived nearby. The only place to walk was up or down the track or in to Cadomin. One Sunday in January Bud & Iris Wendt, George and I walked five miles uphill to Luscar and had tea at Victor Girardis home. Part way home Joe Lavoretti picked us up on his speeder. We were grateful for that ride.

I had been told by my father, A. H. Mahon, CNR Master Mechanic that it was windy in the area. I have never seen such wind as they get through the narrow valley. Complete boxcar roofs sometimes blew off flying through the air. One day we looked out to see a horse trough and woman's old fashioned nightie flying through the air, coming from Cadomin. The wind there blew in circular gusts. You can hear it coming down the valley. Shale sifted in around windows and doors. The table cloth looked as though someone had sprinkled coarse pepper over it. In the morning our pillow slips were black with white marks where our heads had been.

Christmas week the express shed was full of liquor for Cadomin. Groceries from Alberta Trading Co. were shipped to Leyland for Cadomin people. Cadomin was a closed camp and the mine manager objected to people buying outside of camp. Gambling joints were 'closed', officials took the rake off.

January 23 our first child, Jean was born. Mrs. Clyborn from the store south of the station kindly took care of us. Clyborns, Nicholsons had a large store, 50 × 100, previously owned by Hood.

One day Mrs. Wendt and I walked across the McLeod River Valley to Cadomin. On the way home the wind started to blow. Iris held the baby carriage down and I pushed – thankful to get home.

Leyland looking south. Cadomin in distance, 1929.

Leyland Water Tank — 1929.

316

Leyland Station — 1929.

Rocks near Mt. Leyland

(Shipka)

One night when it was about forty degrees below zero, the operator at Cadomin phoned to warn us that some coal cars had started
downhill towards Leyland. Someone had failed to secure brakes.
George ran out and threw the switch to open the track to the Y, as
there was danger of them going too fast to make the curve, and if they
left the rails they would demolish the station. He got CNR merit
marks for this venture. Another night a caboose, Tom Meters was
Conductor, got away and came down past Leyland and uphill before
stopping and rolling back.

317

In February a terrific wind blew for days. The United Church at Cadomin was turned upside down. A chicken house was demolished killing a man who was in feeding chickens. One Saturday morning the whole end of the Leyland store was blown out. Men built a new end taking two days to complete this job. The wind subsided while they were working and started again. We looked out the window after hearing a roar. Flames were belching out of the store, blowing sparks over our station. Apparently wind had cracked the chimney. Cans and ammunition were exploding. The sparks started fire on hill above the station and burned a barn across the Luscar line. George, operators and section men worked all night putting out fires on our roof. Fortunately we had three barrels of water in the station. George's mother, baby Jean and I sat in a boxcar watching this huge fire. We had four suitcases of best possessions with us in case the station burned.

A kind gentleman who used to sell men's suits came along and took Jean and I to his room in Cadomin. Grandma stayed with the suitcases. The backs of my hands had welts from the stones pelting me by the time we walked the mile to Cadomin. The south wall of the station was pitted from the stones hitting it. All outbuildings in Cadomin had pole braces to keep them from being blown over. Houses had shutters on south windows. One night a house lost its complete roof. The CNR water tank was blown out of line necessitating a B & B crew spending eight days straightening it.

We moved back to Edson at the first opportunity. We loved the mountain air and country, but the wind was too much. A month later the wind blew two boxcars loaded with way freight out of a moving train which was crossing the valley to go to Luscar. The Claims Department sent men from Winnipeg to investigate. They thought someone's carelessness had caused these cars to be rolled clear off the track. Only a cement wall across the narrow valley could prevent such accidents. We knew of three men who were picked up in the air by the wind and dropped on gravel, skinning knees and hands.

We spent 20 months in Leyland station and have happy memories of our stay.

* * *

Mannix - Coal Branch Operations

Coal Mining Operation in the Mountain Park Coal Area – (Mercoal, Leyland, Cadomin, Luscar, Kaydee, Mountain Park) commenced in 1911 and coal has been mined by underground and surface methods as follows:

1911–1950	UG & S.	Mountain Park Coal Company Ltd.	7 leases.
1917–1952	UG	Cadomin Coal Co.	7 leases.
1921–1956	UG & S.	Luscar Coal Co.	8 leases.

318

1931–1938	S.	Mt. Cheviot Coal Co., Ltd.	4 leases.
1932–1953	UG & S.	K.D. Collieries Co., Ltd.	3 leases.
1942 – 1946	UG & S.	King Coal Co.	3 leases.

Coalspur Coal Area – (Sterco, Coal Valley, Foothills).

1910–1920	UG	North American Collieries	1 lease.
1910–1923	UG	Yellowhead Coal Co.	1 lease.
1916 – 1930	UG	Beacon Coal Co.	2 leases.
1918–1957	UG	Lakeside Coal Co., Ltd.	4 leases.
1918–1958	UG & S.	Canadian Collieries Resource Ltd.	7 leases.
1918–1922	UG & S.	Stupor, Oakley & Co.,	3 leases.
1918–1950	S.	Sterling Collieries.	2 leases.
1919–1934	UG	Mt. Cheviot Coal Co. Ltd.	1 lease.
1920 1921	UG	Pacific Collieries	1 lease.
1920–1965	UG	Canadian Collieries Ltd.	8 leases.
1921–1923	UG	Bryan Coal Co.	1 lease.
1921–1922	UG	Vitality Coal Co.	1 lease.
1922–1955	S.	Sterling Valley Coal Mine	4 leases.
1922–1932	UG	Val d'Or Collieries	1 lease.
1923–1925	UG	Corona Coal	1 lease.
1924–1957	UG & S.	King Coal Ltd.	5 leases.
1926–1928	UG	Alberta Canadian Collieries	1 lease.
1927–1932	UG	Newcastle Junior Mining	1 lease.
1949–1954	UG	Vitaly Coal Co.	1 lease.
1959–1960	S.	Blackmore Collieries Ltd.	2 leases.

UG – Underground Mining. S. – Strip and surface mining.
XX – Mining, processing and shipping of coal has been resumed from the area with Cardinal River Coal Company being actively engaged in coal operations and Manalta Coal anticipating startup in the Gregg River area.

Mannix Involvement

1922 – The Mannix Company was requested by the Department of Highways, Government of the Province of Alberta, to check the feasibility of a highway route into the Coal Branch area, this was checked and found to be a viable project. (O. Burggren) – Mannix forces were not involved in construction.

1937 – Mannix was successful in obtaining a stripping contract at Coal Valley, equipment enroute from a project completed in Quebec Province to Mannix Yard was re-billed directly to Coalspur, from which point it was moved directly to the Coal Valley area to commence stripping, and continued through into the early 40's at which time stripping commenced in the Cadomin field. In 1942, a large fleet of heavy equipment left Calgary Yard for Cadomin and due to difficulties encountered enroute made stops at Blackfalds, Edmonton and Edson. Arriving at Coalspur, all equipment was unloaded and held at this point until adequate access roads were constructed into the Cadomin Coal area to allow movement of the equipment and commencement of stripping which continued for several years.

L. Pozzi

... Pay or be Thrown off the Train

HARVEY A. SWITZER, Phm. B., by himself – Early in January, 1912, I returned to Edson from B.C. where I had spent the winter with relatives.

I had spent all the previous summer working on the famous (or infamous, depending on your point of view) Edson-Grande Prairie Trail. Along with two partners we took the first outfit from Edson over the Trail, and had planned to return to Grande Prairie the following spring. Working on the Trail, I had a ringside seat to see the great tide of settlers flowing into the Grand Prairie country that summer.

However, our partnership had been dissolved so that my plans were left hanging. I decided to look over the local area where I might find a suitable place in which to open a drug store. I took an all day trip on the train to Jasper, then called Fitzhugh. It was, that winter, only a few miles east of the head of the steel and there was a good deal of traffic in and out; but it did not appeal to me.

On my return to Edson I heard that there was a large camp at Mile 33 on the Alberta Coal Branch where they were driving the tunnel. I decided to go up there. As there was no passenger service I got down to the junction at Bickerdike and waited for a freight going up. About eleven o'clock that night, one came along, and while it was stopped there I scrambled aboard on top of a car of bridge timber, with my blankets in a pack on my back.

Four or five other men had the same idea, so I had company. Although it was January, we had a light shower of rain during the night, but as I had a tarpaulin around my blankets it did not bother me. Along about the middle of the night, the brakeman came along with his lantern and collected two dollars from each of us. We paid it without demur, as it was either pay or be thrown off the train.

We arrived around five o'clock in the morning. The camp was down in quite a hollow from the railway grade and the head of the tunnel was only a short distance farther up the track. I went into the main room of the Stopping Place which was comfortably warm. There were ten inch boards fastened to the wall all around the room for seats. As there was no other accomodation I tried to sleep on one of these, but it was so narrow that every time I fell asleep I rolled off, so I gave it up for a bad job.

I had breakfast when it was ready, and spent the time talking with the men there. Later on word reached us that there would be a train going down around one o'clock. So at that time there were about twenty five or thirty men lined up along the track. We had expected that the engineer, when he came down from the head of the tunnel would stop, or at least slow to a crawl. We were surprised that he 'high balled' right through, as there would be quite a bit of revenue for the train crew. We learned later that there were railroad officials on the train and he did not dare stop.

All the men except myself went back down to the Camp. I started out to walk down to Bickerdike. Along about eleven o'clock that night I spied a dim light which I found was coming from a small shack, housing some eight or ten men in a Tie Camp. I rapped and opened the door, although I had to stoop as the roof was so low.

I talked with the men for a few minutes and they invited me to come in and spread my blankets and spend the night. The place was very small for so many men and the air was terrifically hot and not too sweet smelling. Besides I was quite sure there were lots of 'cooties', so I thanked them and said I would push on.

I walked on until I came to a deserted log cabin which I think was in the vicinity of the present Embarass. The doors and windows were all missing as were a few slabs from the slab roof, letting the moon shine through. It had a dry floor, so I spread my blankets and spent the rest of the night there. The next morning I got up and continued my walk to Bickerdike. I was able to get a train for Edson without too long a wait.

Once back in Edson I made arrangements for my Drug Store. I operated it over the years until now it is operated by two of my sons, both graduate pharmacists. Edson has been my home for all these years and although I have travelled widely, I always returned here.

. . . Time Spent as a 'Political Prisoner'

PETER ADDISON (Baldy) ROBB by his daughters, Alberta Cole and Nevis LaBranche – Baldy Robb was born in the County of Gamrie, Scotland on November 24, 1887. His parents came to Canada with their six boys when Peter, the youngest was about four. They settled in Manitoba.

When barely twenty, P. A. made his way west to participate in the Grand Trunk Pacific boom, freighting supplies for the railroad then being constructed west through the Rockies and for the Branch line.

P. A. Robb — 1924, staking coal at Grande Cache.

Photo — A. Cole, N. LaBranche

Over the Yellowhead Route in 1922. Identified in the photo is Baldy Robb holding the rifle, and Charlie Nelson with revolver. C. W. Niemayer and H. J. Silverthorne were also part of this overland trip   Photo — Courtesy A. Cole, N. LaBranche

running to Coalspur. He established himself on a ranch near Edson. When the overland route from Edson to the Peace River country was opened up, he freighted and packed supplies and mail over the old Grande Prairie Trail.

323

It was during this period that P. A. met the lovely Winifred Edwards, who had recently arrived from her native Wales. They were married in 1915, and after a short time in Edmonton, P. A. took his bride to his ranch at Wolf Creek. It was also during this period that Baldy's avid interest in prospecting resulted in the filing of numerous coal claims, among which was Minehead (Mile 33) and Bryan (Mile 32).[34] A few years later, Bill Rae, then member for Edson-Jasper Constituency, requested Baldy's permission to use the name of 'Robb' for that area. Mile 33 was developed by the Minehead Coal Company, formed by P. A. Robb, Dr. A. E. Porter, and Joe E. Morino. They later sold out to the Balkan Coal Company, in which Alex Susnar was involved.

It is difficult to enumerate the coal claims originally staked by Baldy Robb. Among his effects is evidence of the staking of the claims called Hoppe, on which the present Grande Cache Mine is now situated. The claims at that time were disallowed on the grounds that the coal was 'too green!'

No biography would be complete without mention of Baldy's intense interest and involvement in politics. His tireless work for the Conservative Party, his subsequent disenchantment with their policies, and his decision to join forces with the Liberals preceded the political scandal that held the interest of the West in 1926.

As Deputy Returning Officer for Brule, Baldy was charged on three counts; the first two were eventually dropped but he was finally sentenced on the third count, that of illegally initialing ballots. The conviction was won by the Crown when his final appeal was denied in May of 1926; this after two judges reluctant to pass sentence in the face of the confused jumble of witnesses were replaced. He was released after serving less than a year of his five-year sentence. It may be that a petition from his area signed by hundreds of residents, and requesting his early release was instrumental in his pardon . . . or it may be that the Crown regarded the sentence as excessive in those frontier election battles where the victory of the "right" party was deemed more important by its supporters than the consideration of voting legalities.

Baldy with his typical wry sense of humor explained this sojourn to his children as his time spent as a 'political prisoner.' In present day parlance this might have more than a modicum of truth in it. Correspondence indicates that he ably managed his affairs from his retirement, and that his wife Winnifred looked after four small children and conducted the coal business efficiently and profitably during his absence.

On his return, he moved his family to Robb where he opened one of the several sawmills which he was to operate in the following years. His opposition to the Conservative government, and later to the Soc-

[34] These statements vary with others written in Part 1.

324

ial Credit government continued unabated, as did his support of the Liberal party.

The Robb children remember their big frame house as pulsing with activity and laughter, always with visitors from every walk of life – friends, business associates, old-timers or hungry and destitute travellers. In the tradition of the Coal Branch, friendship and hospitality were freely dispensed.

Mr. Robb's family were disappointed in the flimsy research of one local author who obviously confused P. A. Robb with one "Baldy Rabb", who was charged with bootlegging. Those who knew Baldy Robb affirm that he would have scorned to be involved in such a picayune occupation.

Typical of the many adventures of this pioneer and adventurer was Baldy's participation in the trek over the Yellowhead in 1922.

Baldy and three friends, Charles Nelson, C. W. Niemayer and H. J. Silverthorne started in 1922, in an Overland car on the Edmonton to Victoria route through the Yellowhead Pass. They travelled along the railroad tracks whenever possible. When forced off, they cut a trail through the bush and continued, reaching Kamloops well ahead of their competitors. Here the Board of Trade, forerunner of the present Chamber of Commerce, gave them a tremendous welcome, wining and dining them until the wee small hours of the morning, and splashing their names across the Kamloops paper as the first to cross the Yellowhead. Baldy chuckled as he related how this welcome incapacitated them to the extent that while recovering from it the next morning, the second car, following the right of way they had cut, sped through Kamloops and reached Victoria before them.

. . . *Bought the First Truck in Cadomin*

RICHARD A. CRAIG by his daughter, Mrs. Vivian Melnyk – My father, Richard Allan Craig, was born on a farm near Winnipeg, December 5, 1880. Before coming to Cadomin he had spent most of his life building railroads in Western Canada.

He came to Cadomin in October, 1921 to work in the coal mine. His sister, Annie Douglas and her husband Stewart, were already in Cadomin and he learned of the job through them.

For the first four years he worked at various jobs in the mine – in the rock tunnel, digging coal, in the pillars, then as a driver boss. But my father was not happy working in the coal mine. He was used to working in the outdoors.

The Cadomin Coal Company had been buying their timber for the mine from various sources; from British Columbia, from the Robb area where Baldy Robb and Corey Simmonds operated, etc. My

Hauling logs out of the bush in the Whitehorse.

Seats on the back of Dick Craigs four wheel drive — ready to transport Cadomin residents to a picnic.   — V. Melynk

father on his various hunting trips had spotted timber up the White-horse suitable for mine timber and lumber.

He approached Jack MacMillan, the mine manager for a contract to take out mine timber. After many delays, finally in the fall of 1925 he was given the contract.

He started out by himself with a pick, shovel and dynamite, to build a road up to the Whitehorse Valley. When I look back on it now, remembering the terrain of that country, it seems inconceivable that one man would have the nerve and the ego to undertake such a task.

He worked by himself until he reached the Whitehorse Falls, four miles from Cadomin. Then he hired two men to help him blast and put in the cribbing around the falls. His first camp was built that win-

The First Truck in Cadomin Purchased by Dick Craig.

ter about a half-mile further from these falls. That winter they cut mine timber and hauled it in by sleigh to the coal company.

The next summer the road was continued up the valley another four miles. Here he built a sawmill and eventually supplied lumber as well as mine timber to the mines.

In those days rough lumber sold for $18 a thousand and out of this $2.50 was paid to the government in timber dues. He continued operating in the Whitehorse until 1939.

First of July picnic enjoyed by Cadomin residents at Paradise Valley, up the West Mine Road. All were transported on Dick Craig's four wheel drive.

Photo — V. Melnyk

Dick Craig stands by his first camp on the Whitehorse, a half mile from the Whitehorse Falls.

Dick Craig — 1951 at McLeod River Mill with one of his lumber trucks. — V. Melnyk

My father bought the first truck in Cadomin in 1928. It was a four wheel drive. I can remember the excitement when it arrived by flat car. A sizeable audience watched it being unloaded. This truck was used for many purposes. Besides hauling lumber and mine props, a box was built on the back to haul ashes from the power house, to spread on the roads around Cadomin.

The only two roads out of Cadomin were the one up the White-horse, a distance of eight miles and the other up to the west side of Cadomin – a five mile stretch of road that my father had built for the coal company around the side of the mountain.

As few people had cars my father built seats on the back of the truck and every Sunday during the summer, the people of Cadomin had the pleasure of piling on the back of the truck and going for a picnic . . . either up the Whitehorse or to Paradise Valley on the West Mine Road. As the numbers increased a trailer with seats was pulled behind the truck.

During the years that followed my father did other types of work for the coal company. He built the foundation for the power house when it was enlarged, and laid the foundation for the community hall. One of his biggest tasks as he remembers it, was building the skating rink. There was a strike at the mine and many men were idle. Mr. Chevanaugh, the mine engineer, drew up the plans. Then my father was given sixteen men, none of them including himself skilled carpenters, but in three weeks time they built the skating rink. The rafters were put together on the ground, bolted together, then put in place with the aid of a gin pole and the four wheel drive. This build-ing was remarkably strong. It withstood the force of the winds and heavy snows for many years. The following summer they built the curling rink.

In 1935, my father was given permission to build the first hardware store on the Branch. By that time many people were buying lumber

Craig's Road up the Whitehorse.   — V. Melynk

329

One of the many Sunday Picnics at Cadomin.

from him to build their own houses and he could see the need for a hardware store. At first he thought of only stocking windows, doors, roofing etc, but then decided a full line of hardware was needed. Customers came from the whole Coal Branch to deal at our store.

In 1939, the timber in the Whitehorse being depleted, he leased timber down the Wampus Creek, northeast of Cadomin, towards the McLeod River.

Lumber at Dick Craig's planing mill, about four miles from Cadomin.

Photo — V. Melnyk

Faced with the task of building miles of bush roads he bought a bulldozer. This was the first bulldozer seen in Cadomin and indeed the first to be used in the bush on the Coal Branch. When they started operating there were many who came to watch, amazed at what this piece of machinery could do.

Eventually he bought three bulldozers and with them built many miles of bush roads. I am sure that if they were laid end to end they would reach from Cadomin to Edmonton. This opened up new territory to the residents of the Coal Branch. On his roads people went hunting, fishing, picnicking, berry-picking, or just driving for pleasure. Creeks such as the Deer Lick, the Eunice, the Antler, the Neal and the Gregg River were opened up for fishing and hunting.

Dick Craig

During the berry picking season my father would send sometimes two trucks loaded with people down to the Wampus to pick berries. Two years after timber was cut out of an area, hundreds of acres of wild raspberries would appear. Some Sundays over one hundred people would pile on the backs of his trucks with their lunches and water pails. They would come back in the evening with their pails full of beautiful red raspberries. I am sure that many Sundays over a ton of berries would be picked. People would come not just from Cadomin, but from all over the Coal Branch . . . some as far as Edson to pick raspberries at his camp.

His operations down the McLeod River grew – he bought a planing mill and sold lumber all over the Coal Branch, and to lumber companies in Edmonton, much of which was sold in the United

Mountain Park from top of Cado Mountain, 1974.

Photo — Marcoff

States. He cut around 2½ million feet of lumber a winter and employed around sixty men.

In 1956 as the Cadomin mine had closed and further timber stands in the area were being leased by Northwest Pulp and Power at Hinton, my father with a few of his men went up to High Level in Northern Alberta to look for new timber areas. The next fall in 1957, having obtained a timber lease near High Level, they moved their equipment north. Eventually he sold the business to two of his employees, Manford Nelson and Leno Salvador.

Since then my father has lived in Edmonton and has enjoyed his years of retirement. He is fortunate at the age of 92, in having good mental and physical health . . . perhaps due to the years of hard work in the bush he loved so well. My father was a man of vision. He was held in high esteem by the many people who knew him. I was very fortunate to have had such a man for a father.

. . . The Only Pole Tow Track I Have Ever Seen.

HENRY WASSMUTH by himself – In the spring of 1929 the lumbercamp of Dedoiler & Watson in Embarras closed. I wanted to see the Coal Branch before I returned to Edmonton. I jumped the freight train and found the coal mines were booming. I noticed a real market for the farmer.

In Edson, someone said if you want to work, Fulmer operates a small mill and planer just half mile north of Edson. I worked there and in the evenings walked to see the district. Edson was not easy

Dedoiler & Watson camp in Embarras . . . the logloader.

photo — Wassmuth

country to open up for farming, but the location on the west half of Section 26 impressed me. It would enable me to start a market garden and be a stepping stone for the future.

I worked it and the following winter went to Pat Merrigans camp in Medicine Lodge, and also west of Marlboro.

Roy Broom says: This is the first shack I lived in near Edson. At night it was so cold the water in the water bucket would be frozen solid. I had a job chinking it up. I would get up two or three times a night to stoke the fire.

— Roy Bromm

Then with my borrowed old sleigh and team, I headed for Embarras. I stopped on the farm of Roy Bromm to get orientation. It was about 5 o'clock and I a total stranger.

Roy said, "Is that all the hay you've got?" One bale. I said yes and Roy said to his hired man, "Load one more bale on that sleigh." He then ordered his man to unhook my team, and ordered me into the house for supper. I said I had no money, but Roy ordered me in.

Mrs. Bromm was a real cook and the table was loaded. Roy got to know that I would be another farmer in the district. After supper Roy ordered me to bed upstairs in a manner that left no room for refusal. In the morning my team was fed and Roy said to head for Weald and Jack the Frog. There Jack said I could not make it to Embarras that night, and I could not break loose from their hospitality.

I lost the camp road the next day and travelled the river. The horse on the far side broke through the ice. Finally he struggled up again. Nothing had upset and I reached Embarras that night.

The following Spring I noticed on the way back that moose were so plentiful and did not run from sleigh and horses. Also in Erith I saw the only pole tow track I have ever seen, still in operation.

The farm from a shoestring developed till vegetables and potatoes were shipped to the Coal Branch by freight and in carload lots.

SHERMAN A. AND LUCY A. YELLAND

My father, Sherman A. Yelland, made his first acquaintance with the Coal Branch as a section man with the Grand Trunk Pacific Railway, and later came to be a miner at Mountain Park and Cadomin.

My mother and father were married in California and came to Canada, with their baby, Elizabeth, to settle on a homestead in the Peers area, near Edson, in 1914. Dad farmed in the summer, but in the winter augmented the farm income (and it was necessary) by working at various jobs in such places as Strome, Alberta, Saskatoon, Saskatchewan, and Brule in Alberta. Their first child, Elizabeth, died of diptheria before she was a year old. Their second child, Sherman, junior, was born near Peers. Eventually Dad was working winters in the mines on the Branch, while still working the farm, but then moved the family to Mountain Park.

Dad worked in the Mountain Park mine until 1921, and I, Mary, was born while they were still there. In 1921 we took up residence in Cadomin, and my sister, Flora, was born there. Dad worked at the Cadomin mine right through to his death in the spring of 1952, except for a few months when he left the mine and was caretaker of the Cadomin School. Mother left the Branch in the summer of 1952, when the mine was closed.

All of our family loved the mountains and enjoyed our beautiful setting on the Branch. We spent a good deal of time outdoors, with Mother and my sister and I enjoying hiking and berry picking, and my Dad and brother finding fun in hunting and fishing.

I remember my school days, which started in the old school that later became the Pool Hall, and which concluded in the newer school. Recess was always a pleasant time; in the winter spent in sliding on the hill, and in summer spent in wading in the creek. In my early years in the old school I can remember winter mornings when we spent the first part in action games, because it wasn't warm enough to sit at our desks. School memories would not be complete without a reference to our principal, Herb. Harper, who ruled with some strictness but with a measure of good humour that made him popular.

We did have a swimming hole in a backwater from the McLeod River, and it was enjoyed, except that it never got very warm. The river water was icy, and kept chilling the water we swam in.

My first recollection of a church service was of its being held in the beer parlour of the "Black Beetle", later a rooming house for single miners, and which was destroyed in a spectacular middle of the night fire one winter. Later church services were held in a community church over towards the river from the centre of camp. Then our family attended the United Church when it was built a little up the hill on the west side of the camp. The church was quite a focal point for our family.

My brother, Sherman, now lives in Edmonton, where he works with the Department of Agriculture of the Alberta Government. My sister, Flora, married Donald Pinder, a school teacher, and they live in Victoria, B.C. In 1940 I married the Rev. Dwight Powell, who had been minister in Cadomin for three years, and we now live at Nanton, Alberta.

Mary I. Powell

. . . From Service to the Theatre

REV. C. DWIGHT POWELL by himself — My own residence on the Coal Branch came late, and lasted for a very brief time, three years, but it was so interesting that I shall always be pleased that I had the opportunity to live there.

At the beginning of July, 1936, immediately upon my graduation in theology at the University of Alberta and St. Stephen's College, Edmonton, I was assigned as the minister of the United Church in Cadomin, Mountain Park and Luscar, with my home to be two rooms behind the church in Cadomin. I could not afford both to buy an old car, and pay for its freight to have it shipped to Cadomin from Edson (and there was no road then joining the two) so my travelling was by train when available, and by foot otherwise. The Cadomin Church

335

was located on a "shelf" on the side of the mountain, a few feet above the town, and affording a view out over the whole place.

I remember the first day I rode in on the old, mixed train. Watching the mountain range that we were approaching, and watching my own watch hoping that there was enough time left to get near to that range. What a delight to find that Cadomin lay right in the first valley of the mountains, in a most beautiful country. Many trips up and through those mountains later confirmed the first impression – it is a beautiful country!

The town, itself, had a covering of coal dust over everything, that made it seem somewhat drab at first, but the friendly people and the lively activities of the town (or should I call it "camp" because that was the way everyone referred to it) soon made you forget all of that.

I remember that the Sunday evening church service was set for 6:30 p.m., and wondered about the early hour, until I realized that this was so it could be over by show time in the theatre. Many of the congregation, especially those of the junior choir, moved directly from the service to the theatre.

One interesting new habit that had to be acquired came about because the newspapers came in pairs, with a day off in between, because of the train schedule. One took one's news in large gulps, and then fasted in between.

No one can remember the Coal Branch without mentioning the wind! Some peculiar conformation of the mountains and valleys made a wind tunnel out of the McLeod River valley through Cadomin, and wind came through with incredible velocities. I have been caught out in such a wind when I was unsure whether I could keep from blowing away myself, literally. On one occasion a box car was blown right out of a freight train. On more than one occasion box cars were blown away from the siding, and some distance along the main track.

I remember one night leaving Mountain Park on foot just after midnight to walk to Cadomin, and some three miles from the Park hearing some representative of the mountain lion family howling in the trees fairly close to my route. The hair on my neck actually stiffened, and I could feel some kind of kinship with the ancient, primitive people. If anyone accuses me of being afraid, I would say right here that they are entirely correct.

Times of strike in the mine came with fair frequency as miners obeyed the dictates of their unions, and these caused a kind of excitement, but also a kind of hopelessness as they dragged on. Then occasionally disaster would strike in the underground workings, and a sad farewell would have to be said to a brother.

I have a special reason for fondness for the Coal Branch for it was there that I met and courted the lovely lady who became my wife in 1940, Miss Mary Yelland, daughter of Mr. and Mrs. Sherman A. Yelland.

In June of 1939 I received a new posting within the Church and left the Coal Branch at the end of that month. In later years when I lived in Edmonton I conducted funeral services for many of the Branch people who had moved to Edmonton when the mines closed. In these services we felt drawn together in a particular way because of having shared experiences on the Coal Branch.

C. Dwight Powell

The Alberta Coal Branch Club

Early in 1959 a group of former Cadomin residents in casual conversation, talked about the possibility of forming a club.

The idea grew and on March 9, 1959, a formal meeting was held in the Mewbourne Auditorium in Edmonton. The purpose was the organization of a social club for former residents of the coal mining towns of the Coal Branch, Brule, Pocohontas and Hinton.

Mr. Jim Bush opened the meeting and Mr. William Stene acted as chairman until an executive body was elected.

Suggestions were put forth as to a name and purpose of such a club and finally George Nichol moved that the "Coal Branch Reunion Club' be accepted. It was, but in due course the name was changed to the ACB Club or the Alberta Coal Branch Club.

The first executive was comprised of President, Ray Walker; Secretary, Mrs. Freda Dombroski; Treasurer, Chuck Gowers. An Entertainment Committee that was enlarged to include a Ways and Means Committee was comprised of: Spud Dombroski, George Nichol, Con Doherty, Bob Mitchell, Ed Jenkins, Mamie Stene, Mamie Wrigley, Hugh Anderson and Alf Letendre.

The first social event was a dance held in the Trocodero Ballroom on April 3, 1959, which proved to be an overwhelming success. Membership grew and by May, 1964, the secretary's notes showed a club membership of 1,261. The November 16, 1966 minutes show a membership of 428 members, 185 pensioners.

The ACB Club holds several functions a year including one outdoor picnic. Perhaps the largest event is the New Years Dance held annually a day or two before New Year's Eve. The 1972 dance held at the Polish Hall, one of Edmonton's largest dance halls was so crowded, the 1973 New Years Dance was limited to members and one guest only.

1974 executive members of the club include: President, A. Brennan, Vice-President, A. Anderson, Secretary, V. Palichuk, Treasurer, A. Anderson and Membership, W. Mazur. The clubs membership exceeds 500 in this year of 1974.

— Toni Ross

$50 million coal mine proposed

By TOM CAMPBELL
Of The Journal

Mannix Co. Ltd. of Calgary is proposing to develop a $50 million plus open pit coal mine south of Hinton in western Alberta.

The mine would provide two million long tons of coking coal annually, probably for Japanese markets, and operate for at least 15 years, says a spokesman for Mannix.

The operation would provide about 200 jobs initially in the first years of the operation, but the total of permanent jobs is expected to increase, to more than 300 should the mine achieve full production.

Manalta

The Gregg River Resources Ltd. mine would be operated by Manalta Coal Ltd., a division of Mannix.

Manalta has been carrying on negotiations with Japanese steel companies, but a spokesman for the company says no final agreement has been achieved.

Gregg River will make its application to develop the property at a public hearing before the Energy Resources Conservation Board April 10 and 11 in the Edmonton Court House.

The company did not indicate the capital cost of the

project. But the ERCB esti-
mates it requires a capital investment of $25 to $30 to produce one ton of coal annually
which would bring the two
million ton a year proposal to
$50 or $60 million.